EXPLORATIONS IN ANTHROPOLOGY AND THEOLOGY

Frank A. Salamone
Walter Randolph Adams

University Press of America, Inc.
Lanham • New York • Oxford

Copyright © 1997 by
University Press of America,® Inc.
4720 Boston Way
Lanham, Maryland 20706

12 Hid's Copse Rd.
Cummor Hill, Oxford OX2 9JJ

Library of Congress Cataloging-in-Publication Data

Explorations in anthropology and theology / (edited by) Frank A.
Salamone and Walter Randolph Adams.
p.   cm.
Includes bibliographical references and index.
"This work grew from a panel at the 1994 American Anthropological
Association's Annual Meetings in Atlanta, Ga."-Pref.
1. Philosophical anthropology. 2. Man (Christian theology) 3.
Woman (Christian theology) I. Salamone, Frank A. II. Adams,
Walter Randolph. III. American Anthropological Association.
Meeting (1994 : Atlalnta, Ga.)
BD450.E96   1997   128--dc21   96-49252 CIP

ISBN 0-7618-0660-1 (cloth: alk. ppr.)
ISBN 0-7618-0661-X (pbk: alk. ppr.)

Dedication

Frank A. Salamone dedicates this work to Virginia, his wife, who has kept him going when he wished to retreat to the library to read and hide from the world. He thanks his kids for putting up with his moods and taking an interest his obsession. He also thanks the missionaries who extend their kind hospitality and love to one whose opinions they often don't agree with.

Walter Randolph Adams dedicates this work to his wife, Marilyn Baade Adams, in honor of the 10 years of partnership; to his step-daughter, Michelle Rasey Vancisin; and, to the memory of his grandfather, Walter B. Hannstein, his second cousin, Gwendoyn Ritz, and friends the Rev. Hogan Yancey, Donald Fiester, and Amilcar Fuentes, all of whom passed away shortly before this book went to press.

Acknowledgements

The editors of this volume wish to express their deep gratitude to Mrs. Anna Baidoun, Manager of New Blackfriars, for permission to republish the chapter by Mary Douglas; to Mr. F. Kent Reilly and Dr. Linda Schele for their permission to publish their drawings that appear in the chapter by R. Jon McGee; and to Marilyn Baade Adams for her help in getting the manuscript to its final form. They also wish to acknowledge the cooperation given to them by the contributors, without which this book would not have appeared in as short a period from its conception at the American Anthropological Association meetings in November of 1994.

Contents

List of Tables and Figures

Preface

Frank A. Salamone

This work grew from a panel at the 1994 American Anthropological Association's Annual Meetings in Atlanta, GA. The newly nascent Society for the Anthropological Study of Religion had obtained some panel time. I organized a panel on the relationship between anthropology and religion and asked Walter R. Adams to be a commentator on that panel.

A number of people presented papers and comments at that meeting. The audience was quite large for a non-plenary panel. Part of the reason for the size of the audience was the fact that Napoleon Chagnon had agreed to meet with Father Jose Bortoli to debate the issues that divided them regarding the development of the Yanomami Indians of Venezuela. The panelists had kindly consented to yield some of their precious time to this important issue.

Following the panel, the panelists adjourned for a luncheon discussion. We agreed on the need to pursue publication of the papers and development of this new field. Not all papers were appropriate for publication while other papers were added over time. Walter Adams agreed to serve as a co-editor and he recruited a number of people for the panel. Edith Turner had been invited by the American Anthropological Association to present a special paper and, therefore, could not present a paper on the panel because American Anthropological Association rules prohibit anyone from being on more than one panel. She submitted a paper to us and recruited Mary Douglas.

We have been careful in selecting only the best of the papers at our discretion, for we are conscious of starting a new area of interest and wish to put forward a number of papers from a number of perspectives. Edith Turner, in suggesting I organize the original panel, advised me to focus on treating indigenous thought systems with the respect usually accorded only the major world religions, the so-called Great Religions. All religions, she said, are great to those who follow them.

The papers included in this volume follow that directive. Their perspectives are varied, almost as varied as anthropology itself. The areas covered are equally diverse. But the unifying principle is the respect that Edith Turner demanded. Indigenous systems are taken seriously in this work, including those of Middle Class Americans following a secular icon. As Walter Adams implies in his introductory chapter, we have cast our net wide choosing to be inclusive, rather than exclusive as we begin exploring a new area of anthropology.

Anthropology and theology is not yet shaped, as is reflected by the observation that the authors of these chapters rarely refer to the same scholars and theologians. Indeed, only Emile Durkheim and Victor Turner are cited in two or more of the chapter. We know it is related to anthropology and religion, but we also know it is different from that field. It seeks to understand systems of thought which in the Great Religions are called "theology." The papers in this volume seek to map out the broad areas of this new field and inspire others to follow with their own contributions.

Chapter 1

An Introduction to Explorations in Anthropology and Theology

Walter Randolph Adams

This chapter consists of three parts. The first presents an overview of what we believe the anthropological study of theology entails and how it fits into anthropology in general. The second section describes key points raised in the following chapters and how each paper relates to others in the volume. The last section describes why the chapters appear in this particular sequence as opposed to some other order.

The Anthropology of Theology

Edited volumes are ideal vehicles from which to begin explorations into areas that have not been the subject of intensive scrutiny. Each chapter in such works may not lead logically to the next; the collection of chapters, however, provide multiple facets from which to study an issue. As such, edited volumes are suitable for opening investigations into new topics of study. This volume explores the anthropology of theology, an area of inquiry we believe should become as integral to anthropology as studies of ethnicity, culture change, and cultural institutions are today. The following chapters provide perspectives from which one can approach the topic. We recognize there are other perspectives. Indeed, we hope that scholars with other positions will provide their perspectives and thus further illuminate the subject. If this occurs, this volume will have been successful in making the study of theology a part of anthropology.

To further encourage others to begin explorations into this field, it is beneficial to explain what we believe the anthropology of theology is and how it differs from the anthropology of religion. Most students of anthropology are aware that anthropological interest in religion has had a long history, and thousands of pages have been devoted to its study. Anthropological interest in theology, in addition to being nascent, is different in at least three respects. Two of these differences are suggested in the following definition. The *American Heritage Dictionary of the English*

Language (1970: 1334) defines theology as *"The study of the nature of God and religious truth; rational inquiry into religious questions, especially those posed by Christianity."* Although the definition may come from a dated source, a recent conversation with two theologians indicates it is still valid.[1] The two phrases, "inquiry into religious questions" and "especially those posed by Christianity" require further elaboration for current purposes. They will be addressed in reverse order.

We believe the anthropological study of theology distinguishes itself from the anthropology of religion by permitting and encouraging scholars to study the religions of the cultural others as well as their own. Anthropology is *not* studied by Christians alone; we therefore, believe the anthropology of theology should include all 'modern' religions. Here, the word 'modern' refers to *any* religion practiced on the eve of the Third Millennium.

Earlier in this century anthropologists were distinguished from sociologists by their focus on non-Western cultures. This focus allowed them to observe the behaviors of cultural others 'rationally' and 'scientifically' without calling into question their own philosophical tenets and beliefs. Since the 1970s, however, anthropologists have turned to the study of Western cultures. They began with ethnic groups and the aspects of culture that were exotic to their own lifestyles. It has, therefore, been easy to condemn the colonial process. More recently, attention has turned increasingly to more intimate aspects of the investigator's culture. This is manifested by reflexive anthropology and postmodernism. These inquiries, in turn, have spawned interests into issues that are pivotal to the ethos and world-view of the investigator. The anthropology of theology encourages this process and opens the inquiries into the scholars' own doctrines--both sacred and secular.

The anthropology of theology further distinguishes itself from the anthropology of religion in that it is an "inquiry into religious questions."[2] This approach places more emphasis on semiotics, values, and morality. It is a study of the *meaning* behind central tenets of faith, the systems of *values,* and of *moral* and *ethical* codes.[3] The revelations of these explorations, like psychotherapy, may be disturbing and hence avoided by many. To the courageous, however, the long-term results of the inquiry will be exhilarating even as the discovery process may be uncomfortable.

This quality of the anthropology of theology provides a stepping stone to the consideration of its last difference with the anthropology of religion. Because it deals with *meanings, systems of values, morality* and *ethical codes,* the anthropology of theology focuses attention on religion's dynamic qualities. The problems facing today's inhabitants are different than they were historically. To remain viable institutions, religions must be able to address the emerging concerns of its believers. This is most obviously seen by the rapid development of Pentecostal religions, both in the United States and abroad during the 1980s.

Importantly, however, the anthropology of religion typically focuses attention on institutions. The anthropology of theology, by contrast, can also focus on meanings, values, and moral and ethical codes. These features can change more rapidly than can institutions. The issue of gender-neutral language and how one is to interpret the capitalized male pronoun (He) or its possessive form (His) frequently encountered in *The Bible* (a constant source of debate as a result of the rise of women's rights) is a case in point.

The papers in this volume represent an initial inquiry into the anthropology of theology. Some may prove to be of central significance to the field, while others may be peripheral. We do not know now which will fall on fertile ground. Time will be the judge of their worth. It is therefore important to cast a broad net.

Because we have employed the broadcast method, we encourage the reader to peruse the chapters as a platform from which to pose their own questions into the anthropology of theology. The authors of these chapters should be seen as explorers. As such, they will approach the unknown in different ways. Some are cautious and walk carefully into the void and may be perceived as having accomplished little. Others, however, "walk where angels fear to tread" by rushing headlong into the breach, and may be perceived as "brash" or "foolish." The papers in this volume reflect both approaches. In all cases, as Turner says, "No dogmatic statements can be made and my paper should not be taken in that sense, for I am feeling my way." The same caveat holds for the other papers in this volume, too.

Finally, the parable of the six blind men and the elephant attests that independent explorations into the unknown can engender contradictory perspective and squabbles. This is the case, here, too. We hope these disagreements provide additional facets of inquiry and thus open the field more broadly; or, provide further focus of what the anthropology of theology will be.

The papers in this volume open the anthropology of theology in three ways. First, the definition states that theology is "especially" interested in those religious questions that are "posed by Christianity." We argue that the anthropology of theology should address the religious questions posed by any modern religion. Thus, although most of the papers deal with Christianity, the papers by Dow, Heriot, McGee, Moloye, and Turner broaden the inquiry into other doctrines.

Heriot's paper takes the anthropology of theology a step into the realm of controversy by looking at Christian theology from a feminist perspective. This is a tentative step because, as she says, "feminist spirituality is a social movement and not, as yet, generally an organized church." Because feminist spirituality is derived from Christianity, it also satisfies the criterion of being a 'modern' religion in the traditional sense. However, Heriot notes that feminist theology also obtains fundamental concepts and ideas from non-Western, principally Native American thought. She therefore takes the anthropology of theology into controversial territory by considering, as the editors of this volume have, that modern religion refers to any religion practiced today.

McGee's paper goes yet a step further by opening the inquiry into another modern religion: that of the traditional Lacandon Maya. The papers by Dow, Moloye and Turner take an intermediate step by looking at syncretic theologies. All three papers deal with religious doctrines that some may argue are derived from Protestant thought. However, as Moloye and Turner state explicitly, and is implicit in Dow's paper, traditional Protestant thought did not meet the demands of local populations. As a result, the symbols and their meanings are different in these groups and reflect the different concerns of the believers.

From this perspective, too, we call attention to the papers by Jankowiak and Allen and Kilbride. Both papers focus attention on groups living in the United States and on a practice the morality of which may be questionable to some readers: polygamy. Jankowiak and Allen discuss why polygyny (one male married simultaneously to more than one female) is important to Fundamentalist Mormons, and Kilbride brings forward why the practice may be adaptive for African Americans. Kilbride observes that while male-sharing may be a well-known practice in this population, it has not received open acceptance, and discusses why the taboo should be lifted.

Second, many of the chapters point out that Western culture is secular. Thus, the anthropology of theology should consider explorations into secular religious institutions, too. We offer Hopgood's paper on the "Deaners" because it deals with this type of institution. He demonstrates that secular institutions contain elements that point to fundamental values of United States religious thought. Thus, the line between the "sacred" and the "profane" is not always clear, and what constitutes "secular" and "sacred" is a moot issue. The reader may wish to consider Heriot's paper in the same perspective.

In a way, the papers by Dow and Moloye also deal with secularization. Dow indicates that the emergence of Pentecostal religions in Hidalgo,

Mexico were reactions against the religious elite and their control of the local political institutions. Moloye, on the other hand, discusses how individuals who once held secular offices are now providing religious services. Both of these religious movements, however, occurred in the context of capitalist penetration and resultant social dislocations, the very conditions that, as Moloye reminds us, frequently give rise to revitalization movements.

A third way this volume seeks to expand the anthropology of theology is by posing questions about central tenets of Western "scientism." Some chapters raise questions about the extent to which the social scientific 'gurus' or 'sachems' of yore are relevant to modern religions. Other chapters question whether 'cultural relativism' is unbiased, whether science is scientific or religious, and whether individuals control their own destiny. In short, they raise questions regarding the central tenets of Western scientific and anthropological thought.

The Papers: Major Points and Integrating Themes

The chapters that follow have so many "micro" themes that relate to others that drawing attention to them all would make this chapter long and tedious. Instead, my remarks here serve only to draw attention to some salient features in each chapter and how it links with others.[4]

Robert J. Priest begins with the observation that anthropology has borrowed important concepts from other disciplines, yet has not borrowed any from theology. After discussing the possible reasons for this, he demonstrates that anthropology can profitably borrow theological concepts by using the concept 'sin' as an example. He indicates that many authors have emphasized that 'primitive' cultures do not have the word 'sin' in their lexicon. The same writers, however, fail to note that Hebrew and Greek -- the groups which inspired our concept of 'sin' --did not either. This term, however, is absent from anthropological discourse because Western culture has artificially constricted its meaning. If, however, one defines *sin* as 'moral evil,' the concept is found in all cultures. He uses the Jivaro to demonstrate this point. More important, Priest discusses four areas of inquiry that he believes should be central to the anthropology of theology. These include the 'moral vocabulary' of different cultures, the patterns of cultural symbolism in morality, comparative ethics, and "human impulses and propensities which move people to violate norms and persons." These, Priest indicates, are only the beginning of what an anthropology of theology could address.

Morton Klass' paper continues the discussion that Priest begins. In addition to showing anthropology's "reluctance" to look at theology and theological issues, Klass suggests that the anthropology of theology may wish to study the issue of choice:

> There is certainly much more to be learned or pondered on when we contemplate *sin* as 'moral evil:' As Priest observes, theologians want to know whether such *sin* is indeed 'wilful and deliberate.' Students of *crime* may ask similar questions (e.g., is the individual responsible, or is society?) but the emphasis in *sin* is significantly different--the issue is really not so much 'responsibility' as it is 'choice.' Change *crime* to *sin* and we suddenly find ourselves asking: does an individual in a given society actually *choose* impropriety or 'moral evil'?

He then looks at 'choice in marriage' and demonstrates that 'choice' lies at the heart of other cultural institutions, such as those associated with economics, too. That economics is a moral issue is not new. Indeed, the Reverend Professor John Gessell observed that economists Adam Smith and Kenneth Boulding and activist Richard J. Barnet (1995) have made similar comments.[5] Moloye also discusses this topic in his paper when he discusses the negative consequences of economic policies.

M. Jean Heriot's paper presents the anthropology of theology from a feminist perspective, and, by so doing, shakes the foundations of Western thought. Citing Bednarowski (1992), she says that feminist theologies do so by offering critiques "of the established Western traditions and of Newtonian science as the primary desacralizers of the cosmos and of American culture." Like Priest and Klass, Heriot also suggests avenues of inquiry that the anthropology of theology may wish to investigate. Specifically, she suggests that anthropologists may wish to consider exploring issues of "appropriation, myth making, and essentialism." The issue of appropriation harkens back to Klass' paper because it, too, is fundamentally an issue of choice. Equally important, Heriot notes that

> the feminist spirituality movement offers anthropologists a unique chance to watch the development of a new religion embedded in a contemporary Western social context. It also offers an excellent case study for the patterns and trajectories found in millennial movements in general, for the beliefs and practices of feminist spirituality are millennial in nature as women await the dawn of a new age of equality.

Finally, in the spirit of broadening the anthropology of theology still further, the reader may wish to ponder how a feminist may have explored the phenomena discussed in the following papers.

Edith Turner's chapter, like the previous ones, discusses the uneasiness with which anthropologists have dealt with theology and theologians. More importantly, however, this chapter is the first in this volume that attempts to bridge the gap by discussing the relationship between theology and anthropology in a cultural context. Specifically, she focuses on modern-day Iñupiat culture.

This paper is important for at least three reasons. First, she states that "It has been claimed that in Inuit thought there are categories of spirits...Yet these appear to change as the decades pass; or else emphasis on a category changes or fades." This statement, and her later reference to Michael Jackson's (1989) comment that "ritual experience proves itself to be true and valid IN USE, not as a preordained system or structure..." emphasizes the point that theology is dynamic. As a dynamic phenomena, it cannot be expected to remain the same either from one time to the next, nor from one individual to the next. In all cases, however, a theology has to be meaningful to its practitioners.

Second, to help us understand contemporary Iñupiat theology, she presents a series of narratives that demonstrate that Iñupiat theology means different things to different individuals and other elements of its dynamic nature. Her use of the present tense and her blending of herself within the narrative are strong reminders of her central point that the ritual experience is "true and valid in use" and that to the Iñupiat, there is no clear dividing line between the sacred and secular worlds. For example, she writes, "the story below shows the power of an animal to give itself to humankind and then to reincarnate, thus perpetuating the vital process of cycling of the ecosystem, continually renewing itself and freeing and enlightening all its components."

Equally important, she states that at least one Iñupiat does not associate shaman experience with altered states of consciousness. "One way we may look at the matter is that Iñupiat are able to bring their shamanic and everyday faculties to lie alongside each other in a *normal* world... The situation reflects the *extension* of ordinary life, not something totally foreign to it." At the same time, however, the Iñupiat recognize "an experiential sense of consciousness apart from the body." In many ways, these comments are equally true for the other groups described in the other chapters in this volume, although the authors may not overtly make these statements.

Third, she offers the proposition that the term theology should be defined as "the study of all spirit beings and gods (as Hindu theology indeed does), and include an array of beings distinct from the Christian God." In this respect, she takes the position that the anthropology of theology is the study of any modern-day religion. She notes, however, that Russian Orthodox theologians have had difficulty accepting the concept that traditional belief systems are religions. It is important to note, however, that the inability to accept the concept that traditional belief systems are religions is not a problem unique to Russian Orthodox theologians; indeed, Moloye shows in his paper that Protestant missionaries in Africa have traditionally had the same problem.

Frank A. Salamone, like the preceding authors, also deals with the enmity between anthropologists and theologians. I believe, however, that Salamone draws attention to a central reason for the conflict: Both groups provide similar services to indigenous peoples, and the latter are becoming increasingly rare. Salamone then presents a thorough and well-balanced study of the recent controversy between Napoleon Chagnon and the Salesian Fathers over the Yanomami. His portrayal exposes the differences between the protagonists and illuminates their common features.

Finally, Salamone brings forward two important concepts that I believe are essential to the future of anthropology: First, the rivalry between anthropologists and theologians/missionaries has the unfortunate result of placing the indigenous populations in the position of being a bone for two dogs. This has the result of reducing indigenous populations to a commodity. I do not believe this is the intention of either party. Second, Salamone shows that anthropology and anthropologists are also losers in this squabble:

> Missionaries, typically, spend far more time in the field than do anthropologists. Their language skills generally surpass those of anthropologists and their relationships with indigenous peoples tend to be of longer and deeper dimensions than do those of anthropologists.

It is also true that missionaries engage in "directed culture change." This is one of their explicit goals. Similarly, anthropologists are the providers of unintentional, and undirected culture change.[6] The students of reflexive anthropology bring this aspect of fieldwork into view. We must ask ourselves "Which is worse?" The answer can best be provided by those who are impacted.

James W. Dow analyzes the impact of Protestantism on social and political change in three Otomí communities in Hidalgo, Mexico. In two of the cases (the third is yet unfolding), the change from a predominantly Catholic to a predominantly Protestant community has taken 20 years. He argues that it takes this long "for demographic changes in the ratio of younger to older men to manifest themselves." A central point is that Protestantism has been a reaction against a "traditional, religiously sanctioned hierarchy of authority" in both Europe and Mexico. In Mexico, however, "the authority ... is generated by an Amerindian religion, not by the Catholic Church." I wonder whether this is a significant difference; if so, why is it significant and how is this significance manifested on the population?

Edith Turner's paper on the Iñupiat also deals with the penetration of Protestantism in a local community. In this case, however, Turner demonstrates the dynamic quality of theology by presenting not only how Protestantism caused the traditional Iñupiat religion to change, but also how, because Protestantism focused attention only on religious issues, while the traditional Iñupiat made no distinction between religion and health, important elements of Iñupiat cosmology remained, and are now re-emerging as important elements in their theology. To be sure, the meanings have changed, but this is to be expected, and is necessary if religion is to remain viable for its believers.

Olugbemi Moloye's paper begins with the observation that "cultural adaptation is an attempt to find solutions to the problems of society" and that the revitalization movements often occur as concomitant responses to economic alterations. He focuses attention on the Independent Christian Churches of Nigeria, which he considers to be similar to revitalization movements to support his contention. He argues that such movements are integrative forces that attempt to make sense of the changing environment.

Moloye's main point is that: "the Independent Christian Churches in Nigeria emerged as a rejection of the inflexibility of colonial Christian religion and its failures to incorporate 'Africanness' to its mode of worship as preached by European missionaries in the early part of the 20th century." An important concept, then, is that the message and ideals expressed in the theology have to be meaningful to the believers. He makes this point clearly in the following statement: "Resort[ing] to traditional religion during life crises such as crop failure, pestilence, famine, birth, marriage, sickness and death, is *sine qua non* among Africans and it is during these crises that the missionary religion proved to be the most irrelevant in the lives of the Africans." His paper shows that the Independent Christian Churches have successfully combined the structure of Christianity and retained the philosophical base of the indigenous population. As such, he suggests that syncretic religions may share characteristics of pidgin and Creole languages (see Salzmann 1993; Diebold 1964).

Philip L. Kilbride discusses polygamy among African Americans in the United States. He argues this practice may be adaptive because African American women face a shortage of eligible African American males due to their unemployment, high rates of incarceration and mortality from homicide. Polygamy also may be beneficial to the children because they lack positive male role models. Kilbride argues if churches and synagogues would tolerate this practice, it would also "serve to discard cloaks of secrecy where such practice already exists informally or to unburden disestranged individuals who might otherwise avail themselves to join (or rejoin) religious communities now closed to them." The moral code that prohibits polygamy, however presents a major barrier.

Kilbride looks at phenomena occurring in Africa to help provide clues for anthropological questions. He notes that polygamy is a functional institution among many African groups where strict adherence to traditional Judeo-Christian doctrine espousing monogamy creates a "grave pastoral problem." To deal with similar conflicts regarding other cultural institutions, some Churches have begun to develop "inculturation theology." Citing Crollius (1986), he writes that

> the inculturation of the Church is the integration of the Christian experience of a local Church into the culture of its people in such a way that this experience not only expresses itself in elements of this culture, but becomes a force that animates, orients, and innovates this culture so as to create a new unity and communion, not only within the culture in question but also as an enrichment of the Church universal.

Kilbride suggests the debate on inculturation theology is also pertinent for the United States. This is especially true for groups living under circumstances where deviation from traditional doctrinal practices may, in the long-run, be adaptive.

Many of the papers address the theme that religion should be relevant for specific groups. Salamone and Kilbride raise a question that may be asked frequently by groups to which Western religion has been introduced, "Why do you give us a version of Christianity different from that practiced in your country?" Kilbride's paper offers a possible response: There would be few converts if the theology was not modified to meet the needs of a local group. Indeed, this is precisely the result that Moloye and Turner describe in their papers.

Kilbride also demonstrates that doctrine has to be ready to change within a particular group when environmental (both natural and social) phenomena have adverse impacts on the population that make such changes necessary. This kind of change is already becoming manifested in the United States, as his example of the "wife-in-law" attests. This term refers to "relationships between women who are connected to each other most often unwittingly because they have been married to the same man." The coining of new phrases often requires altering concepts of morality because one needs to determine how to treat the objects to which they refer (Adams 1994).

This and the following paper focus attention on polygamy as practiced by "minority" populations in the United States. Kilbride looks at the institution as practiced by the population as a cultural response to a changing environment that may make it adaptive in the twenty-first century. The other paper, by contrast, studies the institution as practiced by a reactionary and conservative population. In spite of these differences, however, both agree that women may benefit from polygamy because the husbands' authority is not open to question.

William Jankowiak and Emilie Allen argue that Fundamentalist Mormons practice polygamy precisely because it enables the practice of "father adoration." This,

> is a psychocultural configuration that arises from four separate yet intertwined factors: (1) a theology that endows men with a supernatural essence that commands the regeneration of a religious organization...through reproduction; (2) a close-corporate, theological community that confers its greatest esteem on men in either a leadership position as members of the church's priesthood council or who are independently wealthy; (3) a polygamous family system organized around a husband/father, who is the primary focal point, at least at the symbolic level, and who unites the often competing female-centered natal family units into a unified cultural whole; and (4) an American cultural ethos that values emotional familial involvement over a detached, albeit respectful role performance.[7]

These features are found in Fundamentalist Mormon society.

The authors focus attention on essential tenets of Mormon theology and aspects of that belief system that promotes the practice. They state that an immutable tenet of Mormonism is that

> God is a polygamous man who loves all his children but confers on men, and not women, an elevated spiritual essence which insures that 'righteous' living men will obtain a higher spiritual standing. Women's standing, on the other hand, is determined by their performance in the highly valued complimentary roles of wife and mother....It is important to point out that a man's celestial rank is not determined by the number of wives he has or the number of children he reproduces. It is determined, primarily, by a person's ability to live righteously, correctly, according to God's will, with the highest virtue reserved to those who enter into a plural family. In contrast, women achieve salvation primarily by becoming a sister-wife (i.e., a co-wife) in a celestial or plural family.

A woman achieves salvation by upholding "her husband's behavior, especially in front on his children." The importance of this practice, the woman's role in it, and its impact on the children are the subjects of the rest of the chapter.

The authors describe how a man's social standing is based on hagiographies-- the ritualized testimonials performed by their descendants about their "heroic deeds and accomplishments which ultimately advanced or improved the community." These oral traditions "praise the fathers' actions, [and] overlook their shortcomings." Hagiographies have important roles in secular aspects of society. Specifically, they inadvertently help create a hierarchy of relative social worth upon which the virtues of each person (specifically each father) is marked. The relative social ordering of an individual and, by extension, his family also contributes to the practice of attempting to advance or smear a father's reputation.

> The wives have an important role in upholding their husband's image becomes important: In a very practical way, the plural family is held together as much by an image of sharing a common bond as it is with actual memories of interacting with one's father (who embodies the common bond at its highest). It is a bond that needs the active involvement, participation and affirmation of fathers, co-wives and mothers.

The tendency to focus on the mother-child dyad, common in the dominant United States society, is lacking in Fundamentalist Mormon societies because the focus is on the spiritual and administrative authority of the father. Co-wives contribute to the idealization process because they are in competition for their husband's attention, and he becomes the symbolic link between them and the rest of the community, and their key to 'salvation.' The co-wives also cause the children to focus their attention on their father because he has the same role in their lives, too. "This effort, with the child's own desire to bond with his father, enhances the father's stature and esteem." Jankowiak and Allen also describe how the actual quality of the father-child relationship may have an adverse impact on the awe required in the child - father relationship. This, in turn, has an impact on whether the child remains in the religious and secular communities.

R. Jon McGee's paper, like Turner's and that by Jankowiak and Allen, also deals with an oral tradition of religious and social significance. This paper, however, deals with the Lacandon Maya of Mexico, one of the groups that has been least affected by westernization. As such, the Lacandon are similar to the Yanomami described in Salamone's paper. The focal point in this chapter is the presentation of a *tsikbal*. This typically refers to conversation, but in reference to myth telling, it describes a characteristic genre of Lacandon discourse that is different from everyday conversation. In this type of narrative, actions recounted in a myth are believed to be historical in the modern, Western sense of the word, but the narrator makes it clear that he is not describing his personal experiences.

The myth recounts the creation and destruction of the world. Of special importance for current purposes is that the world's destruction is a metaphorical description of procedures used for field preparation and planting of crops upon which the Lacandon depend for food. McGee argues that the "events take the form that they do because they are modeled on the natural environment in which the Lacandon live."

We include this paper for at least three reasons. First, in keeping with the goal of encouraging others to begin investigations into the anthropology of theology, the presentation of the *tsikbal* in its entirety provides the opportunity for the interested reader to begin a study of comparative morality, as Priest suggests. The Lacandon, like other Maya groups, believe that the gods' activities are frequently capricious. They destroy their creations on a whim, not as punishment for human activities. Perhaps the analysis of Lacandon creation myths provide clues to Lacandon morality or lead us to conclusions about the Lacandon perceptions of human nature. Second, McGee shows that myths may provide clues about peoples' perceptions of their environment and their place in it. The information contained in the myth leads one to conclude that perceptions of nature, deities, and morality vary dramatically between traditional and Western societies. Thus, McGee's work causes us to reflect on a problem facing anthropology that Priest describes in his paper. Specifically, Priest observes that anthropologists tend "to underreport the dark sides of life in folk societies and to present idealized or even romanticized portraits of the people being described." The anthropology of theology may begin to reverse this tendency. Finally, as stated earlier, we believe the anthropology of theology should consider looking at religious issues raised in any religion, whether it be Western or non-Western; modern or modernizing populations.

Some of the papers raise other questions that relate specifically to how anthropologists deal with the cultures they study and the impact on traditional culture and its art. For example, does the paper present an 'idealized' or 'romanticized' view of traditional culture? Alternatively, does it document the impact of Western encroachment in tenors that approximate self-flagellation, auto-mutilation and utterances of *mea culpa*. Another question is whether one can document or describe the collision of traditional and Western cultures without moralistic overtones and tendencies so often found in anthropological works.

James F. Hopgood's paper focuses on the "Deaners"--the devotees of James Dean. Like Dow and Moloye, Hopgood refers to scholars who have provided important concepts and foundations for the anthropological study of religion. This chapter offers another challenge to the anthropology of theology by presenting a study of what is, by definition, a pilgrimage, thus a religious event; and, as Turner portrays in her paper, this paper also brings forward the concept that theology is alive and its meaning is obtained through experiencing the event. What makes this paper different from the others is that the object of adoration is quite secular--or is it? Hopgood demonstrates that the secular icons are as rich in their meanings and symbolism as are their sacred counterparts.

We include this paper in the volume because Western society is secular, as Klass and Priest point out. Indeed, as Reverend Hogan Yancey (and others) have said, "our god is money."[8] A component of Western society's secularism is that which one author has called "commodity fetishism" (Taussig 1980) As such, the anthropology of theology may wish to consider including studies of secular institutions like the Deaners. Hopgood clearly demonstrates this aspect of Western society when he observes that "the festival is held on a *weekend* in traditional American Protestant fashion, in deference to the work ethic."

Also of crucial importance to an understanding of the Deaners are his statements that Fairmont has not changed significantly since 1955, and that "Fairmont *itself* is symbolic of another time and creates or recreates an important setting for those seeking James Dean." I received the sense that "small-town America," the 1950s, and the "forever young" ethos so prominently a part of United States society are embodied in Deanerism. Hopgood explores these issues in his paper. A study of Deanerism entails consideration of the system of values that underlies other aspects of United States culture. Many of the papers discuss the separation of Church and State. However, Hopgood's paper and others in this volume give reason to wonder whether the line is blurred and indistinct?

Even more provocative, however, is a comment that Salamone makes in his paper:

> Without doubt many people become Christians in order to gain perceived advantages elsewhere in the world. Not all perceived advantages are material. Many are psychological. Others are, in fact, defensive. Too many of these needs, desires, and expectations are simply out-of-awareness.

By replacing the word "Christians" with the word "Deaners," we are encouraged to seek answers to the questions, "why do people become Deaners?" and "what benefit do they receive from this conversion."

Similarly, we must ask, "What are the values held so dearly by Midwestern, small-community United States culture that appeal to the Deaners? How does James Dean appeal to those values? These are intriguing because there is little solid information about Dean's life and "for Deaners, the life and roles of James Dean are blended into a mythic unity." As such, one may ask whether the stories, accounts, and other sources of information are analogous to the Lacandon *tsikbal* described by McGee and the Iñupiat narratives that Turner presents in her paper. If so, would the hagiographies described by Jankowiak and Allen be equivalent to the Lacandon *tsikbal* and Iñupiat myths?

Hopgood also notes the relationship of Deanerism with the recreation of an ethnic identity.[9] In this respect, this paper ties in with Salamone's issue of what, and who, constitutes "authentic" Yanomami culture--an issue that Adams also raises in his work. Another issue that the anthropology of theology may explore, then, is the role that theology plays in the emergence of an ethnic group. Heriot's paper clearly takes a step in this direction.

Walter Randolph Adams continues a theme implicit, if not always explicit, in the papers in this collection; namely, that "traditional" cultures are dynamic structures. People are always reinventing tradition, always selecting from their heritage those items they deem most appropriate for coping with environmental challenges. The Ojibway are no different from other peoples in this regard. Adams demonstrates how they chose elements from the competing introduced religious traditions (Methodism and Roman Catholicism) to maximize their chances of survival.

Moreover, Adams provides an important reminder to us as well as a corrective to the monolithic view of culture: "...communities are not homogeneous structures. Rather, individuals within communities will respond in ways that they believe may help them survive without fully understanding the situation to which they are responding." In combining "'internal dynamics and external factors," using history, and focusing on both factions in the Ojibway fission provides a contribution to the study of cultural evolution and its relationship to the anthropology of theology. Especially significant is the way that individual Ojibway used the Methodist and Catholic teachings to promote their own 'progressive' or 'conservative' interests.

Mary Douglas' paper provides closure in many ways. She does so, however, by bringing in new things to consider. For example, like many of the other authors, she mentions the impact that secularization has had on modern life-styles. Importantly, she points to an additional stressor: the erosion of the sense of community found in small-scale societies. Similarly, like Klass, Priest, and Salamone, she challenges scholars to begin to think in new ways. However, while the others challenge anthropologists to develop new ways of thinking, Douglas challenges theologians:

> The old tie between conduct and nature depends on a self-conscious, punishing community, and once that is dispersed, the lightning conductor model of divine intervention makes no sense. This is what theologians have to consider.

If religion is to have a place in Third Millennium society (which it should), it is incumbent that theologians fully consider the impact that secularization and living in large urban settings have had, and will continue to have, on society. Like Heriot, Douglas presents a feminist view. Rather than shaking the foundations of Western thought, however, Douglas believes

> We, the women, should look carefully at the reasons given for rejecting ordinations of women. When we do this, we find the defense of hierarchy is a paramount concern. That being so, we are merely setting off the alarms by demanding equality. Instead we should see whether we cannot do better for ourselves by asking for a higher quality of hierarchy.

Her paper provides a framework for doing this.

Her paper also ties in to the papers by Heriot, McGee, Turner, and Jankowiak and Allen by dealing with a myth. Like most of these writers, Douglas does not seek to challenge the myth: "Anthropologists would never ask for a myth to be tested against any facts at all: first it is impolite, and second it is unproductive." Rather, she believes the "task for the women seeking to reform the Church in their own regard is to make use of the myths of gender, of natural signs and of hierarchy, to achieve their ends."

Importantly, Douglas' prescription may be similar to the strategies employed by the cultures discussed in the other papers. Specifically, a careful understanding of a church's structure, its tenets and myths, and crafting them to work for the population in question, may be how missionaries and the recipient culture have adapted religions to their immediate needs. Douglas' paper, then, asks a variant of the question posed in the other works: "why *don't* you provide us with a different version of Christianity?" It is important to note, however, that the word 'us' does not refer to women alone, nor to Christianity alone. Rather, it refers to *any* individual or group who feels excluded from *any* religion. This, then, harkens back to the idea raised at the beginning of this chapter: The anthropology of theology seeks to understand *any and all* religions practiced on the eve of the Third Millenium.

The above pages have highlighted the major points in the papers and have pointed to some themes found in various papers. Culture change is another theme that links many of the papers. Many of them describe how local cultures attempt to adapt to pluralistic environments. This issue is of special importance when some actors are drawn more quickly than others to non-traditional lifestyles. Adams, Dow, Klass, Priest and Salamone explicitly deal with this issue. It is also implied in the works by Douglas, Heriot, Hopgood, Jankowiak and Allen, Kilbride, McGee, Moloye and Turner.

The papers demonstrate that one reaction is to modify cultural patterns and institutions and become part of the global community (Adams, Dow, Kilbride, and Moloye). An equally possible reaction, however, is to become more conservative and religiously fundamentalist (Adams, Hopgood, Jankowiak and Allen, Moloye, and implied in Salamone). Douglas, Heriot, Moloye, and Turner show that groups can also combine elements of both responses, thus becoming dynamic and resilient to the changing environment, while cultural elements that are perceived as fundamental to that group are retained.

A necessary aspect of change is that the ultimate result or outcome of the change cannot be known in advance. An individual may think that he or she knows what the outcome may be, but this is never entirely certain because there are conditions and forces that are also in operation over which one has no control or knowledge. This point is suggested in the papers by Adams, Dow, Douglas, Jankowiak and Allen, and Salamone, and clearly stated in the papers by Heriot, Kilbride, and Turner. In all cases, however, the undercurrent seems to suggest that individuals make the choice they do, with the hope that the path they choose will satisfy the difficulty they face. Yet, at the same time, people must recognize that, the result of such decisions is always a "craps shoot:" The outcome is frequently influenced by phenomena over which the actor has little, or no, control. This concept is well recognized by scholars of biological evolution; but, often is not well accepted by those who have been indoctrinated by the tenets of 19th century rationalism. The reluctance to recognize this point is especially obvious when the issue is the extent to which human beings are masters of their destiny.

The papers by Klass, McGee, Priest, Salamone and Turner demonstrate that the same issue confronts anthropological investigations and investigators. In this regard, the papers by Douglas, McGee, Moloye and

Turner take a 'fundamentalist' anthropological approach that, in many ways, attempt to emphasize traditional culture, or demonstrate its intrinsic value. The other papers, by way of contrast, seek to modify anthropological thought by showing how anthropologists may adapt to the 21st century by modifying their conceptions. For example, Klass and Priest question whether cultural relativity, long considered the hallmark of anthropology, is truly unbiased.

The editors of this volume feel that the culture of anthropology, like the cultures it studies, must change. That is, if anthropology is to survive and remain a worthwhile discipline in the 21st century, mainstream anthropology will have to modify its traditional conceptions. Salamone's paper warns us what can happen if anthropology retains its conservative stance: anthropologists can become anathemas to the very people they wish to protect. Should that occur, the larger public's concept of anthropology's value in the new world order will suffer accordingly. The papers in this volume suggest the same comments hold true also for theology and theologians.

Organization of the volume

This volume provides insights into the width and depth of cultural anthropology. As such these papers represent only a small range of the possibilities available for further research. Some papers contained in this volume are theoretical, while others present ethnographic descriptions that demonstrate the interplay between theology and anthropology.

Because this volume attempts to open a new focus in anthropology, we have placed the papers in an order which we hope challenges the reader to think about the material presented in the previous chapters and to tease out information. We therefore have placed the theoretical chapters at the beginning of the volume. Priest provides a detailed theoretical discussion of how anthropologists might want to look at theology and the questions that may be explored. Klass' paper, although initially a commentary on Priest's paper, provides additional insights on these issues. Heriot's paper provides the same function by raising issues from a feminist perspective.

Turner's paper is also theoretical in nature. Unlike the preceding works, however, this and the following paper reflect anthropological attempts to actively wrestle with incorporating theological issues while conducting fieldwork.

Salamone's paper is theoretical in nature, but it also relates to a specific ethnographic example. Because it is both theoretical and ethnographic, this paper is a bridge between the theoretical and ethnographic papers. While some may think the ethnographic papers constitute a "second part," the tenor of the papers do not lead to such a segmentation. Indeed, both Turner's and Salamone's papers offer both a theoretical statement and an ethnographic description.

Culture contains both "materialist" and "cognitive" dimensions. Because professors of anthropology have stressed that their students be either materialists or cognitivists, it is not surprising that the authors of these papers stress one or the other. The papers in this volume are organized as a progression from those that are predominantly "materialist" to those that are predominantly "cognitive." Alternatively, the reader may wish to regard the order as one that goes from the more concrete and secure to the more abstract and controversial. It is important to note, however, all of them attempt to combine both dimensions and contain elements that readers may regard as controversial. It is likely, then, that one may argue with the specific sequence of the papers.

We chose to move from the "materialist" to the "cognitive" because the ethnographic portion of Salamone's paper clearly highlights a conflict, hence "materialistic" aspect, of the Chagnon-Salesian controversy. Because Salamone also describes the religious conversion of the Yanomami in the context of culture change, it leads to the next paper. Dow describes the process by which Pentecostal Protestantism entered three Otomí communities and the impact Protestantism has had on community political institutions. This paper looks at the moral and ethical standards that allow politicians to behave in a manner that some may believe to be "a-moral" and "a-ethical." Following in the same pattern is the paper by Moloye, which looks at the impact that economic structural adjustment programs have had on religion. This paper focuses much more explicitly on theological (hence cognitive) issues than Dow does. Moloye's paper also serves as a bridge for Kilbride's paper by discussing the historical antecedents for inculturation theology.

The next two papers deal with a behavior that some may regard as a-moral and a-ethical: polygamy in the United States. Following the overall organization of the book, Kilbride's discussion focuses attention on the "material" aspects of the institution, while that by Jankowiak and Allen stresses its "cognitive" dimensions.

The next two papers continues an excursion into the "cognitive" dimension of culture. The first of these, by McGee, focuses attention on the content of a Lacandon myth. His portrayal is tied to the materialist dimension of culture by his discussion of how this myth relates to crop cultivation. Specifically, he argues, "Events in the myth take the form that they do because they are modeled on the natural environment in which the Lacandon's live... [Some] episodes are a reenactment of the Lacandon's cycle of slash and burn horticulture."

There are two reasons for placing Hopgood's paper next. First, his presentation continues the trend from "the more materialist" to the "more cognitive" orientation by bringing forward implicit features of modern Western life. The 1950s as the "ideal" era and the "forever young" attitude are integral to the ethos of the United States in the 1990s. The "Deaners" are the epitome of both. Second, this paper returns the reader again to a critical purpose of this book: to encourage others to explore the anthropology of theology. Although Hopgood's paper is not explicitly theoretical, it has important theoretical implications. We noted earlier that Western society is secular. This the case, we offer Hopgood's paper to serve as a basis from which the anthropology of theology should explore secular institutions.

Adams' paper continues at a theoretical level and describes a culture in general rather than focusing on specific institutions. It deals with the penetration of Western religions (Protestant and Catholic). It also describes the economic and philosophical contexts under which the missionaries operated and upon which they organized their missions. The paper shows that the choice to "become" Protestant or Catholic was a response an individual used to adapt to Western encroachment. The decision to 'become' Catholic or Methodist was based, in large measure, on the extent to one sought to participate in Western culture. This concept highlights a comment that Salamone makes:

> ...it is clear that the message the missionaries send is often not one their audience always receives. Missionaries are well aware that cultural differences in both the encoding and decoding of a message as well as in the 'medium' through which the message travels hinder and distort its reception and interpretation. Too often, however, they tend to think of 'culture' occurring at some 'macro level,' almost as a massive penumbra enshrouding a body of people. It is far more meaningful to visualize 'culture' as being encapsulated in individual interpersonal encounters as well as in the expectations each participant brings to such encounters.

Culture, then, should be seen as both an individual and a collective response to environmental stimuli.

Douglas' paper brings closure to the volume by returning the reader once again to theoretical issues raised in the initial two papers. Her comments, however, are germane to each of the previous chapters. Equally important, while the earlier papers discuss how anthropology and anthropologists may begin to meet the challenges of the twenty-first century and beyond, Douglas' paper does the same for theologians.

Throughout this chapter, we have stated this volume is organized to permit the readers to ponder the philosophical issues described in the preceding articles and to encourage the anthropological exploration of theology. We encourage readers to think about hidden aspects that the authors did not bring to light and to draw their own conclusions and perspectives on the issues raised. This chapter has posed some; we hope that the contents of the following chapters will pose others to you, the reader. In so doing, we further hope that you will present your perspectives on the issue, and in that way more fully expand and define the anthropology of theology.

Notes

1. I wish to acknowledge the help of the Reverend Professor John Gessell and the late Reverend Hogan Yancey, Ph.D. I have greatly appreciated their comments, wisdom and thoughts through the years. Their insights have helped formulate the thoughts contained here, although I, alone, am responsible for any errors contained in these pages.
2. Here, the adjective "rational" found in the formal definition is removed because 'rationality" is a value-laden issue. The question, "What constitutes rationality?" itself, can be a subject of study within the anthropology of theology.
3. To illustrate, readers may recall the fervor that *The Mountain People* (Turnbull 1972) raised when, in the last chapter, the author showed parallels between facets of modern Western culture and the Ik.
4. To be certain that I have correctly presented the arguments presented in their papers, I mailed copies of my remarks to the authors for their comments and asked them to let me know whether I correctly represented their papers.
5. In a similar vein, I am reminded of a comment attributed to John Kenneth Galbraith, who, during a graduation ceremony, supposedly stated, "I cannot ask you to comfort the afflicted; that would be considered eccentric; I can, however, ask you to afflict the comfortable."
6. Napoleon Chagnon (1983: 13ff) demonstrates this point in his work when he shared his food with the Yanomami and otherwise exposed them to elements of his culture.
7. One may want to think about these four elements in relation to Kilbride's paper and ponder the impact that mate-sharing might have, or how African American families may wish to adopt or avoid similar problems if "mate-sharing" becomes established as a part of that culture.
8. I asked the late Reverend Yancey whether /god/ should be capitalized or written with a lowercase letter. He stated that one could do either. As a Christian, he would

prefer lowercase, but stated that United States society operates in a manner suggesting that most would capitalize it.

9. Heriot's paper also raises similar issues.

Chapter 2

Christian Theology, Sin, and Anthropology

Robert J. Priest

Concepts form the tools of our trade. They structure our thinking, orient our research, help us order our data, and allow us to communicate with each other. As anthropologists, we draw our concepts from many sources-- "function" and "structure" from mathematics, "dynamics" and "equilibrium" from physics, "evolution" and "adaptation" from the biological sciences, and "taboo" and "mana" from other cultures. Careful attention by anthropologists to potentially useful concepts from other disciplines is needed.

One such discipline, is that of theology, a discipline with deep historical roots in that part of our own culture with which anthropology is least comfortable. Yet a historical analysis of conceptual developments in anthropology is incomplete without a recognition that those developments occurred in a context where theological concepts were pervasive. In a classic article on the history of anthropology, Irving Hallowell notes that anthropology addresses the same subject matter that religion has traditionally addressed and that anthropologists have replaced priests and theologians as the "class of persons to whom one could turn for authoritative answers to anthropological questions" (Hallowell 1976:22). Hallowell stresses that all cultures have their own "folk anthropologies," that "the traditional Christian world view" provided early western culture with such a folk anthropology, and that "this traditional world view of the West is the historical backdrop against which changes in answers to anthropological questions may be plotted" (Hallowell 1976:24).

The roots of anthropology go back to the encounter of the West with social others. At the time of the discovery of the New World, a whole cluster of closely related concepts were central to Western reflection on the human condition: sin, guilt, conscience, the will, natural law, vice, virtue, envy, gluttony, pride, etc. Christian theology (then queen of the sciences) stressed such concepts. The Catholic practices of penance and, following the Fourth Lateran Council (1215), of annual obligatory confession, required and generated enormous and complex discourses (theological treatises, confession manuals, confessor's handbooks, sermons) on conscience, sin, and virtue (Delumeau 1990: 189ff). Protestants also generated lengthy tomes on cases of conscience, moral law, virtue and vice. The literature of Dante, Chaucer, Milton, Spenser, and many others made abundant use of sin concepts--lust, anger, pride, envy, covetousness, gluttony, sloth--in their reflections on human nature and behavior (Bloomfield 1967). Murals, sculptures, and paintings featured personifications of the seven deadly sins, occasionally locked in combat with seven virtues. In this pre-social science society, theology, sermons, the confessional, art, literature--in short, the whole culture--united in instructing people to reflect on and interpret themselves and others in their every act and motive in the light of such concepts. This is the backdrop against which cultural anthropology was gradually to emerge.

And if we follow Eric Wolf (1969:3) in seeing anthropology "as a form of social action, operating within and against a certain societal and cultural context," then it is anthropology's action with reference to this pre-existent "folk anthropology" which must be examined. Several general points may be made about this action.

First, anthropology has tended to have an adversarial relationship to Christianity. When E. B. Tylor penned the phrase, "Theologians all to expose, tis the mission of primitive man," (quoted in Tylor 1986:17) he was indicating his feeling that the utility of studying primitive man lay, in part, in its use for undercutting and discrediting the views of theologians, Christian theologians. In his article, "Religion and the Anthropologists," Evans-Pritchard suggested that most anthropologists historically have not been religious themselves and have been "bleakly hostile" towards religion in general and Christianity in particular. While anthropologists have not often written directly about Christianity, much of what they have written may be seen as an indirect comment on Christianity. Clifford Geertz writes,

> At the moment when [anthropology] seems most deliberately removed from our lives, it is most immediate, when it seems most insistently to be talking about the distant, the strange, the long ago, or the idiosyncratic, it is in fact talking also about the close, the familiar, the contemporary and the generic. From one point of view, the whole history of the comparative study of religion . . . can be looked at as but a circuitous, even devious, approach to a rational analysis of our own situation, an evaluation of our own religious traditions while seeming to evaluate only those of exotic others (1968:2).

If Hallowell is correct about Christianity being a key backdrop to the development of anthropology, and Evans-Pritchard is correct in seeing the social community of anthropologists as rather consistently adversarial to things Christian, and if Geertz is correct in suggesting that anthropologists make their points in roundabout and indirect fashions, then the relative silence of anthropology on Christianity need not imply indifference or neutrality. Indeed, anthropology may be seen as an active and value-laden form of social action in which the anthropologist, in the words of Weston La Barre (1970:4), conducts "his private rebellion in the arcane language of academic books"--a rebellion against, among other things, Christianity as the traditional religion of the West. And if the oft repeated claim that anthropology has tended to have an adversarial relationship to Christianity is true, then it may also be true that anthropologists have tended to neglect or reject the use of concepts and categories from this older folk anthropology because of their associations with Christianity, rather than because the concepts and ideas themselves have been tested and found lacking for ethnographic purposes.

Second, as anthropology pursued its quest to be a respectable "science" it borrowed concepts, assumptions and explanatory logics from the physical sciences for use in understanding human behavior. Concepts which assumed human freedom or voluntarism, as many concepts from the pre-existent Christian folk anthropology did, were jettisoned as incompatible with a scientific treatment of humankind. Note, for example, Christopher Herbert's (1991:42) treatment of E. B. Tylor and the origin of the culture concept:

> [In] Tylor's *Primitive Culture* . . . rhetorical stress is laid upon promoting "the general study of human life as a branch of natural science"--as a study from which religious values have been wholly evacuated, in other words. ...Tylor predicts that even what appear to be the "most spontaneous and motiveless phenomena" of social life will prove to be subject to laws as definite as those of mechanics; what is disparagingly called "the popular notion of free human will" will be exploded. "The tendency of modern enquiry," says Tylor, "is more and more towards the conclusion that if law is anywhere, it is everywhere" (*PC* 1:2,18,3,24). . . The conclusion to which these juxtapositions of texts point is that the emergence of the scientific doctrine of culture may best be described not as a process of dispassionate investigation of evidence . . . but as a complex and sometimes insidious reconfiguring of moral and religious ideas, in fact of a whole sensibility, at a historical point of crisis.

With this anthropological or "scientific" reconfiguring of ideas and assumptions came an intellectual climate inhospitable to older "anthropological" concepts implying human freedom or voluntarism-- concepts such as that of sin. Thus sociologist Stanford Lyman (1989:119) writes:

The rise and proliferation of the sciences of man . . . have been attended by the fall and the contraction of the idea of sin. Perhaps most significant in this movement has been the philosophical victory in the minds of most educated persons of determinism over freedom. Once man was relieved of full responsibility for his deeds, once dark forces of the mind, of history, of heredity, or of culture were found to shape his thought and shackle his reason, sin with its insistence on the freedom of the will to choose between good and evil had to retreat into the recesses of a suspect theology . . . Through the bloodless language of the new sciences the sins are neutralized.

The general patterns which Lyman points to in this area, may be discerned in the development of the discipline of anthropology as well.

A third factor explaining anthropology's resistance to developing certain concepts and lines of thought is the discipline-wide commitment to relativism. Sol Tax (1978:8) writes:

Whatever propensities and values may unite and distinguish anthropologists, first among them is a view of life that is relativistic . . . We are the only profession, or even community, for which this view of life is definitive. . . It must be kept in mind that anthropology is a free association. Nobody has to stick with it, or with us. Hence the self-selection for propensities and values becomes confirmed by association, . . books, . . contacts with fellow students (etc.).

Sol Tax is suggesting that what the anthropological community shares is not just a scientific method or a specific subject matter but a set of value orientations best summarized as a commitment to relativism. He suggests the existence of a self-selection process whereby those most attracted to relativism are most likely to become anthropologists, but he only hints at mechanisms of social exclusion and control that are also operative within the social institutions connected with anthropology, an important topic we unfortunately cannot pursue here.

One effect of the commitment to relativism has recently been pinpointed by Robert Edgerton in his book *Sick Societies: Challenging the Myth of Primitive Harmony* (1992) as a consistent tendency on the part of anthropologists to under-report the dark sides of life in folk societies and to present idealized or even romanticized portraits of the people being described. Furthermore, relativists are not inclined to dispassionately consider the use of concepts and categories (such as those stressed by theology) which put the focus squarely on the moral dimensions of human life--which focuses research attention on people as moral agents who act in ways moral and immoral.

When anthropologists do fieldwork, they listen as people talk about the moral rights and duties of husband and wife, father and son, mother's brother and sister's son. They listen to gossip about the moral failings of others, about those who are stingy with food when they ought to be generous, of those who are lazy and do not contribute their share. They overhear parental admonitions, warnings, and moral harangues at youth whose transgressions threaten to dishonor their family's reputation. Sentiments of gratitude, of disapproval, of resentment, of love, of feeling hurt, and of obligation or responsibility are the stuff of day-to-day interactions and discourse. Interpersonal conflicts with their accusations, expressions of indignation, jealous defense of marital rights, and expressions of guilt, remorse, and shame are universally present.

Yet anthropologists have fairly consistently refused to utilize an analytical vocabulary appropriate to the sociocultural interpersonal order as a moral order. They have borrowed concepts from physics, mathematics, and the biological sciences to the exclusion and neglect of other equally viable concepts, concepts that, if used, would call our attention to the moral dimensions of life. I suggest that the anthropological value commitment to relativism has served to block conceptual development in the direction of the ethico-moral dimensions of life cross-culturally.

Those few anthropologists who have attempted studies along these lines invariably stress that their efforts involve an unusual departure from normative anthropology. Thus Fürer-Haimendorf begins his *Morals and Merit: A Study of Values and Social Controls in South Asian Societies* by wondering why anthropologists, unlike moral philosophers, "have rarely concentrated on the investigation of moral ideas and their effect on behavior." He continues, "Few accounts of anthropological fieldwork deal specifically with problems of morality, and ethical values are usually discussed only in connection with such subjects as religion, kinship, and social controls" (1967:2). More recently, in his introduction to *The Anthropology of Evil* (1985), David Parkin suggests that "While moral philosophy is big industry," anthropologists are characterized by a "reluctance . . . to study other people's ethical systems" and by a "shyness to say what they understand by morality beyond that it is a form of socially sanctioned behavior" (1985:4).

Perhaps the best known historical contribution of anthropologists to moral reflection has been the assertion of the relativist dogma that there is no basis of appeal to any ideals or values beyond those already affirmed within a society--that there is no such thing as inalienable human rights, for example, only such rights as any society may choose to give. It is somewhat surprising, then, to find the American Anthropological Association invoking a concept from moral discourse (the notion of "rights") as the focal theme of its 1994 annual meetings in Atlanta. Anthropologists now wish to invoke moral language, something they rather often have condemned others for doing, and they do so without ever having worked very hard to generate systematic understandings of the arena of ethics and morality in other cultures. And so, we as anthropologists selectively latch on to one particularly ethnocentric strand of moral thinking in our own culture, one way of conceptualizing morality, and elevate it to a preeminent position at our annual meetings. I suggest that what we need instead is a broader research agenda focusing on the moral dimensions of life which would give broader intellectual foundations for anthropologists who would wish to invoke, or simply understand, moral language. The time would seem to be ripe for this.

Let's take one representative concept from theology, and look briefly at it, the concept of sin. When anthropologists do refer to this concept, they typically do so in ways which distance themselves from its use, suggesting for example that this is a concept employed by missionaries—a concept opposite to relativism, which is what anthropologists stand for. Thus, in his 1975 presidential address to the American Anthropological Association, Walter Goldschmidt (1979:296) stated, "Missionaries are in many ways our opposites; they believe in original sin." If sin somehow represents a pivotal missionary concept, then what is the concept that orients anthropologists in an opposite direction? The answer would seem to be relativism. Cohen and Eames' anthropology text (1982:376) makes this explicit:

> The premises of missionary work are directly opposite to those of anthropology. As cultural relativists, anthropologists begin with the assumption that any cultural system is as good or bad as any other system.

Missionaries on the other hand, they explain, condemned "native customs" as "sinful." Roger Keesing's anthropology text also contrasts anthropologists and missionaries and pinpoints the use of the concept of sin as what he finds particularly objectionable about missionaries, "The concept of sin must rank with smallpox among our most damaging exports" (1981:40). Similar comments appear often in the literature.

But a more positive usage of the term has not been completely absent from anthropology. Marcel Mauss taught a course on sin and expiation at the Collége de France (Dumont 1970:140). Robert Hertz (1922), Irving Hallowell (1939), Evans-Pritchard (1956), Fürer-Haimendorf (1974), and

Burkhart (1989) have all written articles or chapters on sin with many good insights.

But even when anthropologists use the concept of sin, they may be faulted on a number of grounds. The concept as used in theology is a cover term inclusive of any moral wrong-doing, including criminal acts, though not limited to them. Modern secular western culture has tended to drop the language of sin as cover term (using other terms such as crime for many acts, such as homicide) and only employing the term sin where no other term can be employed. That is, the term sin, in secular culture is a residual category speaking of what religion (or God) condemns but which society does not act to sanction. Most anthropologists seem to have followed this secularized usage. It should not surprise us then, to discover that not many cultures have concepts which call attention to a special class of moral transgressions which are unsanctioned by humans, only by the gods. And if we insist on limiting our usage of sin to such a residual category, then we will conclude that the concept has only limited utility anthropologically. But if we return to an older usage of sin as cover term for moral evil we will find comparable concepts perhaps in every culture.

The English word sin, as dictionaries indicate, is a religious term--a term with reference to God. And so, when Fürer-Haimendorf (1974) examines many cultures to see whether those cultures have words for "sin," he, like many missionaries, concludes that these people do not even have a word for sin, from which he concludes that neither must they have a sense of sin. When missionaries from amongst my own students make such pronouncements about the languages of given cultures lacking a word for sin, my immediate response is to reply that neither did the Hebrew or Greek languages (the languages of *The Bible*) have a "word for sin," if by "a word for sin" we mean a word with the exact same range of meaning as our English word sin. What the Hebrews and the Greeks had was many words for moral evil--none of which was used exclusively in religious contexts. That is, words from everyday life speaking of moral fault or failure--words which were used of failure with respect to persons and human laws were also used to speak of failure with reference to God and his laws. Thus in Hebrew *chata'* (חָטָא) meant "to miss the mark" and was used of slingshots missing the mark as well as of human acts violative of moral relationships. It is often translated into English as sin. *`Avar* (עָבַר) meant literally "to cross over" and was normally used in a literal and non-moral sense. But when the law or a command (of God or king) was violated it was like someone stepping over a moral boundary or line, and so `avar was used of this moral delict-- and translated into English as transgression or sin. *`Awah* (עָוָה) means "to bend or twist" and is used both of bent or twisted physical objects and of "twisted" moral character--translated often as iniquity or sin. Altogether some 20 Greek and Hebrew words with root images of disgust, rebellion, treachery, of going astray, of harm, etc. are translated as sin, iniquity or transgression in our English *Bibles*. None of these were used in an exclusively religious sense. But over time "sin" became an exclusively religious term--a term speaking of moral failure in relationship to God. Then anthropologists and missionaries, with no sense of the culturo-religious history of these terms, tell us the startling truth that many cultures do not have a word for sin--failing to recognize that the very cultures from which we derive our term "sin" did not have "a word for sin," but many words for sin, none with the precise range of meaning of our current English word sin.

It is best then if we think of sin, not as a metaphysical concept, but as a sensitizing concept, as a working tool orienting us to comparable areas in other cultures. Just as many anthropologists have recently been studying emotion vocabulary, so one can study the vocabulary of moral evil. In my own fieldwork I discovered the Aguaruna-Jívaro of Peru to have a rich set of concepts applied to moral evil.

At the most general level is *pegkegchau*--bad. Anything ugly, deformed, dirty, bad-tasting, damaged, or worthless is *pegkegchau*. But when used of people it is almost invariably a term of moral reprobation. Stinginess, theft, adultery, incest, laziness, slander and every other reprobated behavior may be condemned as *pegkegchau*.

Tudau is another term of moral disapproval, carrying exclusively moral connotations--used to characterize anyone engaged in active transgressions such as that of incest, bestiality, wife-beating, adultery, sexual exhibitionism, theft and above all, complaining about the food one's wife or mother has prepared. But it is never used of less active character traits such as stinginess, gluttony, or laziness--though these are morally condemned.

To be *yajau* is to be cruel, brutish, malicious, and without normal moral scruples. Anyone who beats his own mother, wife, child or dog from anger is *yajau*. One who is *yajau*, I was told, maliciously kills his neighbor's animals, offers his own sister to a passing stranger, molests women at night and draws or carves images of female genitals on earth or tree. A woman who kills her own infant in anger, who beats her children, or who is constantly actively pursuing sexual affairs is *yajau*.

Katsek has the underlying idea of ruin, harm, damage, destruction. It is used when one accidentally breaks a pot or burns down a house or when a dog or chicken threatens to contaminate one's food. But it is also used of adultery, theft, lies, homicide, fighting and most disapproved behaviors--with the implication that these acts are damaging to others or to the community at large. *Katsek* tends to be used with strong affect, frequently accompanied by vigorous exclamations of dismay, alarm or indignation.

An animal born with an extra leg, a baby chick with two beaks, two bananas in one banana peel, someone with a clubbed foot, six toes on a foot, with one eye, a deformed ear, a hare-lip, etc. is *detse*. *Detse* clearly carries with it the idea of failure to conform to some ideal form. But the term is also used to characterize individuals who fail to conform to moral ideals--to appropriate Aguaruna character traits. Thus perpetual liars, thieves, disobedient children, women who actively pursue affairs, and men who continually approach women's beds at night are also stigmatized as *detse*.

Tsuwat literally means "something filthy," but is invoked continuously as a term for moral evil. Slander is referred to as *tsuwat chicham* (dirty speech) and the slanderer as *tsuwat wenintin* (one with a dirty mouth). *Tsuwat anentaintin* (the dirty hearted one) is one who, to outward appearance, has correct moral sentiments, but is inwardly malevolent. One who commits adultery or steals is said to be one who "works filth" (*tsuwat takaamu*).

Tsumain means "disgusting" and is typically used of foul smells, of decaying corpses and feces, and of any creature which comes in contact with such items--notably vultures, possums, maggots, flies, and dung beetles. But *tsumain* is also used of any especially reprehensible moral act, particularly of a sexual nature. Incest and bestiality are particularly stigmatized as *tsumain*, but so is any man who is overly desirous of sex--even if with his own wife.

Antuchu literally means "doesn't listen," but it is used to characterize anyone who is disobedient or who refuses to attend to moral correction and instruction. Anyone who habitually violates right order as set forth by parents and ancestral tradition is *antuchu*. A sexually promiscuous woman may be characterized as *kugkatan antuchu*. *Kugkatan* is a compound word joining the word for an enticing smell (*kug-*) with the word for penis (*katan*). Sexual desire, in Aguaruna culture is rather consistently symbolized in terms of attraction to an attractive odor. Thus a sexually promiscuous woman is characterized as *kugkatan antuchu*, as one who "doesn't listen because of the enticing smell of the penis."

Space does not permit further exploration of terms. But what is clear is that the Aguaruna have a very rich vocabulary of moral condemnation--as rich, one suspects, as that of the ancient Hebrews.

A coherent, sustained research agenda designed to produce cross-culturally valid understandings of humankind in relation to the moral dimensions of life is currently lacking in anthropology. Such a research agenda would need to include a systematic study of:

1. <u>The moral vocabulary of diverse cultures</u>. This would include broad cover terms for moral evil as given above (see also Evans-Pritchard 1956:177-196), but also detailed vocabulary for more specific moral domains. Take the domain of over-eating in Aguaruna culture, for example. Aguaruna vocabulary with respect to gluttony is extensive. *Suji* literally means stingy, but is most often applied to those who fail to share what food they have and who eat more than their share. It is a serious charge to accuse someone of being *suji*. *Yawetchau* and *mijamchau* are used both of gluttony and of insatiable and unrestrained sexual desire. With the negative suffix -*chau* added to the root *yawet* (tired, worn out) comes *yawetchau*, literally, "one who does not tire." The notion, informants noted, was of "one who does not tire of eating or of sex." Again, when the negative suffix -*chau* is added to *mijamu* (calm) we have a term *mijamchau* suggestive of desire which cannot be satiated or calmed. The underlying idea is that of insatiability, both sexual and oral. The phrase "*mijamchau yutanum*"--"insatiable in eating" is sometimes used to make it clear if oral gluttony alone is in view. *Chakumin* refers to those who eat loudly and quickly with mouth open like a pig or other animal. Though explicitly referring to a style of eating, this term implies gluttony since anyone who eats in this unrestrained fashion is deemed gluttonous as well. *Ushu* refers to strong hunger but is most commonly used not of simple hunger but of gluttonous hunger. "*Ushu aipa*," "Don't be a glutton," parents tell their children. Those who eat a lot, especially of valued food items like meat, eat quickly, and finish off everything given them, are *ushu*, gluttons. *Etsemjau* is a narrower term than *ushu*. *Etsemjau* speaks of gluttony for one item, meat, and may be translated as "meat-glutton." Meat is the primary source of protein, and a relatively scarce commodity. Norms governing the consumption of meat are extremely rigorous. Meat should never be eaten by itself. The ideal way in which meat is eaten involves eating a small piece of meat accompanied by a large bite of manioc or plantain. Children are vigorously scolded for not eating in this manner. If a child fails to eat in this way, and eats its allotted meat too quickly, a parent scolds, "*apatua yuata!*" -- "Eat it joined together!" or more simply "*apatuata!*"--"join it together!" To eat pure meat, to eat large quantities of meat, to eat it prior to its being adequately cooked (out of impatience), or to eat it while all alone, is to merit the charge of being a meat-glutton, of being *etsemjau*. In Aguaruna mythology and belief being

etsemjau is closely linked to being a cannibal. To accuse someone of being *etsemjau* is a very serious charge.

2. Patterns of cultural symbolism in the arena of morality and moral discourse. Filth imagery frequently appears in moral discourse in cultures around the world. It often accompanies moral interdictions. Thus English-speaking parents may interdict certain books or words as "dirty." Those who violate norm may themselves be treated as dirty. For example, the Aguaruna insist that the incestuous have maggots on their fingers and in their mouths and so cannot be allowed to eat or drink communally with others. Since communal eating and/or drinking is central to almost all social events this denial of commensality, under imagery of filth, effectively removes such transgressors from normal life. Filth appears in discourse, mythology, ritual, and religion in cultures around the world in ways which closely link it symbolically with moral evil. This linkage of sin and defilement/impurity/filth has long been stressed by theologians. Paul Ricoeur's *The Symbolism of Evil* (1967) draws on such theological traditions in his superb exploration of the linkage of impurity and moral evil. Yet systematic explorations of filth symbolism in relation to the moral are virtually non-existent in anthropology (for exceptions see Burkhart 1989 and Priest 1993).

Again, moral discourse in cultures around the world invokes imagery of debt in contexts of moral failure, or of moral obligation. Often such imagery is central in cultural contexts where morality is conceptualized with reference to interpersonal reciprocity rather than with reference to laws or abstract universal ethical principles. While guilt as defilement suggests removal by purification rites, guilt as debt suggests removal by gift-giving.

Various other patterns of cultural symbolism with close ties to morality and moral discourse could be pinpointed. For example, moral discourse often invokes imagery of animality or cannibal gluttony as symbolic of excessive desire not under moral constraint. Or again, the primary place where witchcraft and the evil eye exist is in moral discourse. And while both have certainly been well-studied by anthropologists, it is worth stressing that they have not often enough been studied with reference to moral discourse as a whole, of which they are a part.

3. Comparative ethics which explore universal and discretionary features of ethical systems. Of relevance here is the extensive treatment historically by theologians both of natural law and of the distinction between *synderesis* and *conscientia*. *Synderesis* was that part of conscience which recognized *a*

priori, intuitively obvious, fundamental moral principles. Theologians differed over whether such moral principles were innate or learned. But they agreed that such moral truths as the idea of natural law (i.e. the idea that there is an objective difference between right and wrong) or of justice (that similar actions by similar agents under similar conditions merit similar reward or punishment) were *a priori* and intuitively obvious truths--as against second order principles which were contingent on circumstances, reason, and cultural conventions. The first order moral principles of *synderesis* were thought to differ from second order moral principles, by:

> priority, independence, universality, and certainty ("anyone who were to doubt them would upset the whole natural order and strip himself of his humanity") (Greene 1991:217).

Conscientia combined the infallible major premises of *synderesis* with contingent and fallible minor premises as the basis for practical action. The variable and fallible nature of conscience was due, then, to variability and fallibility in the minor premises, not the major.

Whatever the weaknesses of such theological reflections, they nonetheless raise important issues worth exploring today. Potts (1980:71) concludes his treatment of conscience in medieval thought:

> many . . . debates have turned out, in retrospect, to be cul-de-sacs, resting from the start upon assumptions which, once rejected, have made the debate seem largely irrelevant . . . . The medieval discussion of conscience is not in that category; . . . the questions do not have to be rejected: at most, some re-formulation is required.

The questions here raised by theologians are worthy of being explored. Furthermore, anthropologists, due to their subject matter, are ideally positioned to explore these issues: that is, to explore universal and variable features of ethical systems. Yet anthropologists have, with but few exceptions (for one notable exception see Shweder, Mahapatra, and Miller 1990), contributed remarkably little to such an exploration.

4. <u>Human impulses and propensities which move people to violate norms and persons</u>. Meyer Fortes (1983:23) writes:

> I do not think it would now be denied that aggressive and destructive propensities are deeply ingrained in the nature of man . . . . [T]heir prevalence in human society from time immemorial is well-established. . . . And the problem of controlling these propensities has been perennial.

But while an occasional anthropologist such as Bronislaw Malinowski, Robert Edgerton, or Meyer Fortes, acknowledges the pervasive presence of such "deeply ingrained propensities," and while Fortes feels confident that others will not deny this truth, the fact remains that anthropologists (with the partial exception of Freudians and sociobiologists) have not generally been interested in researching and exploring such asocial impulses or propensities.

Theologians, on the other hand, have had no such inhibitions. Under the rubric on the seven cardinal (or deadly) sins, theologians of an earlier era, generated extensive analyses and reflections of destructive, "sinful," human impulses.

Envy was one such sin. But if in an earlier era under the tutelage of theologians envy was widely recognized and discussed as a perennial problem of human nature, under the reign of the social sciences people "found envy an increasingly embarrassing concept to use as an explanatory category or in reference to social fact" (Schoeck 1969:12). In his classic study of envy, German sociologist Helmut Schoeck said that his examination of the subject indexes of major anthropological and sociological journals turned up not a single reference to envy, and argued that the social sciences have "repressed" the concept of envy, disguising the phenomena of envy with concepts such as ambivalence, aggression, tension, rivalry, etc. (Schoeck 1969:9-11, 17, 134-59). Schoeck (1969:128) hypothesizes:

A disinclination to concern oneself with envy may also be connected with the following: Almost without exception all research concerning man has, when faced by envy, seen it as a serious disease.

That is, Schoeck suggests that social scientists have a peculiar aversion to acknowledging the presence of asocial or "evil" impulses or propensities within people, an aversion not generally shared by theologians.

In his classic article on envy and envy avoidance, George Foster (1972:165) agrees with Schoeck that envy seems to have been a taboo topic in anthropology and the social sciences. But although Schoeck's book and Foster's article clearly demonstrated that envy is a universal and pervasive reality and that envy and the fear of envy are central to all sorts of social and cultural patterns, envy remains marginal to most anthropological treatments of culture.

Gluttony was also a cardinal sin. But while theologians taught us to think about food in moral terms, anthropologists developed other lines of thought. Thus, as I commenced fieldwork in the Amazon, in accord with my anthropological training I thought of food in terms of subsistence strategies, technology, and resources for meeting nutritional requirements (carbohydrates, proteins, fats, etc.) in the ecological setting of the tropical rain forest. Yet soon I encountered a moral discourse focusing extensively on gluttony *vs.* restraint--gluttony not as a sin against the self (as many overweight Americans might conceptualize it) but as a failure to exercise restraint on behalf of others. In a well-developed vocabulary of gluttony, in myth, in ritual, in food taboos, and in family and interpersonal relations, the evils of gluttonous impulses were highlighted. Indeed vocabulary and symbolism from the moral arena of food provided the templates on which moral discourse concerning homicide or sexual transgression was modeled (cf. Priest 1993:172-243). Anthropologists have not generally explored the types of things explored by theologians under the rubric of gluttony. But this cannot be attributed to a lack of such moral realities or concerns in the societies studied by anthropologists.

At least one sociologist (Lyman 1989) and one psychologist (Schimmel 1992) have recently contributed books on the seven deadly sins (see also Fairlie 1979; Capps 1987), suggesting that a revisiting of these older theological concepts has the potential for adding to, and correcting, their disciplines' present understandings of human realities. There is every reason to suppose that anthropology, too, could benefit from interaction with these older discourses about the dark sides of human nature.

Other research topics of relevance to an adequate cross-culturally valid understanding of people in the moral dimensions of their lives might include an examination of: the relations of religion to morality (both in terms of sanctions and justifications of morality)[1], the many ways in which ethico-moral ideals and standards are transmitted and inculcated, social responses to transgression (punishment, shaming, social exclusion, etc.), morally relevant sentiments (empathy, love, anger, indignation, guilt, shame, honor, etc.)[2], the various actions which transgressors who harm others or violate rules take to frame or deal with their transgressions (excuses, justifications, apologies, prestations, confessions), etc.

Most of these topics have been understudied by anthropologists. When such topics have been studied they are often studied as a marginal part of some other research agenda. Seldom do such occasional treatments of certain of these topics give evidence that the author is adequately interacting with the relevant broader literature. Seldom, if ever, do we find anthropologists attempting to master the full range of topics essential for an adequate understanding of people as moral beings--topics such as those outlined above. One searches catalogues from departments of anthropology in vain for courses which attempt to pull together such understandings in a single focused setting. A coherent, sustained research agenda designed to produce cross-culturally valid understandings of humankind in relation to the moral dimensions of life is currently lacking in anthropology.

All of these closely related topics have extensive overlap with subjects treated historically in theology. It is my contention that such subjects have been under-investigated and underdeveloped by anthropologists, in part, because of a reactionary stance towards Christian "folk anthropology," that any effort to study such topics while by-passing theology will weaken the enterprise--while a more positive, less adversarial, relation to such historical domains in our own culture as theology has potential for strengthening anthropology as a discipline as it endeavors to construct better understandings of people in the moral dimensions of their lives.

Notes

1. My comments earlier about anthropologists going astray in linking "sin" too closely to religion should not be taken as denying that there often is a close link between religion and the moral. The question of whether and to what extent moral norms carry religious sanctions and are justified with reference to religion and the supernatural is a very important research question. But it is a sub-set of a larger set of issues, not the end point of research where research ceases once any discontinuity with Western Christian concepts is discovered. It is the latter to which I objected.
2. Philosophers interested in metaethics or normative ethics have long sought for some universal core to ethics and have looked for that core in certain universal moral rules. Increasingly many philosophers are abandoning this quest as a dead end, and suggesting instead that better candidates for moral universals are certain universal moral dispositions. Richard Shweder (1990:210) would seem to agree. He writes:

What are the good candidates for moral universals? For one thing, there are certain feelings, the morally relevant emotions--repugnance, shame, anger, guilt, indignation, shock, dread, pride, empathy, and the feelings of being "lowered" or "elevated," "dirtied" or stained, sanctified or cleansed. Those feelings form part of a rational response to a perceived transgression and may well constitute an ultimate aim of moral codes--to preserve and enhance the spiritual dignity of persons.

Chapter 3

Crossing the Great Divide: What Anthropologists Might Learn from Theology

Morton Klass

When for the first time one contemplates the fusion of theological and anthropological insights, it is astonishing how many issues call out for discussion, clarification, and illumination.[1] Let me address, to begin with, what is arguably the most significant one of all: Why has the discipline of anthropology, in its inquiries into the institution of religion, been so reluctant to seek advice and even guidance from theology and theologians?

Reluctant is perhaps too mild a term. Consider the following:

> Ordinarily in a scientific work the conclusions of theologians are ignored. They are somewhat more relevant in the case of primitive religion... (Goode 1964: 249)

> [T]he only systematic and serious criticism of ...preanimistic and magical theories has been made by the well-known Austrian priest and theorist, W. Schmidt. Many of his strictures are quite pertinent. But he is so obviously a Catholic apologist that their force is thereby greatly diminished. In spite of his admittedly great critical powers one is, *quite naturally*, deeply suspicious of his treatment of the facts... (Radin 1957: 76 italics mine).

> Divine revelation as an explanation of religious genesis has no place in this book, and under ordinary circumstances all theological interpretations of the origin of religion would be dismissed from consideration as *irrelevant or prejudicial* (Norbeck 1961: 22 italics mine).

Anthropologists are not usually quite so inhospitable to scholars who labor in other vineyards: we have consulted biologists and psychologists, economists and political scientists and even philosophers -- along with students of literature, music, dance and the graphic arts. Moreover, we continue to do so even when we find the results of the consultation somewhat unsatisfying. Why not theologians?

Perhaps we feel that anthropology -- an academic discipline with pretensions to being a science -- might lose repute in the eyes of other academics if word of such association got out. There can be, so it appears the feeling goes, no rapprochement possible between theologians and us -- that is, between the conclusions arrived at by adherents of particular religious belief systems -- and those engaged in what is supposed to be a rational scholarly enterprise. In addition, as I have suggested elsewhere, anthropologists, like other contemporary scholars, clearly adhere to the "scientistic" assumption "that a *scientific* explanation or interpretation invariably takes priority over, or is superior to, all others" (Klass 1995: 10; and see Beattie 1964: 203).

Whatever the sources of this neglect, it is certainly high time we changed our behavior -- and so Robert J. Priest's challenge in his paper in this volume is a welcome one; truly a wake-up call. By introducing theological perspectives on *sin*, for example, he is able to show us dimensions and aspects of the concept hitherto unconsidered by anthropologists and perhaps, given our mind sets, inherently inaccessible for us.

Thus, Priest argues, anthropologists, like other non-theological scholars, have assumed that the term *sin* refers only to that which receives condemnation solely from religion (or God) and not from society. What then of the things *society* disapproves of and acts to sanction? These are perceived, Priest observes, as *crimes* -- not *sins* -- and are reported on as such by anthropologists, presumably under the rubric of *law and order*. Why not, Priest asks, put aside the question of whether the behavior under consideration is or is not divinely and/or socially sanctioned, and focus instead on what in a given society is perceived to be a "moral evil" -- that is, a violation, presumably wilful and deliberate, of accepted propriety? Using this perfectly proper and perfectly acceptable definition of *sin*, Priest embarks upon a most illuminating analysis of the varieties and complexities of *sin* among the Aguaruno-Jivaro.

It would be useful to compare Priest's approach with that of another anthropologist -- one who avoids the term sin completely, and sees only *crimes*. In his examination of "the social function of anxiety" among the Saulteaux (a branch of the Ojibwa) of Manitoba, Canada, A. Irving Hallowell observes that, among the Saulteaux, "Disease situations of any seriousness carry the implication that something wrong has been done. Illness is the penalty" (Hallowell 1949: 377). This "penalty" is, in his view, "a social sanction":

> In this society, certain classes of sexual behavior (incest, the so-called perversions in heterosexual intercourse, homosexuality, autoerotism, bestiality), various kinds of aggressive behavior (cruelty to animals, homicide, cruelty toward human beings, the use of bad medicine to cause suffering, rough or inconsiderate treatment of the dead, theft and a number of ego injuries like insult and ridicule, failure to share freely, etc.), behavior prescribed by guardian spirits, the acquisition of power to render specialized services to others (i.e., curing or clairvoyance), all fall under a disease sanction (*Ibid.*:378).

Thus, for Hallowell, all of the foregoing are essentially "crimes" and -- since the Saulteaux lack courts or police or other state institutions for the punishment of crimes -- "insofar as individuals are motivated to avoid such acts through fear of disease, anxiety performs a distinct social function" (*Ibid.*: 379). Given this perspective, Hallowell can go on to explore the psychological dimensions of the anxiety precipitated by disease: how do we determine who has performed a proscribed act and by so doing brought disease among us?

But are these acts in fact *crimes* or are they really *sins*? Some, seeking a safe middle ground, might want to argue that the acts are a mixture of crimes (i.e., homicide, the use of bad medicines, etc.) **and** sins (i.e., bestiality, cruelty toward human beings, etc.). Perhaps -- but it is surely most significant that (as we learn from Hallowell's own account) *the Saulteaux themselves* consider **all** these acts to be sins! That is, while never actually using the dread word itself, Hallowell does note that the source of illness is, for the Saulteaux, "bad conduct" *(madjiijiwe baziwin)*, adding: "'Because a person does bad things, that is where sickness ... starts,' is the way one informant phrased it" (*Ibid.*: 380). Clearly, for the Saulteaux, if not for Hallowell, these acts all fall under Priest's rubric of "moral evil" -- the wilful violation of accepted propriety. Hallowell has in fact provided us with a detailed description of sin and its consequences among the Saulteaux, but he sidesteps the issue thoroughly and completely, preferring to deal only with the legal and psychological consequences of such actions.

And so again we find ourselves wanting to know why -- if *sin* is so clearly a useful concept -- anthropology has so neglected it? I suggest it is because the term smacks of the cloth: with *crime* we are on firmer, more secular ground but, as we have seen, we lose a lot.

There is certainly much more to be learned or pondered on when we contemplate *sin* as "moral evil:" as Priest observes, theologians want to know whether such *sin* is indeed "wilful and deliberate." Students of *crime* may ask similar questions (e.g., is the individual responsible, or is society?)

but the emphasis in *sin* is significantly different -- the issue is really not so much "responsibility" as it is "choice." Change *crime* to *sin* and we suddenly find ourselves asking: Does an individual in a given society actually **choose** impropriety or "moral evil?"

We might also inquire as to why the Saulteaux classify so many seemingly disparate acts under the single rubric of *sin*. Or **do** they, in fact? Might not someone like Priest have detected varieties of sins among what Hallowell has lumped together as crimes? And -- again -- what motivates people to perform such acts, given the inevitable penalty (illness to the transgressor or to a member of the transgressor's family) and the inevitable exposure and shame (the shaman's guardian spirits will identify the sinner who will be forced to make a detailed public confession before the illness can be cured)? Why, under such awful circumstances, do Saulteaux continue to *choose* "bad conduct?"

The issue of *sin*, we begin to see, takes its place within much wider anthropological disputes. For Priest, for example, it contributes to the "relativist" debate: is there, in his words, any "basis of appeal to any ideals or values beyond those already affirmed within a society" -- can there be "inalienable human rights," or only "such rights as any society may choose to give"?

There is of course much more to the "relativist" debate. Anthropologists have differed among themselves (and differed even more with other social scientists) about whether "cultural relativism" precludes any possibility of judgment about practices observed -- human or animal sacrifice, genital mutilation, discrimination and inequality and servitude, and so much else. A wide-ranging discussion is long-overdue -- at a scholarly symposium, perhaps, and/or in a volume similar to this one. If such a discussion is initiated, let us hope that theologians are invited, along with the usual crowd of anthropologists, sociologists, historians, and philosophers!

But let me here return to the subject of *choice*. Are sinners hapless victims of the gods (as in the case of Oedipus, and perhaps Job[2]) or are they responsible for their actions: Do they choose "bad conduct"?

Oddly, this is an area where anthropology may have something to contribute to theology! In recent years, there has been much debate among anthropologists about the nature and significance, when present, of "choice in marriage" and "choice in economic activities." The subject matter (*marriage* and *economics*) may seem at first glance far removed from the concerns of theology, but the underlying issues are, I believe, quite relevant.

The issue of "choice in marriage" precipitated much contention in a complex debate among French, British and American anthropologists.

Opinions differed sharply and even confusingly about, particularly, whether choice was present or even possible in the arrangement of certain kinds of marriage in certain societies. Thus, in his book *Structure and Sentiment* (1962), Rodney Needham took issue with George C. Homans and David M. Schneider on the implications of the views of Claude Lévi-Strauss on matrilateral cross-cousin marriage, as set forth in his classic work *Les Structures élémentaires de la Parenté* (1949).

Needham declared that Homans and Schneider so misunderstood Lévi-Strauss that, Needham felt impelled to say, "[their book's] conclusions are fallacious, its method unsound, and the argument literally preposterous" (Needham 1962: 1). He particularly objected to what he perceived as their inability to distinguish between "preferential" marriage (in which choice is possible) and "prescribed" marriage (in which it is not):

> The term "preferential" implies that there is choice, and in the context of marriage that there is a choice between a number of persons ... who may all be married. In this situation there may be a preference for one or more persons within the range of possibilities.... The term "prescriptive," on the other hand, has quite different connotations. In this case the emphasis is on the very lack of choice ... this marriage is obligatory (1962: 8-9).

To Needham's obvious discomfort,[3] however, Lévi-Strauss took issue with Needham, arguing that, from his perspective, there was in fact no significant difference between "prescriptive" and "preferential" (1969: xxvii-xxxv).

I have no wish to re-open that particular controversy; I refer to it here because the underlying point of contention is the presence and absence of choice. For Lévi-Strauss, it doesn't matter whether or not choice is present (for him, the only thing that matters is the presence, in any form, of *matrilateral cross-cousin marriage* whether preferred or required). The other scholars, however, are arguing about *choice*. Homans and Schneider, as Needham intimates, are really interested only in cases where such marriages may be opted for, while Needham is primarily interested in the cases where such marriages are prescribed and not optional.

The underlying issue here is: Why and how are spouses chosen? In a prescriptive system, there is no choice -- one marries the person (mother's brother's daughter, or whatever) the system prescribes. But what of the societies in which the individual has (or *thinks* he or she has!) the possibility of option? The debate between Needham and Homans and Schneider really comes down to the question of why, in such societies, we find people -- supposedly with "free choice" -- significantly frequently choosing one particular category of spouse over all the others.

Is it not clear, from the foregoing, that the observer's position on *choice* (like the observer's position on *sin vs crime*)_most materially affects one's observations and conclusions? Needham -- perhaps understandably, given his disinterest in choice -- seeks to limit or circumscribe its very applicability. He argues that the characterizations "preferential" and "prescriptive" should be used *only* in discussions of unilateral cross-cousin marriage (1962: 57). I have myself challenged this, arguing:

> [O]ne is reluctant to see the terms permanently restricted to the presence or absence of a single marriage rule....

> There is no reason, indeed, why these terms could not be utilized in examining the rules of other institutions and cultural rubrics, whenever what is under consideration is the limitation of choice -- the possibility of alternative (Klass 1966: 952).

Indeed, the question of "choice" is at issue in discussions of other institutions, most particularly that of *economics*. The problem for many students of economic anthropology (see, particularly, M. J. Herskovits [1952]) was that the formal study of economics was predicated upon an assumption of the universality of choice in economic transactions.[4] Karl Polanyi therefore proposed a "substantive" definition of economics -- "an instituted process of interaction between man and his environment which results in a continuous supply of want satisfying material means" -- to facilitate the examination of societies ("reciprocative" and "redistributive") in which choice was not present, or only *minimally* present (1957).

Let us observe that in all of these disputes remarkably similar questions arise: is there really such a thing as "free choice" in human behavior? What are the implications of the presence or absence -- in any human institution -- of the possibility of option or choice? If, in a given society and in a given institution *choice* is not conceived of as *possible* -- what are the consequences of taking unacceptable alternatives?

Following Priest's lead, we may raise additional questions. Would it not be unfair to speak of "moral evil" where it is agreed that choice is not present? For example, does a vampire "sin?" Take another step: If a prescribed marriage between cross cousins is a miserable one, whose "fault" is it? Are the implications of "choice" (its presence, absence, or limitations) the same for economic transactions, marital arrangement -- and for the commission of sins and crimes?

There is much else to be gained from a proper colloquy between anthropology and theology. Ethnographers are certainly interested in recording "native" accounts of "divine revelation" (as to origins, conduct, morality, etc.), but they have given astonishingly little attention to the nature of "revelation" itself.[5] Is "revelation" in a given society, for example, conceived of as "perfect" (i.e., the true and unchangeable divine edict) -- or is "cumulative" (subject to change or emendation by the divinities themselves)? Is the universe understood to be improving or "progressing") or is it continually and remorselessly "degenerating?"

When engaged in such inquiries, one must of necessity interview the theological personnel of the society under study, and this may lead to further explorations of how theological perspectives illuminate other aspects of culture. There is nothing new or surprising in all this: Do we not believe that, in field research, we should begin by consulting the "native sociologist?"

And, of course, we should not be surprised to discover that the "native sociologist" -- in this case the "native theologian" -- can represent many contending schools, just as in our own society, where there is indeed no one authoritative source of theology any more than there is of sociology or anthropology. Thus, Priest derives his theological perceptions from Christian theology -- which is fine, but there is also Jewish theology -- and Muslim and Hindu and Buddhist -- to name just a few!

Clearly, Robert J. Priest has opened the discussion: I look forward eagerly to the ensuing debate.

Notes

1. This paper began as a discussant's commentary on Robert J. Priest's paper, "Christian Theology, Sin, and Anthropology." Inevitably, as it was revised it wandered afield, but I want to express my gratitude to Robert Priest for the stimulation and inspiration his most interesting paper provided.
2. For an anthropological exploration of the similarities and differences between Job and Oedipus, see Fortes: *Oedipus and Job in West African Religion* ([1959] 1981).
3. See Needham's *Postscriptum* to the edition (1969) of the English translation (edited by Needham!) of *Les Structures élementaires* in which Lévi-Strauss asserts that Needham is in error – that, for Lévi-Strauss, both "prescription" and "preference" in fact "correspond to slightly differing ways in which man envisages the same reality" (1969: xxxi-xxxii).
4. How else could there be a "law of supply and demand"?
5. I pursue this charge in much greater depth in my book *Ordered Universes* (1995). See Chapter 2, for example.

Chapter 4

Feminist Spirituality, Theology, and Anthropology

M. Jean Heriot

In the fall of 1994, I heard a counselor, "Ryan," advise a woman in her fifties, "Sally." Sally was in deep despair about her current life situation: she lived alone and felt great loneliness. She was also angry about a forced early retirement and the ageism apparent in her ongoing job search. Ryan himself was the woman's contemporary: about fifty-something in age. He appeared somewhat callous in his response for he claimed that: "as we get older we must be prepared for the reality of loneliness in this culture--it's just a fact of life." When questioned by Sally about his stance, he predicted that the isolation would get worse rather than better as the baby boomer generation grew older. Many women and men know all too well the reality to which Ryan refers, but must his prediction come true?

As the difficulties associated with "modern life" escalate, more and more people are looking for alternative solutions to the problems posed by Sally. While many lay people and scholars alike feel helpless to change our social system,[1] members of a new religion, the feminist spirituality movement, have been seeking ways to address Sally's plight as well as the despair engendered by contemporary life. Feminist spirituality, originating in the United States of America in the early 1970s (Eller 1993a), is based on three over-arching strands of thought: 1) a critique of Western patriarchal culture; 2) a critique of Western Christianity; and 3) a revisioning or remaking of central core Western beliefs through the creation of new (or "revived") goddess(es), rituals, and myths centered on the empowerment of women. At its heart, practitioners of feminist spirituality believe that women will eventually be able to change the patriarchal social order to an egalitarian one in which connections among individuals, the social and physical world, and the divine (usually referenced as a goddess) are developed and enhanced. In this paper I briefly define the movement; explore the ways in which this movement draws on insights from a growing number of feminist theologians;[2] examine how these theological reflections are transformed, in ritual practice, into a fundamentally troubling paradox; and discuss how the discipline of anthropology is referenced by feminist spirituality. At the close of the paper, I draw on insights from feminist spirituality to critique the "typical" anthropological approach to the study of belief.

As an anthropologist who has studied the movement for the past five years, I have been able to observe the ways in which members of the movement frequently draw uncritically on both theology and anthropology. Recently, I have also become a religious studies scholar in training for an ecumenical ministry. This perspective has allowed me to see how practitioners of feminist spirituality do functionally offer profound commentaries, critiques, and alternative solutions to the problems faced by women such as Sally. In this paper, then, I situate myself in the nexus between a social science research perspective which asks questions about the social meaning and function of these religious beliefs and practices and a theological perspective which asks how do individuals organize their lives such that the divine becomes a part of who they are and how they live. In my own work on this movement, as anthropologist and religious scholar, I make the deliberate attempt to join my anthropological skepticism with my bedrock conviction that it matters what we believe.

The Socio-Cultural Characteristics of the Feminist Spirituality Movement

In May of 1991, I began a year's full-time systematic observations of feminist spirituality groups in upstate New York,[3] conducting participant observation and in-depth interviews with several ritual groups. Since then I have continued to observe the movement in two other settings: Princeton, New Jersey, and the San Francisco Bay area of California. From these ethnographic observations, I can offer a number of generalizations about the women who participate, the contexts in which the gatherings occur, and the theological frameworks invoked. But, first, I must also say something about what feminist spirituality is not because I have found that the movement is generally confused with other similar, but different contemporary religious movements.[4]

Though feminist spirituality arose partially from neopaganism, most researchers now consider the two movements as separate (Eller 1993a; Neitz 1990). Neopaganism is the term given to the resurgence in modern witchcraft practices, some of which are known as *wicca*. Scholars trace the beginnings of modern European and American witchcraft to the writing of Gerald Gardner who claimed to have received training from a witch coven that had survived in secret in England, passing down ancient practices from generation to generation (Eller 1993a:51).[5] After Gardner published *Witchcraft Today* in 1954, neopaganism spread rapidly across the British Isles and into America.   Its basic beliefs are earth based, with practitioners celebrating a number of earth holidays, including full moon ceremonies, solstices, and equinoxes.   While feminist spirituality borrowed many of these rituals, its use of these rituals is different.   Among the more important differences are the following contrasts as developed by Eller (1993a) and Neitz (1990).   In neopaganism there is usually a formal initiation ceremony after a period of study; in feminist spirituality, there is no formal initiation.   Practitioners in feminist spirituality are located solely by their choice to affiliate with one or more groups.   In neopaganism practitioners are both male and female, and most ceremonies require that there be males and females present to represent male gods and female goddesses respectively.   In feminist spirituality, practitioners are usually women only (Eller 1993a).

Finally, in neopaganism there are usually hierarchical distinctions made among the practitioners while in feminist spirituality there are generally no hierarchical distinctions.   Instead, the overwhelming emphasis is on the equality of all.   The newest practitioner is thus able to contribute simply on the basis of her experience as a woman.

Feminist spirituality, while it shares many beliefs and practices with some practitioners of the New Age movement, is not "New Age."   It is, however, not easy to separate the two movements as there is a great deal of overlap not only in belief systems, but also in adherents.   When I first began research on the movement, I saw feminist spirituality as one aspect of the "New Age" movement.   However, as I continued to do research, I found many problems with that characterization based on my observations.   I also discovered that, in general, non-feminist scholars tend to place feminist spirituality in the context of the New Age, while feminist scholars see the movement as separate (Bednarowski 1992; Eller 1993a).[6]   I separate the two movements since my research indicates that New Age practitioners tend to be focused on a dualistic separation of mind and body.   New Agers view the goal of humanity as the transcendence of the material world.   Neither of these trends is representative of feminist spirituality which attempts to transcend the mind/body split by honoring the physical aspect of women's bodies including such biological processes as menstruation and childbirth.   In addition, feminist spirituality adherents want to see changes in the social order that are manifested in the here and now, though they often have only a vague conception of how those changes will come about.

Finally, feminist spirituality is not the same as the Christian Woman-Church movement described by Ruether (1985; 1993). In the Woman-Church movement, women and men stay within the Christian tradition and attempt to reform its beliefs and practices. But feminist spirituality practitioners eschew the use of Christian terms in their practices, even if, as is often the case, they also belong to Christian churches. Instead of the Christian trinity of god the father, Jesus Christ the son, and the holy ghost, feminist spirituality practitioners reference in their rituals various manifestations of the goddess.[7] She is often seen as a kind of earth mother, as the creator of the universe, as a caring and awe-inspiring manifestation of power. She is also usually seen as an immanent, accessible divine figure who both exists in the external world and as a kind of divine "spark" or presence within each woman. This "goddess in everywoman" (Bolen 1984) contrasts sharply in the speech of these women with a Christian transcendent, inaccessible divinity. Loosely characterized as the divine feminine, the goddess may be thought of by practitioners as a single deity, though more often than not, the divinity actually referenced in any ceremony is plural.[8]

In saying what feminist spirituality is not, I have also given some information on what it is: it is a religion based on some form of belief in the divine feminine; it is based on rituals that were developed to honor the cycles of the sun, moon, and earth, and the cycle of seasons; it honors women's bodies as well as their souls; and its practitioners usually gather in small, non-hierarchical groups consisting only of women. Other aspects of the movement's belief system will be discussed in the sections on "New Theological Insights" and on "Ritual Practice."

Who are the women who participate and how big is the movement? In general the women are white, well-educated, and of middle class origins according to Eller (1993a): a finding borne out by my research as well. Though numbers are difficult to estimate, some observers indicate that members of alternative religious traditions, of which feminist spirituality is but one, may constitute as much as seven percent of the general population (Albanese 1988) and as much as twenty-five percent of the San Francisco Bay area population (Lewis 1992:3). Among the many alternative belief systems, it is even more difficult to estimate the numbers of feminist spirituality adherents because so many have the perception that they should keep their activities secret from the dominant patriarchal society surrounding them. While there are no good estimates, my fieldwork in three states (California, New Jersey, and New York) and my observations in two others

(Mississippi and Oklahoma) indicate that the movement has large numbers of followers and that it is growing.

New Theological Insights

The theologian Bednarowski defines the work of theology in broad terms (1989; 1993) and believes that theological interpretations should not be reserved solely for "the explication and interpretation of specific doctrines, particularly Christian doctrines" (1989:x). Instead, she argues that theology entails the examination of the ways in which humans order "reality in light of that which the particular system understands as the ultimate measure all things--that which is the measure of all else"(1989:x). Thus she analyzes several nineteenth and twentieth century religious movements (for example, Christian Science and Mormonism) for the ways: 1) in which they order their world religiously, and 2) how they answer questions "about God or ultimate reality, about evil, human nature, the world, death, and the requirements for living a moral life" (1989:xi). She situates these theologies in cultural context and addresses how these movements built on earlier theological interpretations and offered new answers.

In my estimation, as well as her own, Bednarowski's approach is unusual because she is willing to expand her definitions of theology to include what ordinary people have to say about theological reflections (Bednarowski, personal communication, Nov. 11, 1994). She refuses to tie her interpretations solely to traditional theological avenues and to traditional means of interpretations. Thus theology reflects "the creativity of the human spirit, attempting to find its way in the face of ever new problems and crises arising in life" (Kaufman cited in Bednarowski 1993: 211). Bednarowski's eclectic approach is valuable in interpreting feminist theologians who move beyond the Christian and Jewish beliefs espoused by most contemporary American religious practitioners.

McFague has offered a typology to distinguish between the two main categories of feminist theology. She terms those feminist theologies who remain affiliated with established Christian or Jewish traditions "reformist" (McFague 1982).[9] Other feminist theologians, in her view, are "post-Christian" because they take the "revolutionary" stand that Christianity is no longer relevant and that it cannot be reformed from within (McFague 1982; see also Eller 1993b:172). Often overlapping with "revolutionary" feminist theologians are writers associated with the feminist spirituality movement. Representative theologians in this latter category include Starhawk, Zsuzsanna Budapest, and Mary Daly (Eller 1993a; 1993b). In addition, reformist and revolutionary feminist theologians may not appear, from the perspective of traditional theological interpretations, to even be "theologians." This perception is due to their eclecticism which frequently draws on art, music, and other forms of aesthetic expression. Bednarowski thus expands the category of theology to include the work of contemporary feminist artists who openly acknowledge their ties to feminist spirituality.[10]

While the reformists and revolutionary feminist theologians differ in their religious affiliations, they are alike in attempting to create "the resacralization of the cosmos and the re-imagining of the sacred," while offering critiques "of the established Western traditions and of Newtonian science as the primary desacralizers of the cosmos and of American culture" (Bednarowski 1992:168-69). These feminist writers stress the achievement of equality for all and the empowerment of women by the transformation of hierarchy, dualism, and economic exploitation to equality, connection, and some, as yet unspecified, better way of economic production and distribution.[1112.]

I focus here on the theologies of "revolutionary" feminists who have, according Eller, helped create feminist spirituality (1993a).   In my observations of the movement, the writers I have heard cited most frequently include: Margot Adler, Jean Bolen, Zsuzsanna Budapest, Carol Christ, Mary Daly, Riane Eisler, Clarissa Pinkola Estes, Maria Gimbutas, Judith Plaskow, Rosemary Radford Ruether, Starhawk, Diane Stein, Merlin Stone, and Barbara Walker.[12] Though all these writers are associated with feminist spirituality in the minds of the women I interviewed, they are representative of a wide spectrum of interests including Christian theology (Ruether), post-Christian theology (Budapest, Daly, Christ, Plaskow, Starhawk), and anthropology and history (Bolen, Eisler, Gimbutas, Stone). Furthermore, a number of these writers are also associated with neopaganism (Adler, Z. Budapest, Starhawk) and/or with "how-to-do-it" books about ritual (Z. Budapest, Starhawk, Stein, Walker). Each year more and more texts are being published in the field (see MacNichol and Walsh 1993).   The Canadian film series which includes "*The Burning Times*" is also cited quite often and shown in women's gatherings. From these, I have chosen to focus here on two authors whose works are intended to introduce women to the practice of feminist spirituality: Riane Eisler's *The Chalice and the Blade* (1988) with its accompanying guide, *The Partnership Way* (Eisler and Loye 1990); and Shirley Ranck's *Cakes for the Queen of Heaven*.[13] Eisler (1989) and Ranck (1986) begin by focusing on the acknowledged fact that women have less power than men in most societies worldwide. As a result, they argue, most history, archeology, and anthropology is suspect because it represents the dominant, male and more powerful point of view. Drawing on the archaeological work of Maria Gimbutas and others, these authors present a revisionist history of the world. For example, Eisler's book speaks of a time in human history when harmonious, tribal societies highly valued women and women's powers to bring forth new life. She claims that these egalitarian, earth mother worshiping "chalice" societies prevailed world-wide until just 7,000 years ago (Eisler 1988:43). At that point in time, Indo-European invaders who worshiped a sun-god swept across Europe with the "sword" or "blade" and brought in their wake hierarchy, dualism, war, and the repression of women (1989:43). She summarizes this transformation as follows:

The one thing they [the invaders] all had in common was a dominator model of social organization: a social system in which male dominance, male violence, and a generally hierarchic and authoritarian social structure was the norm. Another commonalty was that, in contrast to the societies that laid the foundations for Western civilization, the way they characteristically acquired material wealth was not to be developing technologies of production, but through ever more effective technologies of destruction (1989:43).[14]

The details of this history vary in other accounts, sometimes the invaders arrive at an earlier point in time, sometimes the development of patriarchy is viewed as developing from within society, but the general outlines of the revised history remain (Eller 1993:157). Eisler (1989) and Ranck (1986) concur that at one point people in general worshiped the divine in the form of the "goddess" and that the worship of the "goddess" was based on societies in which men and women were equal. It is important to note here that both Eisler and Ranck argue that there were egalitarian state-level societies which existed prior to this invasion. This claim is contrary to most anthropological assessments of the development of the state which presuppose that state level societies are intertwined with the development of both hierarchy and inequality.

Eisler claims that modern society is now at a turning point where it may be possible to shift the social world from its current dualism to a partnership world (Eisler 1989:198). Of this transformation, she notes:

The most dramatic change as we move from a dominator to a partnership world will be that we, and our children and grandchildren, will again know what it means to live free of the fear of war. In a world rid of the mandate that to be "masculine" men must dominate, and along with the rising status of women and more "feminine" social priorities, the danger of nuclear annihilation will gradually diminish. At the same time as women gain more equality of social and economic opportunities--so that birthrates can come into better balance with our resources--the Malthusian "necessity" for famine, disease, and war will progressively lessen. (Eisler 1989:198-199)

The sociologist Eller sees such writings as a contemporary form of myth making (1993a:157). She lists the key elements of these myths as:

> ancient goddess worship; a patriarchal revolution, and the incipient return to female-centerness. In this economical, mythic way, theological teachings are also transmitted: women are creative and powerful, and endowed with special bodily gifts (menstruation, childbirth, and lactation) that are properly valued in a goddess-worshiping religion (1993a:154).

Eller also notes that many women apparently "believe" these accounts irrespective of any "outside" validation of their "truth."

Similarly, I have found that most practitioners of feminist spirituality are not particularly interested in the archeological or historical evidence which might be used to either support or refute these claims. In general, practitioners are all too aware that aspects of "patriarchy" influence their lives, the telling of history, and the doing of archeology. Since all "established" sources are deemed under the control of patriarchal concerns, they summarily dismiss all attempts to discount this revised history.

Together Eisler, Loye, and Ranck present women with powerful alternatives to traditional Judeo-Christian theologies. Eisler's revised history and predictions of transformations to come change women's place in the religious landscape. For women who were raised in Christian contexts where they were told countless stories of Eve, the temptress who wantonly brings Adam's fall from paradise into travail and woe, the goddess offers a radically different view of the place of women *viz-a-viz* men. Women here are the creators of a different life: not only do they bring forth new life in the form of children, but they also are the harbingers of a new social order in which women (and men) will transform war, poverty, and social injustice into peace, an equitable distribution of goods, and social justice.

These theological reflections rest on changing images of power. For the past two decades, feminist theologians have been discussing shifting the power bases of American society from one which operates under a model of "power over," that is the power to force individuals to comply with the dictates of patriarchy, to one of "power with" (Starhawk 1987).[15] The latter concept is based on an egalitarian model of power, one in which power is "traded and shaped together through negotiation, struggle, mutual concern and respect" (Cooper White 1995:31). In feminist spirituality "power over" is associated with men and with male dominated societies, while "power with" is associated with women. Thus feminist spirituality calls for the transformation of Western society from a system that operates under "power over" to one that operates" under "power with." The theologian Starhawk also included the concept of "power within." Power within speaks to women's need to claim their own inner voice and wisdom. In my view, the movement's greatest strength, and paradoxically, its greatest weakness lies in its efforts to empower women. Its rituals and its words do serve to break, for many women, a patriarchal way of looking at the world.

Ritual Practice

Examining the theological basis of the revisionist history tells us something about how the adherents of feminist spirituality construct their alternative visions. However, the writing alone does not tell us what these women do when they meet and it certainly cannot address the ways that the practices of feminist spirituality change the views of its adherents. Theological reflection must also be tied to action (Adams 1976). Ranck's work (1986) is especially helpful in this respect since the curriculum is specifically designed not only to present the feminist spirituality revisionist view of history and the movements beliefs in the goddess(es), but is also designed to have participants perform specific rituals. These rituals are intended: 1) to help the women form bonds among themselves; 2) to cause women to breakthrough any latent conditioning that they might have to traditional roles for women which inculcate that women are somehow "less than" men; and 3) to change the women's perceptions of themselves as "less than" men. Included in the exercises are opportunities to tell stories about how patriarchy has influenced one's life and to explore how belief in a goddess in both contemporary practice and history might change women's place in the social order.

Courses based on Ranck's book, *Cakes for the Queen of Heaven*, model the feminist spirituality vision of equality: women sit in a circle; leadership for sessions is usually rotated among all the participants; songs and rituals affirm that women have the power to undertake the work of transformation in their personal lives and in society as a whole. Women are told that their grey hair is a symbol of power; that their bodies can, and indeed should have, many shapes; that to menstruate and to bear children is a highly prized and valuable experience. Furthermore, this validation of women's experiences is underpinned by the link to the goddess as a divine entity whose powers are tied to the earth itself.

Though space limitations preclude an in-depth portrait of the ritual practices of the movement, the essence of these rituals can be captured in the following description of a Summer Solstice gathering I attended in 1993.

In the large backyard of a holistic healer's Victorian home, about forty women gather. They arrive separately and in small groups of friends or close family members, bringing food for a potluck, blankets to sit upon, candles, poems, and drums. The hostess, Marilyn, is barefoot, dressed in a brown sheath dress, wearing feathered earrings and a circlet of flowers in her hair.   She carries a staff of multi-colored ribbons. Though most of the participants are white and middle class, one African American woman enters bearing a large drum, dressed in long white garments with a brightly colored embroidered hat. The ages range from young to old: college students attend as well as college professors.   Also present are storytellers, artists, counselors, librarians, grandmothers, wives, lesbians, the curious and the experienced.   From my fieldwork I knew that members of at least four different women's ritual groups participated in the event.

The setting itself reflected the ubiquitous beauty that I had come to expect of upstate New York: rolling hills, covered in green; a gray sky devoid now of the clouds that had spilled an afternoon's rain; a long green stretch of grass whose moisture seeped through the blankets and beckoned our toes.   The hands of women were present as well in the food preparations and in the circle of stones that encased a circle of fire.   Around the perimeter, at the four cardinal directions, flickering candles rested in paper bags of sand casting glimmers of moons and stars through the cut-aways.

The evening's rituals included invocations to goddesses of the four directions, Native American ritual blessings, "casting the circle" or ritually making the circle of women around the fire into a sacred circle, drumming, singing songs from American and Native American sources, dancing, poetry reading, and meditation.   Each of these events has multiple layers of symbolism, but I will draw to the readers attention several important features of this ritual gathering.

First, the event was given, organized, presented, lead, and enacted solely by women.   No men were present and none had been invited.   The leadership was shared, and though particular women did led each segment of the ritual, no one person was the clear leader and no one person dominated the gathering. The shared leadership showed most clearly in the closing ritual as each woman who sat in the circle was asked to speak about her hopes and dreams as she lit a candle.   There was no "front," there was no altar: the focal point was a centrally placed circular fire.   Finally, all the ritual words, singing, drumming, and chanting were designed to speak of the power of women and the nature of women's connections to one another and to the divine. Capturing simply this perspective, one of the more popular ritual chants repeated this refrain:

We all come from the Goddess,
And to her we shall return,
Like a drop of rain,
Flowing to the ocean.

The theology implied here is a participatory one in which people, like drops of rain, come from divinity, partake of divinity, and return to divinity. That divinity is imaged, imagined, spoken of, and invoked as female.

This event was but one of many that believers enact. A typical practitioner will attend rituals that honor the cycles of birth and rebirth in both seasons and in women's bodies. She may attend full-moon rituals which involve drumming, chanting, and dancing, all embodied in one of the primary metaphors of the movement: that is, a circle of women moving. In her home, she may create an altar on which she places stones, rocks, and other symbols of nature, a nature usually seen as somehow connected with her own capacity to create life. Her past may be represented by pictures of loved ancestors, her present may be referenced by a symbol designed to bring her that lover or job she desires, and her relationship to the divine may be symbolized by a goddess figure, including often a reproduction of the Venus of Willendorf. The latter, often discussed in physical anthropology classes as a fertility figure, becomes for her a symbol of a divine feminine which she may or may not take as "literal" or even as her primary interpretation of the divine. Nevertheless, that Venus or other goddess is likely to be on her altar and to symbolize "something" powerful for her.

What is that "something" powerful that these rituals, circles, gatherings, and goddesses come to represent for these women? As an anthropologist, I, and other observers of the movement (see Eller 1993a), argue that at its most basic level these practices represent the metaphoric transformation of women from "less than" powerful to more fully empowered. By remaking divinity in the image of women, women are then able to create and model an alternative "world view" at both a cognitive and emotional level. This modeling allows women to "see" the ways that the patriarchal Western world view has held them in its sway. Many women say that they had never realized until they participated in such gatherings that the language of the Christian religion taught them that they were "less than" males. They may have seen women in roles of authority in the classroom or on the job, but many had not seen women in roles of power in religious gatherings. They also see, touch, feel, hear, and smell ritual creations that have been designed by women for women.   These creations, as anthropologists have long known, have the power to break the ordinary and transform the individual participants into a new state of community, of communitas (Turner 1969). So women participants in the movement image, invoke, create, and remake the divine in ways that express something that they believe speaks to an essentially feminine way of being.

The Essentialist Views of Feminist Spirituality

The understanding of cultural history and religious ritual represented in these texts and practices reflects an essentialist view of gender, creating a primary mythic motif.   Women are presented as more peaceful, less hierarchical, and less dualistic, by nature, perhaps because of the primary relations they have with their children.[16] Furthermore, just as the values associated with women's ways of doing and knowing brought peace and prosperity in the distant past, so too, will contemporary society be changed as women gain power.   While social scientists have begun to explore the previously unaddressed questions of whether women are more egalitarian in general as evidenced by the cross-cultural record and whether women do create different forms of religion when they hold power (Sered 1994), I want to explore a paradox arising from the nexus of feminist theological views and feminist ritual practice.

For many feminist spirituality practitioners the belief in the fundamentally egalitarian nature of women seems to have the ring of "truth" as seen from the perspective of their own lives.   They apparently do not see themselves as capable of violence.   Yet, they routinely practice a form of cultural appropriation that can be viewed as either "violent" or at the very least misguided.

According to some outside observers (Eller 1993a; Rose 1993), the widespread appropriation of the cultural traditions of other religions without giving thought to the disservice such borrowing may do, marks these women as colonialists.[17] Practitioners draw on a wide variety of rituals, myths, songs, prayers, and practices from other religious traditions, usually without asking for permission. Apparently they assume that such appropriations are either totally harmless or, if that if asked, that the practitioners of other religious belief systems would be happy, as a matter of course, to share their insights.   This widespread appropriation bears much closer examination given these women's commitments to an egalitarian social order.

The women who constitute most of the adherents of feminist spirituality tend to be white and of middle class origins. Their appropriation of "ethnic" practices reflects the white Euro-American world view that cultural differences are only "superficial" and that all knowledge, including sacred knowledge, should be readily available.[18] In the early days of the movement, the cultural appropriation was most likely to come from European religious groups. Thus, the rituals borrowed where actually interpretations of pre-Christian European traditions, be they Druidic, Celtic, Greek, or Germanic in origin. Other borrowing came from the appropriation of Goddess symbols from non-Christian world religious traditions, such as Hinduism. During the decade of the 1990s, feminist spirituality groups frequently began to incorporate rituals from Native American traditions. Among these appropriations were the use of chants, drumming, invocations to the spirits of the four directions, purification rituals such as smudging, and healing rituals such as the use of sweat lodges. For example, when I was observing the movement in upstate New York and in New Jersey, I saw women's spirituality gatherings that included Navajo chants, the use of "Native American" medicine wheels, and Native American sweat lodges held in the backyard of women's homes. In practice, feminist spirituality practitioners now include appropriations from religious traditions from across the world, past and present. Controversial appropriations even include the use of "milk and honey" rituals which some observers see as a remaking of the Christian communion service of bread and wine (Small and Burgess 1994). Thus, practitioners of feminist spirituality who espouse a world-view stressing equality for all, in practice seem to subvert that equality by their wholesale appropriations.

One reason for this apparent cultural insensitivity has to do with the paramount importance placed on gender relationships as the determining factor influencing behavior.[19] From this perspective, to achieve equality means, first and foremost, a shift away from gender imbalance. One strategy for change, according to practitioners, is the belief that changing themselves spiritually is a prominent step in transforming society itself. Thus, any religious method which can help facilitate these changes is worth pursuing, and women in the movement seem more interested in the pragmatic adoption of rituals that "work" rather than in worrying over who might be harmed by their appropriation. Because women themselves are thought to model a more egalitarian model of living, everything they do which is emotionally "authentic" is thought to foster that end. This creates the following paradox: equality for all rests on an essentialist view of gender relations which posits that women are, by their very natures, better equipped than men to create an egalitarian social order.

The Irony of Anthropological Critique

In the following discussion, I can only touch on the interplay of these theological issues with anthropology.[20]   As with any religious tradition, questions abound as to what constitutes belief, how one will live one's beliefs, and how one will deal with the inevitable paradoxes. Furthermore, the ideals of any movement are never perfectly embodied in practice. In the case of feminist spirituality, I think the issues of appropriation, myth making, and essentialism are bound to be raised again and again. White feminist scholars have already encountered criticism from feminist scholars of color for their failure, at times, to understand issues of power tied more to class and ethnicity than gender inequality per se.[21] As the feminist spirituality movement spreads and becomes more visible, its practitioners too are becoming the targets of increased criticism.

Anthropologists could have much to say about this movement on many fronts, such as: What relationships of power are embedded in appropriations from other cultures? What happens when rituals are taken out of one cultural context and used in another? Could claims that matriarchies existed in the past ever be substantiated? Are women "naturally" more egalitarian in nature than men? What kinds of myths and rituals foster belief?

In a sense the feminist spirituality movement offers anthropologists a unique chance to watch the development of a new religion embedded in a contemporary Western social context. It also offers an excellent case study for the patterns and trajectories found in millennial movements in general, for the beliefs and practices of feminist spirituality are millennial in nature as women await the dawn of a new age of equality.[22] If the movement continues to grow, observers will increasingly point to what they perceive as defects and faulty assumptions. I myself have noted some of these (see also Heriot 1994) and will doubtless encounter others as my research progresses.

However, let me turn from the multiple ways that anthropologists could critique feminist spirituality to the ways in which the discipline of anthropology suffers from a similar kind of ethnocentric "blindness." During my more than twenty years of schooling and practice in the anthropology of religion, I have rarely seen anthropologists address the question of religious belief from a non-ethnocentric perspective. This failure, I believe, stems from anthropologists' attempts to remain at a scholarly distance from the religious beliefs they study (see also Wafer 1991:94). In so doing, they set themselves apart from what is often the central core of cultural traditions. Indeed, as the process theologian James Luther Adams would claim, "some sort of religious faith is found among all people," even among atheists, agnostics, and social scientists (1974:92). Similarly, though couched in far different language, the latest work by the anthropologist, Morton Klass (1995), makes a similar point. Klass argues throughout his book *Ordered Universes* that the anthropology of religion has remained to a large extent ethnocentric because it is rooted in the Enlightenment separation of reason from religion. Klass, while being careful to remain neutral as to his own stance *vis-a-vis* religious belief, repeatedly raises the possibility that anthropologists have failed to portray well the religions of the groups they study because they are locked into this Western rationalist view of religion.

In addition, until recently anthropologists have retained control over much writing about belief (especially "alien" beliefs) even though their experiences of religious traditions are usually from the "outside." Combining this power differential with ethnocentrism means that anthropologists should not be surprised by the "native" "believers" critiques of anthropology which have suddenly become much more prevalent (Allen 1987; Beck et al. 1977; Deloria 1992; Rose 1992; Treat 1994). Believers rightly point out the inherent problems with setting oneself up as the interpreter of a religion with which one has no deep "believing" connection. These power issues are deeply troubling and have been, to a large extent, unaddressed.

Other reasons for continued ethnocentrism in the anthropology of religion stem from the conventions of anthropological writing and contemporary postmodern theory. For instance, Marton (1994) has argued that perhaps anthropologists have had religious experiences but they have failed to write about them because they have an "unconscious" reaction to the legacy of Castañeda's writing. [23] No one wants to have the entire academy condemn them for perceived "flakiness." In addition, contemporary anthropological theory remains steeped in postmodernism. While this theoretical perspective has made considerable contributions to anthropological theory and writing by raising questions about the multiplicity of "voices" and knowledge bases extant in all societies, postmodernist theories, in general, do not portray religion well. This situation arises because religious beliefs provide a fundamental challenge to postmodern skepticism; that is, they provide a "certainty" of belief which operates to undermine the postmodernists' dissolute and dissolving world. According to the philosopher, Mary Midley (1991), postmodernism entails both a theory of knowledge and a morality, despite its own frequent claims to the contrary. By pointing out the bases upon which the various postmodern world views and morality rest, religious belief traditions serve to make postmodernism only one among many world views and not, as its practitioners frequently claim, the privileged "new" interpretive framework (see Klass 1995; Paden 1992).

Finally, with respect to the discipline of anthropology, it maybe, as Ewing has recently suggested, that the refusal to believe has "prevented [anthropologists] themselves from transcending the contradictions embedded in a situation in which the imposition of one's own mode of discourse interferes with the project of representation" (1994:572). Ewing notes that the refusal to believe has kept anthropologists from "going native." She further identifies the refusal to believe as one of the "last" taboos of anthropology. Careful herself to "neither claim nor deny belief" (1994:573), Ewing explores the consequences of this taboo against belief in anthropology in terms of the continued power imbalances it establishes.

I find it striking that Ewing notes the taboo and its consequences; and yet, at the same time, she offers examples of her own continued doubts about the validity of certain religious experiences.

It seems to me that while anthropologists can note the existence of this taboo, the power of the taboo represents such a high order of forbidden "sacredness" that even to discuss the presence of the taboo can be threatening. For it appears that when the anthropologist does openly break the taboo (especially in writing), if one does states that one "believes," then one places oneself outside the discipline. For example, even when an anthropologist like Stoller goes so far into belief as to become a sorcerer, he eventually comes to distance himself from the event in the writing (Stoller and Olkes 1987). He and his wife tell the readers of *In Sorcery's Shadow* that Stoller is no longer a practicing sorcerer by the end of the book. Similarly, Wafer (1991) plays with the readers of *The Taste of Blood* by offering tantalizing glimpses into trance states in Afro-Brazilian Candomble, which become reframed as postmodern discourse. These methodological and rhetorical strategies imply that every anthropologist who crosses the divide between belief and unbelief, and who chooses to stay on the side of belief, has placed herself or himself outside discipline.

Such a state of affairs in a tradition that prides itself on its holism provides anthropology with its own paradox: namely, that our ethnographic efforts at understanding religious traditions are doomed, in our informants' eyes, from the beginning of the study by the anthropologist's failure to believe. What does this say about the relationship between the theologies of feminist spirituality and anthropology? In one sense it means that there will not be a relationship at all. That is, anthropologists will either not study the movement because it is not distant enough from middle class society or anthropologists will join the ranks of the critics. I, however, would like to see that a dialogue was achieved as anthropologists thought more about the relationship between the goals of the movement and its practices, about the critiques it offers of Western society and the solutions it presents, so that the divide between religious belief and anthropological practice was not continually remade. That divide, in effect, does remain the last and greatest taboo of anthropology as it is practiced today, and ultimately it perpetuates the same kind of power imbalances that seem embedded in the feminist spirituality movement.

In closing, I know that a woman like Sally needs better advice than, "well, your loneliness is a product of your culture and you will just have to endure it." The feminist spirituality movement offers more to Sally than that pessimistic viewpoint. It also calls into question a number of assumptions about Western society and the ultimate goal of social reform. At the same time, the movement has limitations of which most members seem to be largely unaware.

Notes

1. See Rosenau (1992) for a discussion of the ways in which this despair affects postmodern social science researchers.
2. For summaries of various feminist theology positions, see Christ and Plaskow 1979; Bednarowski 1992; and Plaskow and Christ 1989. For a comprehensive bibliography of feminist theology see MacNichol and Walsh 1993. Even though spiritual feminists commonly use the spelling "thealogy" to reflect the divine as feminine (Eller 1993a:4), I will use theology throughout the paper for purposes of clarity.
3. This ethnographic research was partially funded by the Society for the Scientific Study of religion. Further research funding for writing came from a subsequent postdoctoral fellowship at the Center for the Study of American Religion at Princeton University.
4. Much of the following discussion is drawn from the work of Cynthia Eller (1993a), a sociologist, who wrote the first extensive social science account of the movement.
5. For an ethnographic study of English witchcraft see Luhrmann (1989).
6. I am currently writing a book on my ethnographic research on both movements, feminist spirituality and the New Age, entitled *Women's Encounters with the Sacred* (Heriot n.d.; see also Heriot 1994).
7. In the Christian and Jewish traditions there is now a widespread movement to reclaim the feminine side of the Judeo-Christian god. That feminine side is usually referenced as divine wisdom, as Sophia. For work discussing Sophia see Johnson

(1993) and for a text that illustrates how Christian women are re-imaging their faith, see Chinnici (1992).

8. For a more in-depth discussion of the feminist spirituality goddess, see Eller 1993a.

9. Eller (1993b) notes that members of Judaism are less likely to split completely from their faith tradition, though she does not as yet present an explanation for this phenomenon. For this reason, in the subsequent discussion I confine my remarks to the Christian and post-Christian feminist theologians.

10. This approach broad can be seen in other works on feminist theology. See especially Anderson and Hopkins 1991 and Gadon 1989. For a critique of the ways feminist spirituality practitioners use art see Eller 1993c.

11. I discuss the problems which result when a utopia is only partly envisioned in my forthcoming book, *Women's Encounters with the Sacred* (Heriot n.d.).

12. Information on the major works cited stems from questionnaires given to the women I interviewed and from my observations of the movement. For complete citations on these authors see MacNichol and Walsh (1993).

13. See Eller (1993:156) for a discussion of the ways in which Eisler's work transcends the feminist spirituality movement. I concentrate on the ways in which this work was used in a feminist spirituality group. Eller notes that *The Partnership Way* (Eisler and Loye 1990) and *Cakes for the Queen of Heaven* (Ranck 1986) provide the two major study curriculums for teaching the sacred history of the movement (1993a:153). In my field research on feminist spirituality, I have attended classes given by Unitarian Universalist congregations based on the work of Eisler (1989), Eisler and Loye (1990), and Ranck (1986). I have also attended a new course, "Rise Up and Call Her Name" (Fisher 1994), sponsored by the Unitarian Universalist Women's Federation. "Rise Up and Call Her Name" extends the work of Ranck who drew on European goddesses to a global understanding of goddesses. While I have found that the Unitarian Universalist Movement provides one important institutional home for the feminist spirituality movement, other institutional homes are women's programs associated with women's studies departments at colleges and universities across the country and in programs associated with the YWCA (Young Women's Christian Association). Many groups of women meet in homes and have no larger institutional affiliation and thus are part of the rapidly growing small group phenomenon in American society. See Wuthnow (1994) for sociological discussion of this shift in American society.

14. Catal Huyuk (in what is now Turkey) and Crete are the two examples are cited by Eisler (1989) in her discussion of women centered cultures which predate the Indo-European invasion. According to Eller, there are only three archeological sites in ancient societies on which the evidence for women's social status as equals is based: two southern European sites and one located in present day Turkey (Catal Huyuk) (Eller 1993:160-161).

15. Only recently has there been a recognition that the concept of "power with" also implies a connection to a community of faith and accountability. Cooper-White, a Christian feminist, in her discussion of this form of power terms it "power-in-community" and defines it as a power that goes "beyond the individual and

the relationship" to something much larger which "finally approaches what Jesus referenced as the "Kingdom of God" (1995:31).

16. The focus on essentialism is part of a larger debate in feminist literature. See Fuss (1989) for a scholarly treatment of the question and Pollitt (1993) for a journalist's perspective. The belief that child-bearing and child-rearing is an inherently egalitarian activity is widespread in feminist circles. See Heriot (1996) for a discussion of the pervasive quest for essential definitions of personhood in American concepts of the fetus/child.

17. See also Eller 1993a. In addition, at the 1994 American Academy of Religion meetings, I heard papers on the issue of appropriation in three different sessions (for example, a paper by Tracy Pintchman on feminist spirituality; one by Paul Johnson on New Age shamanism; and one by Diane Bell on New Age appropriations of Native American practices). My discussion of appropriations is drawn from these and ongoing observations made as feminist spirituality practitioners attempt to grapple with these issues.

18. Klass (1995) provides both a succinct the foundations of this world view in his book, *Ordered Universes*. Critiques of this Western viewpoint can be found among many Native American scholars writing about their own religious traditions. See Allen (1986), Beck et al. (1977), Deloria (1992), and Sarris (1993).

19. See Eller 1993a for an objective discussion of the various positions found in feminist spirituality on this subject. For an indication of how widespread this particular revisionist history is becoming, see a recent news article entitled "Almighty Goddess" (O'Connell 1994).

20. Other relevant theological questions which have not been discussed here are also important. For example there is an ongoing debate on whether women's religious beliefs are more immanent than transcendent (see Wessinger 1993). This debate needs more cross-cultural input as does the debate on women's "essential" nature and women's moral perspectives (Gilligan 1993; Belenky et al. 1986). Yet another area of intense interest surrounds the concept of ecofeminism (see Ruether 1992; Gaard 1993; McFague 1987).

21. For criticisms made by women of color see Anzaldua 1990; Hooks 1990; Lorde 1984; Minh-Ha 1989; and Mohanty, Russo, and Torres 1991. For womanist theological perspectives see Williams 1989.

22. See Eller 1993d for a discussion of the movement's potential for social change.

23. Carlos Castañeda wrote his first book, *The Teachings of Don Juan: A Yaqui Way of Knowledge* (1968), while he was attending graduate school at the University of California, Los Angeles. His second book, *Journey to Ixttalan: The Lessons of Don Juan*, was based on his doctoral dissertation (Philip Newman personal communication, 1994). These two books were extremely controversial, though Castañeda claims they were based on ethnographic fieldwork. Other anthropologists often discount the works as 'fiction.' His subsequent works are completely discounted by anthropologists (Marton 1994).

Chapter 5

Theology and the Anthropological Study of Spirit Events in an Iñupiat Village[1]

Edith Turner

   Two theologies came face to face in 1890 at Ivakuk, an Iñupiat village that had already suffered disruptions due to contact with the commercial whaling industry. The incoming Episcopal church was quite certain of its message: the shamanism prevalent in the village was heathen and invited demonic spirits to its aid. There began a century-long effort to eradicate it, culminating in the latter half of the twentieth century with success. Then the Whites left, handing over to a strongly Christianized Iñupiat clergy and congregation. However, politics, in particular the need to resist White political and land depredations, produced a turn-around at the end of the twentieth century. Several indigenous leaders, unswayed by Christian conservatism, started to revive a number of the old rituals.

   Meanwhile in metropolitan America and England, liberalism began to influence the Christian churches in taking a negative view of what they had done. Apologies for attacking Alaskan cultures appeared in the press. The two religions now had a chance for rapprochement.

   This example throws up many complex issues, particularly for anthropologists. First, if an anthropologist discusses theology, does she do it coolly at a distance, or with an eye to discussions *with* theologians, say about the validity of shamanism? When considering a meeting on common ground of anthropology with theology, we note that in seminary theology and among the young in religious studies in America there is a broadening of awareness of other religions and a new sense of moral responsibility, in other words, liberation theology.

   From the point of view of basic Christian theology, anthropology has recently become respected because it gives clues to the meaning systems of societies that the churches wish to convert. A notable example is the article in *Theological Studies* (1986) by Gerald Arbuckle, S.M., "Theology and Anthropology: Time for Dialogue." This article, which well represents the thinking of the Catholic Church today, starts (p. 429) by quoting Paul VI as claiming the mission of the Church

> to evangelize man's culture and cultures (not in a purely decorative way as it were by applying a thin veneer, but in a vital way, in depth, and right to their very roots).... Evangelization loses much of its force and effectiveness if it does not take into consideration the actual people to whom it is addressed, if it does not use their language, their signs and symbols....[Paul VI *Evangelii nuntiandi* 30 and 63]

My reaction to this as an anthropologist of comparative ritual and religion is not delight but fear. So indigenous religions are to be studied "to their very roots" in order--I can't help feeling--to alter them radically, at their roots. This mission is now termed "inculturation" and is highly approved in Catholic circles. The article was supposed to be a friendly overture to anthropology. It is sad, because it looks as if Christianity cannot let people be. Cultural survival itself, then, will require to be radical, and on the other side, the dogmas invented by Christians may have to be uninvented.

Another concern of interest to anthropologists emerges from Arbuckle's brief history of anthropology in his article. He defines anthropology as an atheist functionalist science: within anthropology "the possibility that supernatural beings could exist would not even be considered" (p. 432). This has largely been true. Arbuckle grants Evans-Pritchard, Mary Douglas, and Victor Turner (pp. 435-445) some insights into symbolism, and agrees that "symbols form the very heart of a culture" and "symbols carry meaning in themselves" (p. 435). Let us reexamine this. If, as Arbuckle says (p. 134), symbols lead one into contact with a mysterious reality (beautiful statement--but wait), then symbols are strictly secondary. As I perceive it, there do exist certain poetic metaphorical symbols like this, but the so-called "symbols" of actually operating religions are often not "representative" but are themselves spirit things, numinous objects, primary. Native Americans, Africans, and many other cultures, have long recognized this. However, the "symbol as metaphor" school in anthropology persists, and we see that much of the present teaching in seminaries (some of it based on a reductive version of Victor Turner's work), is becoming rationalistic in a way not suited to the experience of many peoples around the world. This is a strange circumstance, and one that needs examination.

Because a number of anthropologists themselves are experiencing mysterious material happenings in their researches, we now have the ironic circumstance that it may be this group of anthropologists who will restore the faith of a rationalistic church--and that of other religions too--in the experience of the people.

Meanwhile it is to be noted that the liberal overture of theologians toward anthropology reflects the Episcopal/Iñupiat discussion mentioned at the beginning of this paper. However it is not clear on which side the *main* body of the discipline of anthropology might line up in the Iñupiat efforts to revive their shamanistic heritage. Mainline anthropologists treat both the church and shamanism with objectivity. Many of them still claim their discipline to be an impartial, scientific tool, at its best when outside all matters of religion. Is this the best way to study religion?

We can see there are many questions here. In anthropology as in theology, thinking is changing, toward a respect for the anthropology of experience, even religious experience, whether indigenous or Western. Anthropologists now are permitted to experience, themselves. And here is a paradox: to experience what the field people experience and be outside of it at the same time one would truly need to be a shaman, in the body and out of the body, as it were. In fact this has always been the specialty of the most gifted anthropological fieldworkers.

How then should one address this non-neglected but necessary topic of anthropology and theology? From experience I conclude there is no clear unambiguous way. Theology (the discipline which began as Christian) first took form as a monothetic, marmoreal, self-enclosed system. We see the following statement in *The Encyclopedia of Religion*: "All theology is required to be faithful to the apostolic confession of faith" (Rev. Congar, Order of Preachers, 1987, 14:461). Yet this statement is by a "revolutionary" in the Church, defending and revitalizing the early religious experience of Christians as against the enormous outpouring of words by the schoolmen. These discussion are not our concern here, only to observe that theology, like psychology, is appearing in a variety of forms.

As for liberation theology, its influence has spread into many fields. This "theology" is not theology at all, but the necessary and praiseworthy widening of moral responsibility for the poor and disenfranchised of the world.

What then about my own fieldwork in the light of the discussion of theology? I have written about spirit healing in Africa and a kind of para-shamanism in the Arctic. Would it be in keeping to compare the theology of, for instance, the Inuit healer Claire with Christian theology? Do I hold with some of Christian theology anyway? When I say the creed at Mass I say, "I believe in all religion," then I take communion.

Here is a proposition: it is possible to change the meaning of "theology" to that of the study of all spirit beings and gods (as Hindu theology indeed does), and include an array of beings distinct from the Christian God. Each culture knows different ones. "Know" is the word here, just as Jung "knew" God, and did not "believe" in him.

With regard to a possible Iñupiat theology, the tendency of theology to classify becomes a problem. For instance, Russian Orthodox scholars refuse to dignify the pre-contact spirit knowledge of the Iñupiat with the term "religion." To them "religion" is purely Christian or refers to the higher religions, not to the minimally organized work of shamanism, which they judge to operate purely on a personal level and in no way to constitute a moral system. (According to liberal Christian scholars, theologies may also be found elsewhere, see Tracy's "*Comparative Theology*" 1987:446-455.) So then the field of theology is supposed to concern moral systems? There might well be an interesting field in tracing how the experiencing of gods and spirits in different cultures does promote moral systems.

Anthropology has hitherto found theology foreign to itself. Any "logy" about "God" might not the way to look at the religions of the world. Like indigenous peoples, we see our material as given to us, given in experience, not in pre-decided "logical" terms. Critical anthropology is unlikely to come to terms with, for instance, high Catholic theology backed by an anti-feminist pope. The two would never mix, only collide, and both would founder under a hopeless weight of words.

But I propose something much gentler--the childish voice that says that the emperor has no clothes on. This is the voice of indigenous humanism, which is also our anthropological humanism. We here are the indigenes, we anthropologists. We now have the color of our field people, and even in the crowd at the Association meetings one can sense it as a kind of universal color. However complex and mixed, it is not like anything else, it is field people color. Now what is that?

It is something about which we may find common ground with theology. Is it "ethics"? Not ethics, those are just moral systems again, though extremely valuable. Poets know this thing, as does the prizewinning Don Mitchell (1993); and the odd myth-teller Miles Richardson (1994) has the touch. The reader might begin to understand what it is. Books like *Bridges to Humanity* (1995), edited by Bruce Grindal and Frank Salamone, the special issue on humanism in *Anthropology and Humanism* (1994), *Anthropological Poetics* (1991), edited by Ivan Brady and myself, and other writings, circle around the mystery--as is correct, because one cannot come at it direct, that common ground. It is in fact what arises when one honors the human being and her religion in the faraway places of fieldwork. So through the human being out there is a way open where the fresh unjaded soul can go, on a journey out of this world, as the shamans say. It is to the realm of the theology of small indigenous groups, labeled "folk religion" or "magical ideas." But they are not ideas. Nothing can keep the magic imprisoned as an idea in the head, or a concept in the head, a thought. It is active and exists in process.

How to make up a theology for that, construct a tower of theory on that? It does not hold up in towers, in structures, but exists in present action. Can we term the study of these events "social science"? Old guard scientists and theoretical Marxists do not conduct *participatory* studies of magic or of anything irrational. But such studies would not be foreign to the truly brilliant scientists, the brain studies people, the particle physicists, the chaos theory people. The anthropology of religion too will gradually become a science belonging to the alliance of all the planet's peoples, not excluding even Serbs, Hutus, Ghadafi, Farrakhan, Russian communists, or Middle Eastern males. We can put ourselves at the service of the planet--the way it is, not the way it ought to be. Shakespeare, I think, was a much better person than God, he had a sense of humor and a tenderness about "mortal men," as he called them, and an ability to depict people better than anything the leaders of the higher religions could do. The leaders have just been after obedience, not very concerned with people themselves. "Obey God's will." Or one should love the virtuous in a person and disappoint him by not having any part with his drinking and smoking.

Anthropology then has its own beloved mission. It is seditious, not good. We are just fascinated, as everyone on the planet is fascinated, by the oddities of everyone else.

Caveats in the Anthropological Study of Indigenous Religions

With remarkable regularity we find that indigenous religions have their roots in spirit experience and in the rituals taught people by spirit entities during those experiences. At this primary level ritual has strong efficacy. As Michael Jackson teaches in his book, *Paths Toward a Clearing: Radical Empiricism and Ethnographic Inquiry* (1989), ritual experience proves itself to be true and valid *in use*, not as a preordained system or structure. In the case of my field friends, the Iñupiat, their work in spirit matters has validity in use. Ritual has effectiveness through its performance, the fact that it is performed with the body. For instance, *muktuk*, delicate whale tidbits with a sacred character, are actually **eaten**, plentifully eaten. This has fundamental importance where consciousness of the whale's spirit is concerned. Roland Littlefield (1992:97) has a term for this: "hylotheism" ("hylo" means "matter"), that is to say, a perception of god as matter, god as identified with her creation, god *as* the earth. Such a connection with matter, as food for the body in the case of *muktuk*--as well as being symbolic--brings the people into connection with the cosmological cycle of giving and taking, using and being used. It takes place in a process system, working itself out as it goes, and is said to arise from spirit experience, not from a system of preexisting structures.

It has been claimed that in Inuit thought there are categories of spirits (Merkur 1985, writing about Canadian Inuit elders' accounts of long ago). Yet these appear to change as the decades pass; or else emphasis on a category changes or fades. However if occasion arises and a particular event concerning spirits comes to the fore, it is then that a definite category may stand out in its full dimension and be well understood. I will attempt to describe such events among the Iñupiat for certain classes of spirits that appear to have been at work in the village of Ivakuk[2] during the decade 1987-1996. These are animal helpers, shamans' spirits, the whale spirit (*inua*), the eagle spirit, souls and their experiences at death, good and bad ghosts, reincarnating souls, the spirit helpers of healers, and the spirit figures experienced by Iñupiat Christians. It must be borne in mind that we are dealing with elusive imponderables here. Not many Natives on the North Slope like strict categories. If we are dealing with one category, the others are altogether absent and are not of present concern. Theologies, systems of spirits are *not* a preoccupation, and this is not for lack of intellectualism, but in keeping with the very nature of the subject matter.

As I saw it, spirit perception and spirit experience came in flashes during the vicarious events of time. This "flash" characteristic again shows the elusiveness of our subject matter and teaches the need for the utmost caution in the matter of ethnographic documentation. No dogmatic statements can be made, and my paper should not be taken in that sense, for I am feeling my way.

The Village

The scene is the village of Ivakuk, a long way north of the Arctic Circle on the North Slope of Alaska--a wild country. The people of Ivakuk, 700 in number, live in frame houses in a nucleated village with modern streets, village store, power station, school, clinic, and two churches. They obtain two-thirds of their food from subsistence hunting, an activity they pursue on ice, sea, and land. Their main food comes from the bowhead whale.

When the missionaries first arrived in 1890 they abolished the people's old religion, calling it devil worship; while traditional healing itself remained. They built a church and a school, replacing the old underground houses of the people with thin frame houses, which were "cleaner." Christianity taught them obedience to a high god and to those who were bringing them not only the English language but many valuable connections with the outside world. The missionaries instituted a school, and beat those who spoke Iñupiat within the school precincts, or they stuck plaster over the children's mouths. The very idea of shamanism was taboo. Yet in spite of itself the church became a fertile ground for the people's own sense of spirit things. The field material I cite shows the mixing of these tendencies.

The Villagers' Working Conception of Spirituality: Clues to Iñupiat Theology?

"Eskimo spirituality:" this phrase was often used by the people about themselves and would be heard in the context of significant events and experiences. Furthermore the phrase betrayed a nationalist tinge. The consciousness of the people of their uniqueness in this respect helped to maintain their will to survive as a culture.

In the house of Clem Jackson, Iñupiaq traditionalist and patriot of the village of Ivakuk on the North Slope of Alaska, I sat with the family as they gathered around a supper of polar bear.

"Come and eat," said Clem. It was good hearty meat, like beef but darker. "Eat the fat, eat the fat. That was what made my daughter so strong." He added, "My son Kehuq's animal helper is a polar bear, a ten-legged polar bear. Polar bear helpers grow to a gigantic size, then develop three more pairs of legs to become the ten-legged polar bears known as *kiniq* or *qoqoqiaq*. Kehuq got his polar bear helper from his ancestor Kehuq."

"Ah, the one who was a shaman," I said, thinking. We began discussing animal helpers.

"You may think you have one," said Clem. "Does it come to you? Does it touch you? Do you see it like you see this?" He took hold of the salt shaker in front of him.

"I don't see a helper the way you see that," I said.

I was curious about the way people see. "Is there any difference in the way your great-great-grandfather Kehuq saw the ten-legged polar bear and the ordinary way of seeing?"

"He rode on it," said Clem simply. "Like you ride on a horse. It was real. *You* call it magic. It's ordinary."

"No, I don't think it's magic. It's real." And I meant it. There were other experiences I had had which cautioned me against sneering. Then I said, "But suppose--say a White lawyer or construction engineer went down on the ice, could he see and touch a polar bear helper?"

"No."

"What's the difference?"

"The old ones were masters of the ancient science."

From what Clem said there is not another *kind* of seeing. There is the power to call the animal helpers, those beasts who actually exist. Also the shaman can fly out across the tundra like a ball of fire, or she or he can travel under the ice. Whites tend to call these ideas "myths" (a word that sometimes connotes "lies") or "legends." The Iñupiat have asked me not to use such words about their history.

Evidently at least the Iñupiaq Clem does not associate shaman experience with altered states of consciousness. One way we may look at the matter is that the Iñupiat are able to bring their shamanic and everyday faculties to lie alongside each other in a *normal* world. A human being may learn to develop more power, usually through dancing, and may learn the ancient science and study the continuum between the human and animal world. Thus he or she then commands a wider sensorium. Even the shamans' flight up through the skylight is real. There do seem to be gateways like this, certainly, but the difference is that through the gateway it is perfectly real too. The situation reflects the *extension* of ordinary reality, not something totally foreign to it.

Clem often reproached me like this with unbelief, but owing to those earlier experiences of mine I did actually believe him. He couldn't believe *me*. Others too questioned me, and I stood my ground on the matter.

What was going on here? I saw signs that the Native culture was fighting back, consolidating an opposition to us Whites. Our anthropological analyses of symbolism have premised that such statements as Clem's are symbolic, that is, are to be regarded basically as clues to "meaning," or constitute "the world views and beliefs of participants." Often the statement is made by anthropologists that the issue of the reality of the claims is unimportant, for the work of anthropologists is the interpretation of symbols. However, interpretation in that sense fails to grasp what it might feel like to experience ghosts or have pain actually taken out of one's body. The question has been discussed in publications in the anthropology of experience (Desjarlais 1992, Jackson 1989, Stoller 1989).

In addition, the neuroscientist Charles Laughlin (1994) is recognizing that there is a real problem about such happenings, like those that Clem accuses me of labeling "magic." These events constitute in fact the very reality of experience. Laughlin considers them a matter of "apodicticity"--literally "beyond speech," with the dictionary meaning of: "of the nature of absolute certainty." Using Husserl (1931), Laughlin examines the subjective experiences that an individual has undergone that only the individual can know. Science has hitherto classified any claims to such private experiences as scientifically unprovable. Moreover the events often cannot easily be put into words. Yet people do try to use words, knowing they are insufficient. Pain, for instance, is such an experience; the "I know" conviction is another; or what Clem says the shaman Kehuq experienced. Laughlin is calling for this class of material to be included in serious anthropological study. It is a quietly revolutionary call.

More material about the shaman Kehuq is known. It well illustrates the matter. It appears that when Kehuq was a young man and first became a shaman, his initiation occurred through a vision. One day Kehuq was out alone on the tundra when he heard the sound of paddles up in the air. He looked up and saw a boat floating in the sky. It landed, and Kehuq saw within it a couple of otters running to and fro, and a shaman with one big eye, who danced and gave him pleasure. The vision disappeared, and by the time Kehuq reached home he remembered nothing about it. (This was surely a matter of "apodicticity," literally "beyond speech," representing a distinct experience, but one that cannot be put into words.) Late that night Kehuq started up naked and left the tent for no reason. They brought him back, but for four days he was crazy and could not eat.

When he recovered Kehuq found he could dance. When he did so he was possessed by the tutelary shaman's spirit. Kehuq then taught the people the shaman's songs and also showed them how to carve the shaman's face in wood. He was now gifted with full shamanic powers.

The same type of initiation was common amongst the countless shamans who in former times served the various Inuit peoples with healing, foresight, weather control, and hunting success. This was the spirituality abhorred by the missionaries and disbelieved by the Whites--and only recently it is regaining respect as our understanding of the complexities of consciousness grows.

The curious matter of Kehuq's four day "state of fugue," as psychiatrists might term it, is found, with the same creative results, in several other contexts in Inuit life. The healer Claire had at least four bouts of this "fugue" syndrome in her life, "and every time my healer grew stronger," she said.

Others in the village experienced it. The father in Jean Briggs' account (1970:254-255) of the Canadian Inuit experienced something similar. The so-called Arctic hysteria might be associated. Like ritual itself, that curious link with the body, this physical phenomenon seems to have more to do with religion than with psychiatry.

Thus the shaman and his helper spirit together have become a key interdependent factor working in Iñupiat spirit life. The healers of today descend in an unbroken line from these former masters. The entry and indwelling of a spirit at a crisis event in a person's life is then a strong item in this "ur-theology." Whether or no it causes some religions to mistrust it, this feature is true in its context and we have to guard against chauvinism in our attempts to find logical consistency throughout all the world's religions.

The Whale and Eagle Spirits

"The Iñupiat perceive their world as an ecosystem of which they are an integral part" (*The Iñupiat View* 1979:4). The story below shows the power of an animal to give itself to humankind and then to reincarnate, thus perpetuating the vital process of cycling of the ecosystem, continually renewing itself and feeding and enlightening all its components. The whale spirit and the eagle spirit are both dominant spirits for the Iñupiat.

The Whale

This principle spirit being--a very solid animal and one that galvanizes the whole village into action--comes into play at the migration season, and at intervals during the year.

On Halloween Day itself it so happened that the whaling families gave out their whale tail meat at a large gathering--so that "the whale would come next year," in April or May. The whale would know if it had been thus properly honored. "Be quiet," the women would command the children. "If you don't, the whale will know." This event took place in the Bingo Hall. Cardboard was spread upon the floor, and the best of Iñupiat activities took place there, that is to say, meat distribution. This was obviously a matter of the body, and surely to do with the spirit. It was not worship, it was spirit understanding in practice. Dora Nashanik was the dominant character on this occasion, the wife of the whaling captain who had caught this particular animal. Dora is the most bodily person I know, ready to hug you at an instant, a big and hearty person. She distributed all the gathered meat until it was gone.

Then we come on to the early new year, before the whaling begins. On the night of the first full moon, Margie, the wife of Clem (also a whaling captain), and his daughter took a ritual bowl of water and went out into the moonlight. Margie raised the bowl and asked the moon god to send whales. It is said by others that when this is done a tiny whale drops into the bowl. The idea of a moon god goes back also to the ancient account of the sun goddess who was raped by her brother, the moon god. This account was given by word of mouth. As for the whale, as well as being its natural self, it can take this tiny form, its tail can appear in a shaman woman's mouth, the tail appears in the faces on carved masks--it is "refracted" many times in the culture, as Evans-Pritchard might have put it. And as the time of whaling drew on, the whale spirit was given much attention.

My friend Annie, also a whaling captain's wife, talked to me about it. "The whale is *different*. It knows, it talks to other whales, it knows if you a good person, if there is no quarreling. The whaling captain leads the prayer for a peaceful safe whale hunt." The whale chooses its beneficiary. It relates.

At whaling time I was unwilling instrument to the ice closing in dangerous circumstances. I had perforce harbored an English BBC filmmaker in my house. At the beginning of his visit I was down on the ice in a tent when the wind rose and we had to leave in a hurry. The ice shifted and all the water disappeared. Everyone in the village knew that until the moviemaker left, the whale would not bring a north wind and open the water. The whale was aware of the possible offense of moviemaking. The very day the Englishman gave up and boarded the plane for the next village the water opened and there were whales. This, like the other material here, was documented in my journal. So the whale knew, as Clem made sure to tell me.

Finally, when Clem himself caught a whale and finished cutting up and distributing the meat, there took place the ritual of the head. The men of his family drew around this huge head and painstakingly levered it toward the edge of the ice. The head, Clem explained, was the seat of the spirit of the whale, and if it returned to the water it would gradually grow a new parka, a new body--it would literally reincarnate. I watched the work of *niakuq*, that of putting back the head. At the moment that the head finally teetered on the edge, and fell in, the men shouted, "Come back!" And at that moment I became aware that the ice was indeed empty, a huge spirit had gone. In its absence, by hindsight, I understood that a spirit had been there. Now, mere piles of whale meat were lying around on the ice, different stuff.

Iñupiat call the animals, "the masters." They are the causers, they initiate the movement of cycling in the cosmos. They desire human spirituality and sacrifice themselves for it.

The Eagle Spirit

In January 1988 the people renewed a long lost celebration of the eagle spirit's gift to humankind, called *Kivgiq*. At Barrow where the event was held, the word "eagle" and "spirit" were rarely used in conjunction for fear of the Christians, though that is what the celebration was all about, the reaffirmation of a primal event in which the first humans learned from the spirits shamanism, music, drumming, trade, and a form of writing. The main dance at the *Kivgiq* celebration portrayed the respect that the primal hunter of the eagle showed for his quarry, so that in response the eagle lived again and carried the hunter on a shamanic flight to the eagle mother, whose heart could be heard beating loud for her son. Far away in the mother's house the hunter was taught the arts of civilization, sledding, trade, a way to give messages, and how to make a drum that sounded with those same heartbeats.

Four years after the first revival in 1988, the words "eagle," "eagle's gift," and "spirit" at last surfaced in the writings of Whites and Iñupiat concerning the *Kivgiq* celebration. Through the means of *performance*, their own religion was growing again. Animal dances were added to the yearly *Kivgiqs*, after a seventy years ban, and string puppet acts were performed-- with the weird effect of reality that these produce. After that first performance of the new *Kivgiq*, in spite of its relative understatement, the spirits seemed to have heard and the whales heard. In Ivakuk we caught five whales in April and May 1988. The people had performed *Kivgiq*, they had been dancing, bodily, and they had shared their whale meat and exchanged valuable gifts. It seems to have worked.

The power of the whale and the eagle are again shown in medias res, not as a structured part of a system. In the missionary days the rituals for the eagle spirit seriously offended the missionaries, who on behalf of their own god would brook no competitor.

This class of spirits, that of the animals who give themselves to the humans, seems to be somewhat different from that of "animal helpers." The principle of self-sacrifice and reincarnation appears in both the whale and eagle protohistories, and confirms the over-arching principle of cosmological cycling, that deeply creative process which manifests itself in the doing. Cosmological cycling was first discussed by the anthropologist Ann Fienup-Riordan of Anchorage in her book *The Nelson Island Eskimo* (1983). Fienup-Riordan shows how the Inuit basic philosophy is a process philosophy, to be viewed as a universal cycling in which humans are part of a food chain. This is also seen as a spirit cycle. Animals come to deserving humans to teach them spirituality. If the humans treat them with respect, replacing the soul parts of the body--the head, or bladder, or sometimes nose--back to their elements to regrow the fleshly integument, then the hunting power of the human also grows. The entire animal kingdom takes part in this cycling, and all parts of the universe. Everything in the universe has its *inua*, spirit. This is diametrically opposite to the Christian pyramidal cosmology of God on top, humans in the middle, and animals at the bottom. The contrast has also been well shown in the findings of Gary Gossen (1974) among the Maya people of Mexico, and the same concept is to be found in most of the Native Indian communities of the two Americas. Its origin may be traced among the hunting peoples of northern Asia. Ironically it is to be feared that the later developed hierarchical Christian cosmology, the pyramidal one, bastardized in capitalism, and beheaded and nonreligiously extended in scientific Marxism, is what is ruining the ecology of the planet. One may ask, how is it that the people who have the simplest way of finding their subsistence, that of hunting and gathering, should develop an ethic that preserves the ecology, whereas during the subsequent march of history, through herding, hoe agriculture, advanced agriculture, and scientific industrial civilization, we should have diverged from the all-over democracy of the healthy globe to greater and greater hierarchies, higher and higher pyramidal structures? These now have seriously damaging consequences, as with the forestry clear-cutting practiced by powerful business firms in the tropics, and nuclear dumping by many nations in the formerly clean places of the deserts and the north. It is the very danger that is making us turn and examine the old self-sustaining systems and see what is behind them. I argue that it was that philosophy--theology if you will--that consciousness of the unity of all things, of cosmological cycling, of the *inua*, that was the core and essential element of survival for the Iñupiat--not utilitarianism--though they are a fully practical people. Because of need their ears were open to the message of the whale or caribou, "I will come to you if you are a moral person."

The Soul or Spirit

To help picture the Iñupiat knowledge of the soul we have Claire's description, based on her experience:

"You can see if a person's going to die. The person's soul looks like a still boat on a still sea, going out, far away. You have to bring it back so that the person doesn't die."

This soul can also be seen by the healer as a long line of light coming out of the fontanelle and speeding rapidly away. A shaman can follow it. Her or his spirit will have to travel fast and catch it before it has gone too far.

Netta, an old healer, related that on one occasion she died, and found herself looking down from above at the people bending over her body. Then she returned into her body and recovered. This entity, the Netta from above, would be the same soul that Claire mentions. Netta had yet other experiences in which her spirit traveled all the way to the far mountains, where she found herself on a green jade floor surrounded by the scent of flowers, among her dead ancestors. She was told, though, she had to go back (in the Iñupiat language). Similar experiences were reported by Claire and other Iñupiat and they corroborate many accounts in other parts of the world. (I myself have briefly felt myself looking down on myself in this manner.) It is the classic near-death experience.

The Iñupiat use the word "spirit" for this. On one occasion I was sitting by Netta's bedside when she was sick, during which there were three moments when I thought she was going to die. Afterwards Clem her grandson said to me in his slow voice: "Her spirit went out of her body three times. Three times it went out of her, and Claire brought it back and pulled it down into her stomach. When it leaves it goes up through the hole in the top of the head." I had been watching how Claire had been using her hands to free the blockage in Netta's stomach and bring the spirit down again into the body. She hugged Netta's head, put her own head on Netta's stomach, and used her arms in a containing way to hold the spirit in. Claire succeeded in bringing Netta around on those occasions.

These accounts together show an experiential sense of consciousness apart from the body. There is a range of similar understanding running through public consciousness in the rest of the United States in the churches as elsewhere. Theology is no longer as strict as it was. The bookshelves are crammed with a wide variety of writings, from ecofeminism and feminist deism to a sudden enormous interest in angels.

Spirit at Death

I was sitting next to old Joanna in church, as I always did. We went up to take communion, Joanna walking behind me. I turned after receiving it and walked back to my pew. After a while Joanna returned from her communion, tears running down her face. I tenderly touched her hand to comfort her.

"What is it?"

"I saw Paula, Paula, up there!" she whispered. She pointed up to the sanctuary.

"Oh, Paula!" I said holding my chin in amazement, gazing at empty space. Paula was her sister, dead now for many years. "Why, that's good, Joanna," I said. I thought, so Paula had not gone for ever.

Two years later, when Joanna herself died of cancer, I was back in the village on a Sunday, sitting in the church in the same pew. This time I felt Joanna palpably beside me--not visibly, but she was just *there*. I greeted her fondly; and eventually she was not there any more.

Reincarnating Souls

A knowledge of human reincarnation flourishes in Ivakuk. About half the kindergarten class of 1992 were named after some tragically dead person of the village. Naming is consciously done with an ear to the spirit that might want to re-live in the new child. This kind of "ear" might be termed a kind of divination, and a parent knows when it is successful by the contentment of the child afterwards. The renaming is specially attended to in the case of twins, when one dies. The other takes the spirit of the dead one. Reincarnation is considered desirable, in which it contrasts with the philosophy behind South Asian reincarnation, where the ideal is to go upward to Nirvana or to heaven with the gods, and not to be reincarnated on this sorrowing earth.

Thus the Iñupiat in a shadowy way identify a "soul" that can slip from one body to another. It is not exactly the same as the soul that can slip out of a person when she or he dies, though the point is arguable.

There are many events in which spirit ideas come to life, the flashes that occur often enough to keep a sense of these entities alive. It can be seen how the ideas about each type of spirit run into one another, the whale and its reincarnation, human reincarnation, the soul in the body's illness and death, and the ghost.

Let us look at what may be regarded in two ways, one as a laughable example of hysteria running through the village, *or* a flash from an unhappy and angry ghost.

I was in the elementary school at the class of one of the White teachers, writing family trees with the children. Several little boys accosted me and said, "Did you see the big animal last night? The Thing? It was scary."

"It was near those houses built on graves," said another. "It happened about five in the morning. Peter Westfield saw it, Dionne's son."

"What was it? What was it?" said one kid.

"A big black thing, very fat, seven feet high, large--"

"It had *seven* claws," broke in another boy, bouncing.

The White teacher listened with fond horror. She was married to an Iñupiaq. "It's the full moon just now," she said. "They come out at the full moon."

A little boy turned to me and looked up. "Wouldn't you be scared?"

"Probably not. I had four elder brothers and had to fight them all. I grew up brave."

The teacher told me she had seen on the TV there was a total eclipse of the moon at 2 a.m. in the morning, but she hadn't stayed up to see it.

I left at 11:20 a.m. and went to the store. Clem was standing at the back looking at some hardware.

"Yes," he said. "They're all talking about it." His voice fell into the sing-song wondering tone of the spirit-experienced. "When you build houses over graves, the masters of the ancient science come up." ("What can you expect?" his tone of voice was saying.) "The masters are still there. The sea...." He hesitated. I looked at him, wondering if he would say it. "The shamans. They were the masters."

"They weren't all bad," I said.

"They were like we are, some good, and some bad. Some had too much to drink. Some were *irritated* by what people do." His eyes widened. Then his voice became gentle. "They're going to have to recreate the old science."

I went with some children to Dionne's house. Here the children met up with a tall youth. This was Peter, only twelve. The children stood around in awe as he pointed to some marks that could be seen nearby. These were two long scratches on the ground, six feet in length and six feet apart.

"It's the Domino Snowman," said a small boy. He meant the Abominable Snowman. Other names for whatever it was were "Pokeman," as we have seen, "Hooked Man," "Satan," and "Bigfoot," although "Caribou Man" was mostly used.

Dionne arrived and we went to her house to talk. She unlocked her outer door, then unlocked her inner door. We sat on the sofa. She proceeded to describe the night.

"It was about 5.15 in the morning. I woke from this awful nightmare. I heard something. A voice kept saying--"

"In English?" I asked.

"Yes. It said, `I want to smash the house down.' There were a lot of swear words, obscenities," she said in a lowered voice. "I've been trying to keep such words away from Peter."

Dionne rose and showed me how Peter had lifted the window shade and looked out.

"Peter looked out and saw this black thing, thirty feet high. I screamed! I shouted at it, `Get out of here in the name of Jesus! Jesus! Jesus!' Like that. The name of Jesus! And the thing backed off. It ran down that Honda ATV ramp there and just disappeared."

As Dionne talked she was by no means in a jelly of fear. She said, "Lots of friends have been in to sit with me right through the night. They said, `Dionne, you have faith.'"

While telling me this Dionne up looked at one of the pictures on the wall. It showed Jesus praying at Gethsemane. She also looked at another print showing the Last Supper.

"See, my parents passed away. I'm lonely," she said. "My mother left us three years after my father because she missed him so much."

"I know how she felt," I said. "My husband Vic died four years ago." We hugged each other with tears in our eyes.

In the early hours of the next night I was woken by a huge CRUNCH on the gravel outside my window. It sounded enormous, as if an elephant had landed from a height on one foot. I listened, a little excited, but couldn't work up any fear. What could it be out there? The one crash was followed by dead silence. There was no sound of footsteps going away, no sound of a Honda engine, no rush of wings: just perfect silence. I raised the curtain. The window pane was covered with dewdrops so that I couldn't see out. I listened for a time but there wasn't a sound. So I went back to sleep.

Next morning my housemate said she too was awakened by the sound; moreover she had felt the house shake. She had a strong sense of evil which was very scary, also a feeling of cold. She'd heard me move the curtain but had said nothing. I was pretty impressed by now. I got dressed and went outside and around to the back. There was some very recently disturbed dirt in a sandy yellowy place. The dirt was damp and stirred, and looked as if it had been messed up four or five hours before, not much more. I took out my notebook and quickly drew a picture of what I saw. Two long joined grooves showed in the dirt, about eighteen inches long and about three inches deep. I even fetched the camera and took a picture. I looked for some sign of a big single depression that might have been made by whatever caused the "crunch" sound. But there was nothing, only the scratch marks. A bird was the only thing I could think of, an enormous bird with one foot. But why was there no sound of flapping afterwards? Was it a meteorite? Yet there was no sign of boiled slag, no large object that hadn't been there before, no big depression in the gravel. The sound had come from the surface, not like some underground movement of the permafrost. Was the thing partly material and partly spirit? I myself had felt no evil, just my usual sangfroid. Nonetheless the facts faced me, the sound and the marks.

The Iñupiat were used to such flashes as this appearance. Nevertheless still they marveled at each one; and they certainly did during the buzz of excitement in the village at the appearance of Satan alias the drunken master of ancient science, grown huge in form and in a bad temper.

The Spirit Helpers of Healers

Various spirit ideas enter the world of Iñupiat healing. I myself was learning the techniques in a very elementary way. One cannot stay this side of medical beliefs for such healing. One has to begin to see illness as some kind of substance--then it works. It does seem to work. The illness appears to be a kind of spirit substance, offending inside the body of the sufferer, telling lies to the afflicted and infecting her. Not those germs seen in a microscope, but spirit germs in a sense, yet quite palpable. There could be good ways to ameliorate bad intrusions--again by means of the body.

Evelyn was healing Netta's finger, by patient manipulation and listening to what was inside it. I had already learned that the healer takes the bad spirit into her own body.

"It's not just manipulation, is it?" I said to Evelyn. "You take out the illness."

"Yes. You take it into your own body. Then you have the pain, in the foot, or wherever it was in the person."

"How do you get rid of it?"

"You wash your hands, or blow it out." Evelyn blew from her body upwards. Netta herself, who was a healer, had told me, "Blow it up through the smoke hole."

In another case, Claire had been treating someone with a rash. "The trouble came out of her stomach," she said.

"By vomiting it out?" I asked.

"No. It came out. I myself had the pain in my shoulder, then in my arm, then it appeared as a lump in my hands and fingers."

"What happened then?"

"It just went away."

Often Claire mentioned that something more than germs transferred itself to her--something that could be termed the spirit form of the disease. I have felt it myself, and this is how Claire taught me.

She said, "I have that pain in my rib. It happened when I had a Honda accident. It got my rib here. It's still bothering me after four months."

I said, "Shall I rub it for you?"

She didn't say yes but went to sit down at the table. She put her hand to her back rib on the right and I followed with my hands where her hands showed the spot. Had she broken a rib? Yes, there on Claire's rib was a clenched "thing," about 1 ¼ inches across.

"That's it," she said.

"Yes," and I showed her the size with my finger and thumb. "It's clenched up."

I merely caressed it, as Claire would have done. Around, and on top. The thing seemed to dwell greedily on that rib, scaring the body into believing the body was sick. A lump all right. It was body stuff acting up hard in the wrong place. Now, astonishingly, I could feel that Claire was letting the thing go into my hands. She was letting it go and letting it go. The clenched part was mainly softish and normal now, but I could feel within it a little long section still hard, say half an inch long. And I handled the hard bit a little more. One gets a picture of it inside there. Now there was only the shadow left, and it was gone.

"That's better," said Claire, so I went to wash my hands. She told me later that the pain hadn't recurred.

I wasn't doing it. It happened from...doing the right action? Not exactly. It was from some...some "X" intervening when the two elements were there, that is, the person in pain, and a person evidently able to transmit it away. It seemed to me that the perception of the trouble was not "extrasensory perception," *outside* the senses, but an actual fine sense--existing contrary to expectations--in the fingers, somehow resulting in the transfer of the ailment. This sense perception of the fingers seems actually to exist; and there is a knowledge, a certain awareness in the human consciousness of a link between oneself and the sufferer, empowered by a kind of rushing of one's own consciousness into that of the other. This, whatever it is, is the concrete meaning of "sym-pathy," "feeling-with"; and it follows a palpable path, through the fingers' understanding. In the experience I had, it was something to do with the cast of feelings. When the feelings are open (they cannot be forced) the channels to the other person are open. Somehow nothing happens if the person is not sick; it is the hand's sympathy with the person's sick tissues that opens the way. The "sympathy" that passes is not only "energy" and heat, it is too personal for that. Whatever it is, it is the cause of the "opening" that takes place at the hands' contact with the sickness. That rushing of one's consciousness into the other person I think is exactly the *spirit* in Iñupiat parlance, alternatively "the good Lord," to whom the healers pray. It isn't one's own doing, it's one's own allowing. It can't be forced but is prayed for; "prayer" is of that nature and is mysterious, moral, in that way. A non-egoistic intention is necessary, but intention isn't it. It's the allowing of an opening. The practical part of Iñupiat healing is to create a conversation of bodies by the hands' work. The hands intimately work at the pain, they also reposition the organs, and attract the pain into the hands, which temporarily are "Jesus's hands." The healers sometimes say: "They are God's hands, not mine." The trouble can enter as far as the elbows, where one blocks it off. Then one washes out the bad thing one has drawn into one's hands.

When Claire talked of knowing the sickness and healing at a distance I realized that in healing at a distance there is no bodily touch, but perception might still take place in a bodily way, shown in one case in which Claire, while sitting in her house, felt the same pain in her own body which was afflicting someone outside as he approached the house in search of healing. The sense that achieves that kind of perception appears to be on the same continuum with the fine bodily sense I have just described. However the sense has been able to extend itself until it becomes the visionary "seeing from afar," "telepathy," and the seeing of spirit beings. How it does this is hard to say.

In the case of healing the spirit-being involved is now Christian, owing to the circumstance of the missionaries' abolition of shamanism. The people greatly needed their healers, so this change was the only way the ancient craft could flourish. Thus the spirit helper is "Jesus" or "God."

The Spirit Figures Experienced by Iñupiat Christians

Annie told me how she was on a visit to Wainwright, and went into the church on Sunday along with the people. Then she suddenly found the church quite empty, and realized she was alone there, looking up. Annie told me, "God came, and living water flowed down into my mouth. In! In!" She opened her mouth wide to show me. Her cousin also was with her in the church, and also found herself alone and experienced the same thing.

Now seals are usually given fresh water when they are caught and brought into the house, to honor them, just as caribou are given seal oil--the reversal of liquids being a recognition of the reversals of the ancient world, when everything was upside down. God was giving Annie fresh water when she entered his house. Again we have the syncretism of Christian spirit events with ancient Iñupiat ones.

Annie also told me how her husband John once had sinus trouble and very serious nosebleeds. Annie took him to Providence Hospital, Anchorage. On the way there Sam's face became stiff and white from loss of blood. After many difficulties they arrived at the hospital and Annie left Sam in the nurses' care. Annie stayed at her relatives, and sat up all night unable to sleep, wondering how Sam was getting on, and praying. Suddenly she felt a hard blow on her forehead which sent her head back so that she became unconscious. The relative came by and found her snoring. (Here Annie laughed, put her head back, and snored.)

In the morning Annie and her relative went to the hospital, and there was John with a bucket beside him and a mass of cotton ready for his nostrils. They had already operated on him. John told Annie that in the night he felt he was being lifted up, lifted up. He was going to heaven. Suddenly he felt two strong blows on his side.

"Who did that?" he wondered. His tongue had been curled back in his mouth, and now he was able to get it out. He called the nurse and asked the doctor if anyone had touched him. But none of them had.

"It was the Holy Spirit telling him to come back to life," said Annie. "It was just at the same time that I'd had been sent to sleep by God. He didn't want me to worry."

These accounts were given me in great seriousness by Annie. The spirit forms, God, Jesus, the Holy Spirit, were quite clear when one encountered them, but would in a sense fade and crack if made into strict categories.

Changes in Christian Theology and Christian Apology

The period of the late eighties to the mid-nineties in the village was one of continual coming and going across the so-called boundaries of reality. This was a stage of recrudescence of the people's pride. It was shown in the increase in the festival system and the revival of long-forbidden rituals; in the consciously made connection between the loss of culture and the terrible increase of alcoholism and suicide; and actually through the Christian churches.

At the 1992 whaling festival the Iñupiaq preacher in charge did not put God first in his dedication but the whale itself, saying, "In the old days the whale was our God. Now we are blending this idea with Christianity. We must never forget our tradition, and must always continue whaling." Here was a change in the people's consciousness. In former dedications the Christian God would have been all in all. Now the preacher was foremost in appealing for the perpetuation of tradition, that is, respect for the whale.

From 1988 on, as we have seen, the long-banned Messenger Feast, *Kivgiq*, was revived, depicting the eagle's gift of spirituality, music, and trade to the human members of the cosmological cycle. Animal dances, which horrified the old missionaries above all things, were revived. The old Iñupiat philosophy has been redeveloping, significantly *after* the revival performances got underway.

The churches have become conscious of the different emphases too. On June 9, 1991, Episcopal confirmation day, there appeared in Ivakuk church a surprising figure, a bishop dressed in the usual miter but in a cope which bore the American Indian insignia on the back, that is, the four directions in yellow, green, black, and blue; also mountains were depicted around the lower edge of the garment. This personage was none other than the new Episcopal bishop of Alaska, a young Choctaw Indian, broadly built and tough-faced, Steve Charleston by name. He proceeded to confirm thirty young Ivakuk folk in the church, while the Iñupiat and I sang our usual shrill chants in full harmony, "Ye Watchers and Ye Holy Ones"--spirit beings again.

As the bishop laid his hands on the heads of the young ones he made a different remark to each. He directed his sermon toward them, explaining the distribution of the loaves and fishes (reminding them of their own division of the whale). He ended by saying to them very seriously, "Later on in your life when you're in trouble you'll remember what I'm saying. You'll experience two things following you: the footsteps of your ancestors, your elders, protecting you. And the footsteps of the Holy Spirit." Note the order, the ancestors first and the Christian spirit second. Awareness of the ancestors was returning to at least one Christian church.

A little later in Juneau, Alaska, the state capital, on Wednesday October 30, 1991, the clergy of four churches, Lutheran, Catholic, Presbyterian, and Russian Orthodox apologized to Native Americans for their respective churches' past wrongs against them. The Rev. Larry Olson, pastor of the Resurrection Lutheran Church confessed that: "We have responded with fear, suspicion, arrogance, hostility, and a patronizing attitude that treats your people like children." Catholic Bishop Michael Kenny said to the Natives, "I humbly ask your forgiveness for the blunders, for the times the Catholic missionaries have failed to appreciate the depth of Native spirituality and to affirm the beauty of... Native culture, Native tradition." The Rev. Lew Rooker, pastor of the Methodist-Presbyterian church, and the Russian Orthodox leader also acknowledged their church's mistakes. Another instance of apology came from Pope John Paul II, on August 11, 1993. He apologized for the abuses committed by Christian colonizers against Indian peoples "by authorities who did not appreciate the spiritual values of indigenous cultures."

We may look upon these statements as a part of the swing in the world's thinking toward multiculturalism--and this may be due to the patient efforts of anthropology to widen the public's view.   Thus a link between anthropology and theology has already been effective.

Notes

1. *Acknowledgments* My warm thanks are due to my sponsors, the Wenner-Gren Foundation for Anthropological Research and the University of Virginia, and to Mary and James McConnell and many others for further help. I am particularly grateful to Claire, Clem, and Annie, each of whom was a guide and educator in different ways. The people of Ivakuk gave me unstinted encouragement, help, and affection which I remember with gratitude.

2. Names of people and places have been changed throughout this article.

Chapter 6

Theoretical Reflections on the Chagnon-Salesian Controversy

Frank A. Salamone

Introduction

Missionary scholars such as Burridge (1991), Donovan (1983), Hillman (1993, 1975, 1965), Kirwen (1987,1988a, 1988b), van der Geest and Kirby (1992), and Whiteman (1985), have long challenged interpretations of Christianity based on Western ideas. Their work has highlighted the problem of adapting Western European Christianity for people whose cultures include theological systems based on concepts different from and even hostile to those of Western thought.

Anthropologists, also, have been struggling to reconcile their discipline's assumptions with the dilemmas and challenges that the basic assumptions of Western thought that underlie their field of study may not be so universal as once assumed. This challenge has served to upset a number of anthropologists who feel that their very reason for being has been called into question. I argue that in situations already loaded with anxiety, such as fieldwork, challenges to old ideas only sharpen conditions of confusion which often lead to violent outbursts against those whose world-system is perceived as a threatening challenge to one's own.

The missionary-anthropologist relationship, in this perspective, is but a structural variety of a more basic relationship; specifically, a relationship between those who reside in a community in order to transform it according to some higher authority, termed "God," and those who seek to obtain knowledge in the name of another higher authority, termed "science." Since the missionary is often on the scene long before the anthropologist, he or she often possesses resources essential to the successful completion of many anthropological studies; for example, knowledge of the geography, understanding of local power structures, ties to officials, and access to indigenous peoples. Whenever pragmatism demands cooperation, hostility will normally be repressed. In a complementary fashion, however, whenever an anthropologist perceives that a missionary is obstructing successful completion of a project, overt hostility will erupt. At best, the missionary-anthropologist relationship is one charged with uncertainty, for both share a number of professional and personality traits and it is often their underlying similarities rather than their differences that result in conflict. Both, for example, ideally share a commitment to the welfare of indigenous peoples, according to their lights, and both also have an irrepressible streak of romanticism that dooms them to being forever marginal to their own cultures and societies, never fully at home anywhere and always seeking to be at home somewhere else.

It is a truism that people of good will can, and often do, disagree. Similarly, it is also a truism that love and hate are but two sides of the same coin, that love is inherently an ambivalent relationship. The history of anthropology, in fact, is marked by often violent disagreements. Foremost among these clashes have been those between missionaries and anthropologists. Often that disagreement stems from intense concern for the welfare of indigenous peoples and the best way to promote that welfare. It is important, therefore, that the disputes concerning indigenous interests not shift from the native peoples themselves, but always keep the native peoples in focus. It is also important, though a subsidiary issue, that partisans disagree without being disagreeable.

It is, therefore, commendable that both Napoleon Chagnon and Jose Bortoli agreed to discuss the issues that divided them over the past year or so.[1] This disagreement placed the Yanomami and their plight squarely in the center of discussion and such a discussion offers the best opportunity to air controversial and significant issues of interest. Certainly these are of interest to missiology and anthropology, but they are a far greater concern to both discipline's stated goals of serving the interest of the peoples among whom anthropologists and missionaries alike profess to serve.

The recent dispute, now thankfully laid to rest, between Napoleon Chagnon and the Salesian Fathers, provides a significant case study of a major dispute involving missionaries and anthropologists (For example, Chagnon 1993 and 1994). I became involved in the dispute as a result of my long-time research into the cultures of missionaries and anthropologists as these affected the field situation of ethnographers. Additionally, over time, I extended my research into missionary cultures and their impact on the culture and behavior of indigenous societies.

The Salesian Fathers asked me to go to Venezuela to look into the increasingly bitter dispute between Chagnon and the Salesian missionaries. I alerted Father Edward Cappelletti to the fact that I, also, had been involved in differences with Catholic missionaries during the course of my own field work in Nigeria. While it is true that our differences have generally been patched up and my overall association with missionaries has been cordial, still we do not agree on all issues. The Salesians assured me of a free hand in reporting my findings. They guaranteed me total access to their stations and to the Yanomami who resided near those stations on the Orinoco.

What I discovered was, to a large extent, what I had anticipated. People of good will had allowed themselves to be pushed into positions they felt uncomfortable occupying. Certainly, there were, and are, very real differences between Chagnon and the Salesians. These differences, however, had never seriously interfered with their cooperation over their long mutual history stretching back into the 1960s, an association that saw them cooperate in a friendly fashion on a number of projects (for example, Chagnon, Bortoli, and Eguillor 1988).

The authentic question, then, lay in what *really* lurked behind the explosive events of 1993-94. There were, of course, very serious issues involved in the dispute that had lain festering for years. The roots of the dispute lay in events of 1989-90. However, the Yanomami massacre in August 1993 at Hashimo-thieri provided the occasion for an explosion of invective between the two sides. It is essential to inquire just why this human tragedy involving Yanomami led to a missionary-anthropologist confrontation.

There were two Presidential Commissions chosen to investigate the massacre, one with Chagnon and one with Bishop Ignacio Velasco. The clash between these two competing Presidential Commissions, was an embarrassment to Chagnon. Most anthropologists, including me, instinctively flocked to Chagnon's side when they heard that Bishop Ignacio Velasco ordered an anthropologist from his field site. Further reflection and developments, however, led many to suspend final judgement pending additional investigation.[2]

As Cardozo notes,

> As I understand events, Velasco never ordered anybody out of Parima. He doesn't have that authority. It was the designated 'fiscal' from the Fiscalia General de la Republica who did so (E-mail May 16, 1995).

Most American anthropologists, however, did not discover that fact until much later in the dispute.

The Issues

A number of key issues appear to underlie the dispute between the Salesians and Chagnon. Principal among these concerns is control of research in the Orinoco region of Venezuela. The issue, in many people's views, is whether Chagnon or the Salesians should control research in the sector. Chagnon's statements imply that he would either exclude Salesians from the area or allow them in only if they subject their work to his evaluation.

From this perspective, the entire issue resolves itself into a "Turf War" and the Salesians simply joined with other enemies of Chagnon in a united front. Prominent in this phalanx was the French anthropologist, Jacques Lizot. Lizot and Chagnon have often differed bitterly on theoretical and substantive issues. In addition, a number of Venezuelan anthropologists resent what they perceive, rightly or not, as Chagnon's efforts to establish American research control over a region in their country.

Chagnon himself has clearly stated the issue:

> ... the central issue regarding the future of the Yanomamo: what do informed and concerned citizens think should be the respective roles and authorities of (1) the Venezuelan and Brazilian governments, (2) religious institutions such as the several Mission groups working among the Yanomamo, (3) NGOs, (4) medical researchers and practitioners, and (5) scientific researchers from many different disciplines? All the above now play some role in this process, but the roles are poorly defined and who has what kinds of authority is an open question that, if unresolved, will lead to increasing chaos and increasing peril for the Yanomamo. How should all of these groups, ideally, interact and cooperate with each other? . .. Whatever exists on paper or in theory, an outside observer would be obliged to conclude that in Venezuela the de facto authority determining the future of the Venezuelan Yanomamo rests in the hands of the Salesian Missions of Amazonas. Given the importance of this to the future of the Yanomamo, this apparent abrogation of legal authority and responsibility by the Venezuelan government is something to which serious thought be given and should be widely discussed in Venezuela (1994 Jul-Aug:161-162) [Translation from Spanish by Napoleon Chagnon].

Chagnon's original research, however, was carried out near a settled mission area, that of the New Tribes Mission. Not surprisingly, many missionaries perceived this attack as a betrayal of their hospitality. Although the primary research for Chagnon's "the fierce people" was not conducted primarily at the Salesian stations, the Salesians have aided Chagnon and other anthropologists from their coming to the Orinoco in the mid-1950s.

Moreover, although the story of *Yanomamo: The Fierce People* is familiar to most basic anthropology students, the Salesians are upset that most students do not, however, get to know that events are more complicated than they might appear. The situation described in the book is not, as students might infer, an everyday one.[3] Missionaries have been quick to indicate that Chagnon's description of the Yanomami has not been an accurate one (Finkers 1994, for example). They have been joined by others whom Chagnon once deemed his friends (Asch 1991, for example, and Good 1992, his former student).

Chagnon, himself, at that time and others often was a man under extreme pressure. After all, although Chagnon was the anthropologist who had "opened up" Yanomami research, nonetheless he was out of the Yanomami area from the late 1970s until 1985. Therefore, he sought a means to stabilize his position and assure himself of research access. He concocted a biosphere project with Charles Brewer Carias, a Venezuelan dentist, who had political connections. This scheme would enable him to maintain great control of projects in the Venezuelan Yanomami territory. Unfortunately, Brewer Carias is not a favorite of either Venezuela's anthropological or mission community and this tie did little to heal the rift between Chagnon and members of these Venezuelan communities. [4]

Chagnon blames much of his problems regarding access to research on the Salesian missionaries. Although he had indeed collaborated on projects with the Salesians, he nonetheless regarded them as obstacles to his free admittance to the Amazon area. The biosphere would be closed to all but productive research. As senior anthropologist and director of the biosphere, Chagnon, a proven anthropologist, would decide which research would be in the Yanomami's interest. It would also ensure him access to the Yanomami.

Terence Turner, however, offers a different interpretation of the situation.[5] Turner agrees that Chagnon indeed raises serious issues regarding development, issues of concern to people of good will, missionaries and anthropologists alike. Chagnon raises a significant concern regarding whether the higher death rate at Salesian missions communities is a result of long-term Yanomami settlement having a damaging effect on Yanomami nutrition through their over hunting's leading to resource exhaustion.[6] Chagnon accused the Salesians, in sum, of killing the Yanomami with kindness at their frontier posts. Turner, however, questions this conclusion, asking "Is it that their posts are collecting points for the desperately ill or that Salesian policies are bad?" In short, he argues that it is essential to ascertain the cause of the high death rate at Salesian posts.

In fact, Turner provides the strongest statement on record of any American anthropological opposition to Chagnon. He accuses him of "unconscionable slandering of those helping the Yanomami," "a sociopath who slanders those who help the Yanomami without regard to the Yanomami themselves." Turner views Chagnon as "a liar whose lies damage the Yanomami." Among Turner's specific complaints is the fact that Chagnon's labeling of the Yanomami as somehow inherently "fierce" is still quoted in the Brazilian press in anti-Yanomami articles. While admitting that a person's scientific writing is often distorted in the popular press, Turner point out that Chagnon has never repudiated the uses made of his work. In fairness to Chagnon, it must be noted that he does, in fact, repudiate this misuse in his 1983 version of *Yanomamo: The Fierce People* (Chagnon 1983: 213-214).

Turner repeated many of his charges in a question to Chagnon at the meetings of the American Anthropological Association in Atlanta, Georgia, on December 2, 1994, at the session, *Anthropology and Theology*. Since the question sums up many of the charges against Chagnon, I reproduce the transcript here of the question and of Chagnon's response.[7]

> I have two questions, the first about the problem of who speaks for the Yanomami, the Yanomami leadership, with particular emphasis on the case of Davi Kopinawa. Professor Chagnon has just said some kind words about Davi so he's obviously a nice guy and means well. And I think that's true. He also said that he seems to have all his remarks scripted for him. What he says isn't his own; it doesn't come out of his own mouth or at least his own heart. It comes from Anglos, I suppose. This is not true. I speak as someone who is listed as a co-author of the longest printed text that Davi Kopinawa is down in. That's a text printed in full in *Cultural Survival*. It has an article which I suggest you all look at, if you're interested, called "*I Fight Because I Am Alive*." Now this article, which was partly reprinted in the newsletter of this Association, was dictated to me by Davi. I asked the questions, what I hoped were leading questions to get him to address points that were issued between the Yanomami of Brazil and the government of Brazil about the whole problem of the reserve that was then in question. Davi answered these questions at great length and in terms which I certainly could never have invented. They are terms which are soaked with Yanomami concepts, Yanomami cosmology, Yanomami ideas of diseases, Yanomami ideas of cosmic order and disorder. These are not concepts which were supplied by me or by anyone else to Davi. But Davi has used this rhetoric on other occasions. He has also used the rhetoric of conservationist organizations. He is trying to represent his idea of the interest of his people in terms that we can understand that will be real for us. He's trying to manipulate our rhetoric but, or hence, which I think he sincerely believes are the ends of his people. He is not a mouthpiece for anybody. Now Professor Chagnon has recently said in print in the American Anthropological Association newsletter that I have forfeited all credibility as an anthropologist because I have referred to

Davi Kopinawa as a genuine Yanomami leader, whereas he is only a mouthpiece for NGOs. It's not only a matter of this being false, it's a matter of this undermining the most effective spokesman for Yanomami interests, although it's quite correct to say that Davi is not a chief of all the Yanomami, he's only a leader of one section of the Yanomami, but nevertheless, he is the most effective spokesman for many of the general interests of the Yanomami to the outside world. He is someone who has made a political difference for the Yanomami, especially in Brazil. To undermine him in such an untruthful way, without knowing him and obviously without taking the trouble to analyze the text of his speeches of his publications, directly damages the interest of the Yanomami. And I submit that this is in apparent contradiction to the ethical dictates of this Association in which the rules of professional responsibility which hold above all that we as anthropologists should endeavor not to damage the interest of the people we work with. Their interests must come first unless it's a matter of declaring scientific truth which is not the issue in the case.

SALAMONE: Napoleon, would you like to ...

CHAGNON: You're god damn right I'd like to. I came here in a spirit of conciliation with an interest in advocating the rights of the Yanomami and I'm going to ignore all of Professor Turner's comments, which I think are out of place in the spirit of what we're attempting to accomplish in this meeting today.

The spirit to which Chagnon refers is the spirit of reconciliation which took place publicly at the session, *Anthropology and Theology* at which he and the Salesian representative, Jose Bortoli, agreed to a truce.

On their part, the Salesians in New Rochelle have stirred up controversy and animosity regarding their mailing of anonymous articles. There were two distinct distributions of material. One went to anthropologists listed in the AAA *Guide to Departments*. The other was placed on a table at the American Anthropological Association Annual Meetings. There are various people who might have translated and distributed the Venezuelan articles. No one is, however, willing to go on record claiming or naming these people. Some think that a disgruntled former student of Chagnon sent them. Other Venezuelan anthropologists, however, suggested that Bishop Velasco sent the clippings and then the Salesians sent a mailing out to people on the American Anthropological Association's mailing list. The clippings, sent by Velasco, were translated, either by a Salesian translator or by one of Chagnon's anthropological opponents. Additionally, it is beyond dispute that the Salesians carried a package of materials to the 1993 American Anthropological Association meetings in Washington, DC, leaving this package on a display table with no identification as to their origin. Unfortunately, the Salesians still do not understand the anger most anthropologists feel regarding the receipt of anonymous mailings and handouts.

I asked Father Cappelletti why he did not understand that anger. His response was that the articles enclosed in the package were from reputable sources and those articles were clearly identified. The fact that anthropologists are plagued throughout the year with anonymous mailings from religious sources damning us for embracing the evils of evolution or some other heresy meant nothing to him. Nor did the fact that American academics still remember the evils of McCarthyism and its hidden accusers. Certainly, the subtleties of subjective selectivity in article selection did not impress him. There was no argument I could put forth that moved him to consider how repugnant anonymous accusations were to American academics.

The Salesians argue, moreover, that their action was in response to an Op Ed article Chagnon (1993) published in the *New York Times*, essentially charging the Salesians with inciting the Yanomami to murder him. Additionally, Chagnon attacked the Salesians for selling rifles to their mission Yanomami which these Yanomami used to kill other Yanomami in warfare. Moreover, Chagnon charged that the Salesians had distorted the Yanomami's way of life and were responsible for bringing epidemics into their area. In sum, the article, intentionally or not, was a rehearsal of most of the charges anthropologists had hurled at missionaries over the years.[8]

The Salesians responded in kind. Their mailing and distribution campaign was but part of a concerted effort to discredit Chagnon. They worked with Jacques Lizot who launched a bitter attack on Chagnon.[9] Other attacks followed, most notably that of Timothy Asch.[10] Brother Finkers, a Salesian brother whom Chagnon accused of not rendering medical aid to the Yanomami in an emergency, responded in an article.[11] Some attacks were less open and conducted by people who refuse to go on the record, some in fear of retaliation and others for less noble reasons.

In any case, the Salesians were not "a small minor Italian order" who would take a frontal attack quietly.[12] They enlisted their vast network in support of their efforts and were prepared to escalate their efforts if they saw a need to do so.[13] The Salesians were frustrated with their failure to obtain Op Ed space in the *New York Times* and the refusal of *Science* and other journals to print material on the Yanomami that contradicted Chagnon's position.

In the midst of this furor, the major issues were often lost, misplaced, and redefined according to the interests of those listing the issues. The underlying point, according to Jesus Cardozo, is how well Chagnon gets along with the

Yanomami. In essence, Cardozo sees three discrete issues in the dispute: Chagnon and the Yanomami; Chagnon's accusations; and Chagnon's personality. In common with most other anthropologists, he argues that Chagnon's embrace of the theory of sociobiology be disregarded. After all, Cardozo, himself, is interested in sociobiology and Chagnon's student but disagrees with him regarding his evaluation of the Salesians. He states that Chagnon is opportunistic, noting that his charges appear in the *New York Times, The Times Literary Supplement, The Chronicle of Higher Education* and other such popular journals. All of these articles, however, according to Cardozo, ignore the fact that he was illegally in the area.[14]

Luisa Margolies, who with her husband Graziano Gasparini collaborated with Chagnon from 1986-1989, notes that it is ironic to see Chagnon cast as a victim after his attacks. In fact, Cardozo and Margolies counseled that only by focusing on the attacks could any sense by made of the imbroglio. Indeed, there are facts that help explain the attacks.[15]

First, there have been significant changes in Salesian mission organization. Prominently, there is currently a policy of concentrated planning in distinction to the pre-1976 policy of independent stations. The Salesians, under the influence of Jacques Lizot, have pursued a policy encouraging non-dependent development among the Yanomami. They have advocated a course in which the Yanomami participate in the planning, development, and control of any schemes in their area. The Salesians, in sum, counsel the Yanomami to pursue only those projects that fall into the category of sustainable development. Moreover, the Salesians have warned the Yanomami about the sources and dangers of epidemics. Consequently, the Yanomami have asked to see the permits of any people entering Amazonas because illegal visitors may be carriers of disease or endanger life as do the illegal miners from Brazil, *garampieros*.

These changes have led to modification in relationships between Chagnon and the Yanomami. Perhaps, the most glaring example is a Yanomami letter sent to a government minister asking that Chagnon be kept out of the area. Chagnon blames the Salesians for encouraging the Yanomami to become aggressive enough to write a letter. Cesar Zimanawe, a Yanomami, states that he wrote the letter unaided and not encouraged by anyone else, including the Salesians. The Salesians, however, did publish the letter in *La Iglesia en Amazonas,* their Venezuelan organ (1990:20). Since the letter has led to considerable strife, I reproduce it here.

Mavaquite 7-2-90

Señor Chagnon

Nosotros los de Mavaquita, Washere y Quetipapirei theri y Mishi mishitheri no queremos que Usted venga alto Orinoco.

Porque Usted tenia pleito con Washere y ademas no queremos que Saco en Taritatheri Washewetheri Meishi mishither tierre mucha pelic y sangranto mucho los yanomami en la pelicula asi me contos un amigo.

No queremos que saque meas pelicula.

Cesar Zimanawe

When I personally questioned Cesar Zimanawe, he maintained that he alone had written the letter. He then launched into an attack on those who believe that Yanomami should remain frozen in time so that anthropologists and other Westerners could come to visit them and admire their primitiveness.

"They come here," he stated, "and take their clothes off so that they can be like us. But if we put clothes on to be like them, they object that we are not authentic. I told Shaki[16] that when he first came here he had an old boat with an old motor. His boats got better as time passed. Then he came in helicopters. I asked him why he could improve and we could not? Why must we paddle in old canoes when we can get motors for our boats?"

Chagnon's depiction of them as fierce people has been an essential part of Yanomami resentment of Chagnon. They argue that although there is violence in their society, they are not violent people. As Cesar Zimanawe told me,

I have killed but I am not a killer. I do not like violence. That is why I am now living near the mission station. It is peaceful here and raids are less likely. No man likes to die. It may be necessary to kill and die but I want to live in peace and be with my children. The missionaries always tell us to be peaceful and to settle our problems through discussion.

This comment came in response to my asking him whether the missionaries had sent him to kill Chagnon as he has charged. After laughing at the thought, he said he did not want to kill Shaki (Bee), the missionaries would never ask any Yanomami to kill anyone else. Moreover, he asked, "Why doesn't Shaki come and make these charges to my face? That is the Yanomami way." [17]

Cardozo was at a meeting with the Directora of Asuntos Indigenas who told him that Chagnon's permit was suspended as a result of Cesar's letter. According to Cardozo, Bortoli advised Chagnon to go to the Orinoco and discuss his problem face-to-face with the Yanomami. He failed to do so. In addition, the minister and other Venezuelans, including Yanomami, charge that Chagnon has neglected to donate promised materials. For example, at the end of his 1985-87 fieldwork he did not donate his outboard motor, dugout canoe, and other materials to the Universidad Central de Venezuela as pledged.

Chagnon, of course, has his own reasons for being angry. Beginning in 1985, according to Cardozo, he has claimed that Yanomami films have been distributed that contain pornography inserted in the middle. These films have been shown in the Shabono. Chagnon feels that their was a conspiracy to undermine his integrity. Cardozo, however, does not believe that the Salesians are responsible for this conspiracy.

> In 1985, during my first visit to the Upper Orinoco, in the village of Hauyapiwei, Chagnon said to me that the Yanomami had complained to him about his taking pictures of them because they had been shown a film made by him that showed naked women's vaginas. Chagnon was angry and ranted about who could have spliced pornographic footage into 'one of his films' (presumably those done by Timothy Asch) and shown to the Yanomami. These are the facts as I know them. I have *NEVER* heard of any other information that confirmed or even made reference to the existence of such a film not to its alleged exhibition in a shabono or elsewhere. In fact, whenever I have asked Yanomami and missionaries alike in the Upper Orinoco and anthropologists in Caracas, I have always been answered with incredulous laughter at what people perceive as another one of Chagnon's tales. As far as I know, *NOBODY* has ever heard or seen this film, nor does anyone think it likely that such a film was ever doctored as alleged by Chagnon and then transported with generator, projector, screen and other implements to be shown in a shabono (Cardozo 1995).

On the other hand, however, the Yanomami say that they have seen Chagnon's films, complete with "vaginas," shown in the North. The Yanomami say that other Venezuelans remark that the Yanomami are "just like monkeys." On principle, they object to having their way of life ridiculed and some Yanomami believe that Chagnon's depictions have led to ridicule among their compatriots as well as among people in other countries. In addition, the Yanomami say that he takes too many pictures "is always talking about the dead." In a typically Yanomami aside, however, one of the Yanomami told me, "besides he does not pay us enough for talking about the dead!"

Chagnon believes that the Salesians had pushed the Yanomami into writing the letter. Whether they did or not, it is indisputably true that when Chagnon failed to respond to the letter, which the missionaries delivered to him. They then encouraged the Yanomami to deliver it to the Directora de Asuntos Indigenas to make her aware of the Yanomami's position. They also published that letter in their journal *La Iglesia en Amazonas*. Therefore, when Chagnon wanted to return to the High Orinoco, he was told that there was a problem and that he had to clear that problem before he could carry out any further research. Bortoli, a Salesian missionary, believes that incident was the start of the fighting and confrontation between the Salesians and Chagnon. In this he is in perfect agreement with Chagnon. That confrontation has had some amusing twists.

Interestingly, for example, Chagnon has stated that the Yanomami who speak Spanish are not really authentic Yanomami. That is a charge to which the Yanomami object rather vehemently. They are changing, and it is, truly, the mission that has brought about many changes. However, it is rather naive for any anthropologist to believe that without the mission station the Yanomami would not have changed at all. The real question is whether the manner in which the missionaries have brought about change is compatible with Yanomami culture. Bortoli, in fact, is a great proponent of the process of "inculturation," not to be confused with "enculturation." Nzomiwu"s (1988: 13) sees inculturation as a process related to indigenization.[18]

> For christian theologians it is an incarnational attempt to articulate the christian faith clearly in the thought-forms of the environment in which Christians find themselves but it is not to use such thought-patterns to introduce ideas which change the meaning and substance of the christian message [lower case 'c' in the original].

It is simply wrong-headed to state that only those Yanomami who live in the forest are authentic Yanomami. Such a static and monolithic view of culture has been long superseded in anthropology and missiology. The Salesians believe that if people themselves want to change, then outsiders telling them they cannot change are as guilty of cultural imperialism as those who tell them how to change."In other words," as Bortoli states, "if people want to change, who are we to tell them not to change?"

If the Yanomami are to survive, they must be able to make their own case in front of Venezuelan officials. The days are passing, the Salesians believe, when a few machetes will be enough to allow anyone to exploit the Yanomami. As Bortoli says,

The question or problem for us is to make them very aware of the dangers of certain change because they want to change everything, and they see something they want, they want, they want. We want to make them conscious of the dangers of certain changes. You may have outboard motors but to keep the motor going you have to have money to buy gasoline. And so we have to work more than ever to make them aware of the consequences of change. We are doing that. But even if you speak they to them, they have to touch the experience. And they love when they have made an experience. They come to you to speak to you about it again. You are seeing what they are thinking now and so on. You want to be present in this process.

To that extent that the instillation of this caution among the Yanomami has made the Yanomami more difficult to work among, Chagnon is correct in stating that the Salesians have made his research more difficult. However, this caution is a necessary ingredient in the world in which they live, for the threat of illegal miners and the slaughter in 1993 are very real issues. The lust for Yanomami land among many Brazilians and Venezuelans is very concrete as is the danger of epidemic disease carried into their area by outsiders. The outside world even begrudges the Yanomami the resources and their cost required to fight these endemic diseases.

Teo Marcano, a physician who served for five years in the High Orinoco, summed up the situation in the following manner.

Now we are preparing a system to supplement the health of the Yanomami. There is no continuing health service there. It is very expensive. You have to spend more money on the few thousand Yanomami then among the many people in Puerto Ayucucho. The Ministry of Health has to spend more money among the Yanomami than among other peoples. The Yanomami don't vote. They don't produce anything. When you try to make a proposal to the major foundations, they ask you "For who are the Yanomami relevant?" (Marcano 1994).

Reflections

While peace between anthropologists and missionaries is undoubtedly a very desirable thing, to an anthropological outsider it is clear that the message the missionaries send is often not the one their audience always receives. Missionaries are well aware that cultural differences in both the encoding and decoding of a message as well as in the "medium" through which the message travels hinder and distort its reception and interpretation. Too often, however, they tend to think of "culture" occurring at some "macro level," almost as a massive penumbra enshrouding a body of people. It is far more meaningful to visualize "culture" as being created in individual interpersonal encounters as well as in the expectations each participant brings to such encounters.

Luzbetak (1988:124), among the most anthropologically oriented of all missiologists, states clearly:

> If Christ were not unique and universal, normative and final, most of what the present author understands as mission, whether in non-Christian or Christian lands, would make little sense indeed. A unique and universal Christ is what the Gospel is all about, current radical theologians notwithstanding. ON this\single basic theological premise alone much that an anthropologist may or may not have to suggest will depend.

The *ad hoc* contextualization often made in mission fields because of pastoral concerns frequently adds to the mixed message of the mission. After all, if one "respects" the old ways then why are some acceptable and others not? Why agree that God is found in all religions but refuse to let one be Christian, Muslim, and traditionalist at the same time? Why are the modernization tendencies of Christianity so inherently opposed to traditional relations?

Finally, unanswerably, many indigenous people ask,"Why do you wish to give us a version of Christianity so different from that practiced in your own country?" Even the remotest parts of the world are now well within the world communication network. Without doubt many people became Christians in order to gain perceived advantages elsewhere in the world. Not all perceived advantages, however, are material. Many are psychological. Others are, in fact, defensive. Too many of these needs, desires, and expectations are simply out-of- awareness. Culturally, they are merely taken for granted. The fact that a missionary does not always understand these demands in the cultural terms of the people is not a problem of good-will. It is a problem of cultural translation. Good-will alone cannot avoid mixed messages resulting from conflicting structural and cultural categories.

The missionary-anthropologist Kenelm Burridge warns, furthermore, that

> Official statements of ideals and tolerance collide with new ways of thinking, fresh attitudes to the world, and differing dispositions that require new institutions and structures to contain them. Respect for institutions and respect for persons are not necessarily tied together (Burridge 1991: 200).

A major theme of Burridge's perceptive study is the persistent uncertainty found in even the most positive statements of cultural respect on the part of Christian organizations. Reservations regarding practices opposed to missionary perceived essence of Christianity, usually those involving polygyny, are maintained. I repeat that "the past" is used to promote various agendas and that no imputation of ill-will is necessary to understand the dynamics of the social situation and competition.

Cox (1991), moreover, reminds us that cultures are changing at a dazzling pace and that those missionaries who advocate a return to "traditional" beliefs may, in some sense, provoke modernizing peoples to accuse them of cultural imperialism, as Mbefo (1987), has, in fact, done. Moreover, it is also imperative to note that no culture is a unified object and that people have always used aspects of their cultural heritage to promote their desired goals.

The question at issue is "In what sense can we say that a culture is `authentic?' Who, for example, defines the terms of authenticity (McDonald 1993)? We are long past regarding any culture as consistent and unified. The concept of hegemony has alerted us to consider the terms of discourse and to be alert to who sets those terms.

Unquestionably, we automatically inquire "Authentic for whom?" Similarly, we regard culture as in one sense or other as a communication system. Therefore, we not only seek to discover for whom it is authentic but under what conditions and for what purpose it may be so. The audience equally contributes to its interpretation and social actors, willingly or not, present a particular version of their "culture," or more accurately from their cultural repertoire, to fit their particular audience. From a transactional, symbolic-interactionist, perspective, they do so in hopes of attaining some perceived good and, perhaps, to avoid some discerned evil.

This line of inquiry consequently seeks to discover how a "genuine" or "authentic" culture helps people solve problems. It appears necessary to distinguish in what manner a people distinguishes what constitute problems and how they apply "cultural" solutions to those problems. In that sense, therefore, the concept of "authentic" culture emerges as an adaptive one in so far as it directs our attention to the manner in which people use aspects of their cultural repertoire to adapt to particular self-defined problems. Since culture, so conceived, enables people to adapt to specific settings it is an evolutionary concept in keeping with its ever-changing kaleidoscopic nature.

Any attempt to address these dilemmas takes us into deep-seated regions of the psychology and culture of missionaries. Missionaries deserve the same type of intensive ethnographic work we extend to any other group. Such work would profitably begin through distinguishing the differences found among missionaries in terms of national origin, religion, age, sex, location of work, personality, education, and other relevant variables. This information would move us toward greater understanding of cultural processes.

In fact, the missionary, in league with many anthropologists, is at heart a romantic who does not wish to see "his people" become "too" modern. At the same time, he knows he "cannot retard progress." The message he sends others is often mixed because his own internal message is itself confused. I use "he" consciously, for women missionaries are much clearer in their mission.[19] There are hints that African and Euro-American clergy have begun to move in that direction. So far their efforts have not produced a "paganization" of Christianity. Rather, these efforts have led to a deeper appreciation of its universality. Incarnation theology and a deeper understanding of liturgical reform have led the way toward a true merger of traditions.

Culture is, among other things, a pattern for living and a means for adapting to an ever-changing cultural environment, a position explicitly stated in *Gaudium et Spes* (1965) which asserted that the Church "is not tied exclusively or indissolubly to any race or nation, to any one particular way of life, or to any customary practices, ancient or modern." Therefore, questions regarding its authenticity degenerate into mere Platonic quibbles for those with political axes to grind while the real people who live their own authentic lives somehow realize that whatever gets them through their days is authenticity enough.

Conclusion

At root the Salesian-Chagnon dispute was a fraternal struggle, a struggle between two branches of the family. One branch seeking truth in what is apparent only through empirical methods; the other, through a metaphysical method. Each, perhaps secretly, envies the other his means to certainty while each must deal with his own internal demons and doubts. The conflict was not truly about rifles, depletion of hunting resources, nor the best means, if any, to promote sustainable development. It was about the human condition itself and fear of seeing one's self in the other.

Missionaries and anthropologists in spite of their protests share a number of characteristics. Both, for example, claim spiritual descent from figures in classical antiquity; missionaries from St. Paul and anthropologists from Herodotus. Both witnessed a rebirth of their professions during the Renaissance as new peoples impressed themselves upon European consciousness in a manner previously unknown. Indeed, many "new" trends in both missiology and anthropology had their roots during the classic and

Renaissance periods, including the current missionary concept of "inculturation" theology and the anthropologist's preoccupation with reflexivity. Finally, both established images dominant in the popular mind during the late nineteenth and early twentieth centuries; namely, that of idealistic adventurers who travel to remote and exotic places to serve an aspiration outside of oneself. Once established, that image has been virtually impervious to any changes that have occurred since.[20]

I have written previously of the contradictory relationship that exists between missionaries and anthropologists and of the great debt anthropologists owe to missionaries for much of their work (Salamone 1994, 1983, 1982, 1977). I suggest that one of the reasons for the uncertainty of missionary-anthropologist relationships stems from their theoretical disagreements. Moreover, I further suggest that many of the theoretical disagreements between anthropologists and missionaries are more apparent than real, stemming from motives not deeply related to theoretical issues at all but having more to do with boundary-maintaining mechanisms and self-definition or more material motives. In either case, their disagreements have more to do with power struggles for perceived scarce resources than with abstruse conceptual formulations. Missionaries, typically, spend far more time in the field than do anthropologists. Their language skills generally surpass those of anthropologists and their relationships with indigenous peoples tend to be of longer and deeper dimensions than do those of anthropologist. On the other hand, their purpose in being in the field, in spite of some demurrers, is to change the people with whom they come into contact. Specifically, it is to change their world view, converting both the people and their world-view to their own religion and understanding of the world. Their understanding of the people's cosmology and way of life, therefore, at least in theory, is mainly for the purpose of changing them to their own version of western cosmology and behavior. Generally, anthropologists have looked rather cynically at missionaries and their objectives.

In common with other nineteenth and twentieth century rationalists, Sir James Frazer was a curious mixture of Rationalist/Romantic. Certainly, he shared the contemporary fascination with "exotic" practices. These practices were carefully displayed in their full glory for all to wonder over. Practices from hither and yon found themselves cheek-by-jowl with one another to suit Frazer's grand evolutionary scheme.

Conversely, however, Frazer placed contemporary practices alongside exotica from areas foreign to the European world. His point appears to be to demonstrate that underneath the apparent surface differences there was an underlying communal reality uniting these "strange" practices. That shared reality Frazer attributed to "the psychic unity of mankind," meaning not only that all humans share a common humanity but that given similar circumstances they will arrive at similar solutions to life's problems. Although it is a rather mechanistic view of human behavior and mental processes, it does have the virtue of including the "savage races" within the human family. At times, in fact, Frazer even seems to glance nostalgically at a certain lost innocence no longer within the grasp of "scientific man" of his day.

It is this powerful evocation of "the savage," as well as his generally reverberant literary style, that has enabled Frazer to withstand powerful attacks from within and outside anthropology while influencing professional and amateur anthropologists. My point is that Frazer has inspired missionaries and anthropologists in numerous ways and that a study of their movement away from his direct sway holds one key for understanding the trajectory of missionary-anthropologist relationships. Here I wish to focus on Frazer's treatment of magic and religion and the manner in which exploration of that false dichotomy has developed in anthropological and missiological thought.

For Frazer (1963:11-12), it is clear, magic and religion were contrasting categories, sharing only the fact that they were erroneous ways of thinking about reality. Magic, moreover, differentiated itself from religion as "savages" began to notice the first glimmerings of natural law. To paraphrase Malinowski, who acknowledged his debt to Frazer even while differing with him on numerous issues, "Magic compels, religion requests." Magic was simply false science, based on faulty empirical observation. It would, under the right circumstances, evolve into true science but its basic orientation was scientific not religious. It is true that magic frequently attempted to influence spiritual beings or powers whose existence could not be empirically verified, but both Malinowski and Frazer attributed that as part of the cultural milieu of various people and focused on the procedures used in addressing these beings or powers (Malinowski 1948).

Malinowski's assertion that religion finds its own fulfillment in itself while magic is always for something other than itself, for good crops or a successful voyage, appealed greatly to missionaries who reversed Malinowski's progression and with Wilhelm Schmidt saw the movement from magic to religion as a devolutionary one, as evidenced by Schmidt's favorite example, the Pygmies (Schmidt 1935). They could ignore the fact that science, not religion, was the asserted logical mental perfection of magic and that religion for both Frazer and Malinowski was a dead-end side road.

Some hope, moreover, could be taken from Frazer's conclusion to the *Golden Bough* (1963:826):

The reality in the "grounded world," however, is somewhat different from that of the more logical "typical" or "ideal" one. It is that "grounded world," the phenomenological reality and the use partisan actors make of theoretical constructs which I have explored in this paper. At that level basic behavioral similarities stand out in stark relief from those divergent philosophical positions which biased actors employ to underpin and "explain" them. In sum, I contend that anthropologists and missionaries are truly squabbling siblings who share a Romantic ancestry, as distasteful as the thought may be to many members of either camp.

Brighter stars will rise on some voyager of the future - some great Ulysses of the realms of thought - than shine on us. The dreams of magic may one day be the waking realities of science. But a dark shadow lies athwart the far end of this fair prospect. For however vast the increase of knowledge and of power which the future may have in store for man, he can scarcely hope to stay the sweep of those great forces which seem to be making silently but relentlessly for the destruction of all this starry universe in which our earth swims as a speck or mote. In the ages to come man may be able to predict, perhaps even to control, the wayward courses of the winds and clouds, but hardly will his puny hands have strength to speed afresh our slackening planet in its orbit or rekindle the dying fire of the sun. Yet the philosopher who trembles at the idea of such distant catastrophes may console himself by reflecting that those gloomy apprehensions, like the earth and the sun themselves, are only parts of that unsubstantial world which thought has conjured up out of the void, and that the phantoms which the subtle enchantress has evoked to-day she may ban tom-morrow. They too, like so much that to common eyes seems solid, may melt into air, into thin air.

To the religious mind that beautiful and poetic conclusion evinced a despair with mere rationality and its inevitably logical tragic resolution. The poet T. S. Eliot, after all, was of a rather conservative religious inclination but as Bartholomeusz (1991;340-41) indicates Eliot took what he needed from Frazer, especially the myth of the dying god, and transformed it for his own needs. In Eliot's hands the religious elements in *The Waste Land* stand in stark contrast with science's destruction of the mystery and majesty of the world. I suggest that missionaries used Frazer in a similar manner. [21]

After all, if one "respects" the old ways then why are some acceptable and others not? Why agree that God is found in all religions but refuse to let one be Christian, Muslim, and traditionalist at the same time? Why are the modernization tendencies of Christianity so inherently opposed to traditional relations? Finally, unanswerably, they ask,"Why do you wish to give us a version of Christianity so different from that practiced in your own country?"

As anthropologists point out, inherently the mission situation is structured so that its consequences flow inevitably from the virtually unavoidable actions of its protagonists. The mission protagonists do appear to outsiders as somewhat larger than life. "The Missionary" and the "Indigene" represent types, categories of our Western epistemology. Their "fatal flaws," virtues in other settings, lead to misunderstanding that cause epic suffering. Character truly becomes destiny as West meets Third World and each fails to understand the other in spite of the best of intentions.

The Chagnon-Salesian controversy is part of this overall process within the nature of anthropology itself. It is part of the history of the field that sees it as moving toward a new future for those "savages" entrusted to its care. The missionary, on the other hand views the indigene as an opportunity to spread the word of God and perfect the message the "savage" has received in some primordial manner. That neither the anthropologist nor missionary wishes the "native" harm is part of the tragedy of life itself. That the Yanomami, in common with other Fourth World peoples, needs to be protected from the dangers of development by those who, however well-intentioned, have their own agendas is also part of their own personal tragedy.

It is from the perspective of tragedy that one should view the Chagnon-Salesian controversy, a tragedy rooted in so ancient a transgression that like that which shadowed the House of Atreus it is doomed to continue into the distant future with periods of truce among its combatants. Like Yanomami warfare itself, it is marked by truces, shifting alliances, and betrayals. Like Yanomami warfare also it is often the innocent who suffer, the weak who are most harmed. Finally, like Yanomami warfare it is conducted to gain and control strategic resources, not always material but always precious.

Notes

1. This amicable discussion occurred at the 1994 Annual Meetings of the American Anthropological Association in Atlanta, Georgia, at the session I chaired, *Anthropology and Theology*. Further discussion ensued at Luisa Margolies's workshop on indigenous peoples in Venezuela.
2. For newspaper treatment of the issues see sources in the bibliography.
3. The situation, in brief, is that a Yanomami group came to the area to re-establish an alliance. Two Yanomami villages were established near Protestant missions and the third upstream. A fourth was a previous enemy whose people wanted to stabilize an uneasy peace. The third village provoked the war that Chagnon describes. In sum,

the behavior that Chagnon describes did occur but it was behavior exhibited during a period of extreme pressure under threat of war and during a ruinous epidemic.

4. The Salesians wrote a bitter response to Brewer Carias in 1991, *Consideraciones a un Documento de Charles Brewer Carias*. They signed as "Un Grupo de Missionaros del Alto Orinoco." Basically, the Salesians objected to the unbalanced nature of Brewer Carias's development plans. The very thing which Chagnon who allied himself with Brewer Carias later accused the Salesians of planing! Chagnon has since broken with Brewer Carias and admits he was taken in by his ideas. Luisa Margolies (April 3,1995) wrote "I feel that Chagnon's motivation is far more complex than summed up. He really did not concoct the biosphere scheme. Biosphere movements had been going on for years, generated by the IVIC ecology department (going back 20 years, I believe). Chagnon's friendship (genuine) with Brewer Carias is long-standing. Brewer Carias himself had worked on a type of biosphere project in La Neblina, partially funded by the American Museum of Natural History. Brewer Carias has mining interests in the Amazon, a fact denied by Chagnon, and this has created an enormous conflict of interest.

5. These conclusion are based on a phone conversation with Terence Turner on November 2, 1994. Turner later repeated the salient points at the American Anthropological Association meetings on December 2 in my session on *Anthropology and Theology* and in other sessions, most notably *Missionaries and Human Rights*.

6. Such a position reverses Chagnon's earlier one regarding the sociobiological sources of warfare and places him in Marvin Harris's camp, a reversal Chagnon acknowledged at the 1994 American Anthropological Association session, *Anthropology and Theology*. (See Harris 1984 and Good 1987 and 1989 for the outlines of the debate.)

7. Transcript of *Anthropology and Theology* session, December 2, 1994.

8. I investigated Chagnon's charges thoroughly. I found that the Salesians had never sold rifles to the Yanomami. The Yanomami cooperative SUYAO had sold rifles which they had obtained from the missionaries, the total was either five or six depending on the person relating the tale. All agreed that the Salesians put a stop to the practice, anticipating that the rifles might be used for warfare. In any event, there are hundreds of rifles in Yanomami hands. Most come from Brazil but some come from the Venezuelan National Guard who sell old rifles to the Yanomami. It is not against the law for any Venezuelan citizen, including Yanomami, to have rifles in the bush. Some Yanomami state that Chagnon himself sold a rifle to a Yanomami.

9. Lizot (1994) *American Anthropologist*

10. Asch 1991. Asch and Chagnon broke with each other after years of collaborating.

11. Finkers. Finkers is a remarkable naturalist and ethnographer. The Yanomami bring him specimens of any unusual plant or animal they come across. His notebooks are examples of punctilious recorded and drawn observations. There is little about the Yanomami or their environment that he does not know. He speaks the language fluently and has an easy relationship with them.

12. Donald Delaney, a Salesian, who accompanied me to Venezuela, was adamant on that point. He pointed out just how powerful the Salesians were in many countries,

including Venezuela, where their educational work meant that they had trained many of the leaders of various countries.

13. It was with some effort that Delaney and I persuaded Cappelletti to remain cool and not hire a psychologist to do a profile on Chagnon, for example. Cappelletti ranted that he would spend $20,000 on such a study. He also entertained thoughts of mounting an anthropological expedition to discredit Chagnon's anthropological work. While such displays of temper must be taken with a grain of salt, they do hint at serious contemplation with further action, including lawsuits.

14. Cardozo E-mailed me ". . .although I am very much interested in sociobiology (evolutionary psychology as it is now called), I don't agree with all its tenets. Also, although Chagnon was the head of my doctoral committee, I never took classes from him. I had finished course work when Chagnon was hired at UCSB and he never taught graduate seminars at that time. . . my main qualm with Chagnon's attacks against the Salesians was and is that they (the attacks) are consciously false and slanderous. Whether he was legally or illegally in the area is not the center of the discussion."

15. Margolies (1995) writes "Graziano and I were commencing our project on the indigenous architecture of Venezuela and asked Chagnon to collaborate with materials on the Yanomami shabono. We incorporated Chagnon and Hames into our research projects. From 1986-1989, they worked quietly in Venezuela as our collaborators. Chagnon's problems recommenced in 89-90."

16. Shaki," bee", is Chagnon's nickname among the Yanomami.

17. In fact, no Yanomami has ever killed a European or American. They have more likely been the victims of outside violence and exploitation than its originators.

18. See also John Paul II (1990) in which he speaks of the need for patience in the implementation of the inculturation process. He also warns that inculturation cannot be allowed to threaten what is fundamentally Christian.

19. See Salamone, "Nurses, Midwives, and Teachers - Joans-of-All-Trades: The Dominican Sisters in Nigeria." *Missiology* 5:487-501, 1986.

20. For a discussion of missionary-anthropologist relationships see Salamone 1985 and Whiteman 1985.

21. A recent article about the Jesuit astrophysicist the Reverend George Coyne, S.J., makes an analogous suggestion (Hitt 1994:36-39).

Chapter 7

The Theology of Change: Evangelical Protestantism and the Collapse of Native Religion in a Peasant Area of Mexico[1]

James W. Dow

Protestant Theology and Economics in Latin America

Protestantism originated in Europe as a reaction to Roman Catholicism. Bolstered by its primary theological tenant that the Holy Scriptures held the first authority in matters of faith and order, Protestantism rebelled against the authority of the Catholic Church. Many varieties of Protestantism have arisen since the time of the Reformation, and today Protestant churches are continuing to grow in Latin America where they are again replacing forms of Catholicism (Martin 1990; Stoll 1990; Garrard-Burnett and Stoll, 1993). The theology of Protestantism continues to be a dynamic force for change in Latin America.

The classes of people affected by Protestantism in Latin America changed between the nineteenth and twentieth centuries. In the nineteenth century Protestantism was adopted by the newly emerging middle class. In the twentieth century, however, Protestantism began to spread among the rural lower classes. The change in focus requires explanation. Why do rural populations now adopt religions that once served primarily the urban middle classes? As Martin (1990:206) points out, Latin American Protestantism is now more difficult to understand in terms of the theories of Max Weber, who saw it as a way in which a rising middle class could justify their wealth in theological terms. This chapter shows that Weber was not wrong, but that one part of his theory is more applicable to Latin America than another.

This chapter looks at the adoption of Protestantism in three rural Mexican villages in the Otomí Indian region of eastern Hidalgo. Before the arrival of Protestantism the people in these villages worshiped an assemblage of Catholic Saints. Although the outward appearance of their religion was Catholic, many of the rituals and beliefs had an indigenous origin. For example, in one village a local religious official carried the box for the

Eucharist in processions. However, he people made it clear that the box, containing a sunburst image, represented their Sun God not the Holy Sacrament. This and other pagan deities had not been forgotten despite the village's "conversion" to Catholicism in the 16th century. The influence of the Roman Catholic Church on these people had been largely superficial. They adopted its symbols rather than its theology.

The rituals in the villages were highly organized. Ritual offices called *cargos* were assigned to men for periods of one or two years. A *cargo* holder had many ritual duties and many expenses for entertainment and feasts. After completing his service in a cargo, a man rose in prestige. The prestige accumulated and eventually led to his membership in a group of elders who constituted the supreme governing authority of the village. Such a system is called a civil-religions hierarchy (Carrasco 1963; Cancian 1967), a type of *cargo* system in which the prestige gained from holding *cargos* leads to political power. Other types of *cargo* systems do not have such political outcomes, although, always, a person who holds a religious *cargo* rises in esteem. *Cargo* systems appear to be superficially Catholic because the images of Catholic saints are displayed during the rituals.

The new Protestant movement in this region was Pentecostal.[2] The growth of Pentecostal Protestantism in Mexico coincided with an economic boom that took place after World War Two. The per-capita gross domestic product of Mexico, measured in constant 1970 U.S. dollars, rose from 337 in 1940 to 874 in 1968. It continued to rise to 1217 in 1978, and it peaked at 1410 in 1981.[3] A large part of the economic growth was around Mexico City, located about 100 kilometers southeast of the three villages. Although they were not sought at first for industrial work, rural people, often with an Indian background and practically no schooling, were welcomed as agricultural laborers on the outlying farms feeding the burgeoning urban masses.[4] Migrating workers brought back money to their villages and invested in such things as television sets, pickup trucks, and better houses. Most of these items made a contribution to the productivity of the family through better education, health, and mobility.

Max Weber analyzes the relationship between Protestant theology and economic growth. In *The Protestant Ethic and the Spirit of Capitalism*.[5] Weber explains how Protestant theology provides a new, rational ethos for economic behavior. In another work, *The Protestant Sects and the Spirit of Capitalism*,[6] Weber focuses on the way in which Protestant sects in United States support bourgeois capitalism. He sees this as a continuation of the asceticism of European sects, which, through their other-worldliness, could portray economic success as a sign of grace. Thus, he postulates a psychological link between Protestantism and capitalism. This psychological model has been the source of theorizing about barriers to development in underdeveloped countries. For example, it is used by Annis (1987) to explain why Pentecostal Protestantism has succeeded in rural Guatemala. Although Weber was later unhappy with it (1958:31), the psychological model has influenced the bulk of subsequent research probably because it is more appropriate to explaining the spread of Protestantism in the United States.

However, in a later treatise, *The Sociology of Religion*, Weber suggests a second, sociopolitical link between Protestantism and capitalism (1963: 251). Here he looks at the social and political situations of Protestants and Catholics after the Reformation. Catholics did not have the same economic freedom as Protestants. Their actions were still constrained by papal injunctions. Their behavior was controlled the clergy, whereas Protestants were free from these restrictions. Protestants could pursue economic gain without interference. The Protestant desire for freedom continued in the liberal Protestant theologies that followed. For example, Pentecostals are led directly by the Holy Spirit. Thus freedom from authority is a very basic element in Protestant theology that Weber suggested was a means of overcoming impediments to the growth of a capitalistic economy.

Most Evangelical Protestant sects do have church authorities. However, their theologies still contain the revolutionary element that gave birth the to original church. This element subordinates earthly authority to the inspiration of *The Bible* and Holy Spirit. Thus, Evangelical Protestant churches are generally equipped theologically to wage holy war against any religious authority that might question them.

In Latin America, where the Catholic Church is influential, one might expect Weber's sociopolitical model to apply. However in Mexico the Catholic Church has exerted little control over people's lives since laws in the last century deprived it of its economic and political functions. Yet I maintain that Weber's sociopolitical model is still correct. There are oppressive religious authorities blocking the growth of the capitalistic economy in rural Mexico. They are not Roman Catholic religions but *cargo* systems. *Cargo* systems spend wealth on rituals not on the family. *Cargo* system theology advocates the redistribution of wealth not its investment.

Other theories explaining the rise of Evangelical Protestantism Latin America

The rise of rural Protestantism in Mexico has been explained in many ways. Clawson (1984) attributes its success to its ability to generate local leadership. This point also made by Garma (1984). Turner (1979) contends that people in Mexico convert to Protestantism primarily because of a spiritual experience. However, he does note that in one case a missionary-sponsored medical clinic had a profound influence on the spiritual response of natives. Garma (1992) finds that the Pentecostal community bridges the rural-urban gap to facilitate labor migration. Earle (1992) looks on Pentecostal Protestantism as a social disease infecting rural communities weakened by the stress of economic change. He feels that it does not serve any long term needs or interests.

More general theories explain the rise of Protestantism in Mexico as part of a general rise in the whole of Latin America. Martin (1990) attributes the overall success of Pentecostal Protestantism in Latin America to a confluence of North American economic values and Catholic traditions. Martin thinks that Latin America has trouble with a secular solution to value conflicts created by economic change, so it has developed a native Protestantism that flourishes in the rents created by the pulls of the North American economy. According to Stoll (1990:317-321) the success of Pentecostal Protestantism over Catholic Liberation Theology is due to its ability (1) to speak directly to the poor in terms of magical power, (2) to organize groups, and (3) to remain relatively autonomous. Stoll underscores the connection with North American right-wing Protestants, but also acknowledges that such imperialist connections offer but a limited explanation. Bastian (1985), on the other hand, thinks that Pentecostal Protestantism is most often a local indigenous movement and not the product of North American imperialism. Regarding Protestantism first as a reaction to the power of *caciques* (1985), Bastian (1992a) now sees the Pentecostalism as a way of integrating of the poor with new emerging power structures at the national level. Therefore, he opposes the ideas of Martin (1990) and Stoll (1990) that see Pentecostalism as more revolutionary.

Some authorities have attributed the spread of Protestantism in Mexico to North American missionaries (Stoll 1990). North American Evangelical missionaries were present in one of the Otomí villages for a time but they were not instrumental in the conversion of the communities. In general, the spread of Protestantism in rural areas of Mexico cannot be explained wholly by the presence of North American Evangelical missionaries. Protestant movements in Latin America are now mostly native movements (Bastian 1992a). The major Protestant church in the three Otomí villages and the largest Evangelical church in Mexico, the Unión de Iglesias Evangélicas, has been an independent native movement since it was established before World War Two (Barrett 1982:492). Translating *The Bible* into the native Otomí language was the main goal of the North American missionary who entered one of the villages, but people went back to using Spanish *Bibles* after the missionary left.

A common feature of rural Evangelical Protestantism reported by the investigators in Latin America is that it relieves people of economic burdens placed on them by *cargo* systems. O'Connor (1979:261) writes that Mayo Amerindians in Sonora, Mexico, became Protestants in order to avoid *cargos* in the traditional *fiesta* system. In Ecuador, Protestantism removed the social pressures for ceremonial consumption in a local *cargo* system (Muratorio 1981:525). In the Totonac area of Mexico, Protestants refused to participate in the *cargo* system (Garma 1984:130, 1987:163). In rural Guatemala Protestant families refused to participate in a system that forced them to spend a quarter of their income on *cargo* rituals (Annis 1987:106).

The literature indicates that Protestantism, particularly Evangelical Pentecostalism, relieves people of the economic burden of a local *cargo* system. I have found that opposition to *cargo* systems, is the primary reason for the spread of Protestantism in the three Otomí villages. Thus, Weber's second sociopolitical model is the key to understanding the advance of Protestantism. However, in applying Weber's model one must understand to what Protestantism is reacting. It is not reacting to the ecclesiastical controls of the Catholic Church. It is reacting to a local religious authority.

The Spread of Protestantism within the Eastern Sierra of Hidalgo

The three Otomí villages, San Nicolás, Santa Mónica, and San Pablo, were studied by the author during periods of field work between 1967 and 1990. All three of these villages are in the same ecological zone and have very similar subsistence agricultural economies and migration patterns. The three villages are located in the *municipio* of Tenango de Doria in the State of Hidalgo.[7] The 1989 populations of the villages are shown in Table 1. Economically the villages differ very little from poor rural villages in other parts of Mexico.

Table 1: Populations of the four villages in 1989

Name	Population
Santa Mónica	1084
San Pablo	992
San Nicolás	1471

In this region, the Unión de Iglesias Evangélicas, also known as the Movimiento de Iglesias Cristianas Independientes Pentecostés, exerts a powerful Evangelical Pentecostal influence. It is the largest Evangelical movement in Mexico today, Indian or otherwise (Barrett 1982). This Pentecostal movement has spawned Pentecostal temples in San Nicolás and Santa Mónica. The first Pentecostal temple was built in San Nicolás in 1960. Santa Mónica followed with a temple in 1980. At present, San Pablo is just beginning to experience the influence of the Pentecostals. No temple has been built there, and meetings are held in the house of one of the converts.

San Nicolás

San Nicolás was the first village to turn Protestant. The *cargo* system of San Nicolás is described below as it existed in the 1950's. Then the church in San Nicolás housed the images of four saints. Religious rituals for the saints were held during four annual *fiestas*,. Each saint was attended by a group of annually appointed *cargo* holders called *mayordomos*. Two other *cargo* holders called "Godfather," performed rituals for all the saints. The godfathers held the most prestigeful *cargos*. A man was not appointed to Godfather until he had served many times as a *mayordomo*. Men who had served previously as godfathers formed a group of elders. The elders made the appointments. If a young man stubbornly refused to receive a lower-level *mayordomo* appointment, he was put in jail until he accepted. The elders made all the important decisions and established law in the village. The Judge, the highest civil official, was nominated and controlled by the elders.

The theology of the system created prestige for the *cargo* holders. As each *mayordomo* publicly appeared in the church and later at his house to sponsor a large feast for all people who came, he was recognized as a religious and generous person. The image of religious devotion to a public saint, which was regarded as a protector of the village, and the generous spending of hard-earned wealth led to respect and prestige for the person. In a subsistence-oriented economy, prestige was a better investment than the accumulation of goods or property. The image of generosity reduced envy that could flare into violence against a person. The theological principles that backed up this system stated that humans were dependent on a capricious super-human world and that to survive one should always try to be on good terms with the super-humans. People believed that the saints watched over the people and protected them. The *cargo* holders were entrusted with the sacred duty of maintaining good relations with the saints. Any deviation from the advice of former *cargo*-holders who had been close to the saints was regarded as dangerous.

In 1947, a small plane dropped *Bible* tracts on San Nicolás. One man, Miguel, wrote to an address on a tract and received a set of *Bible* lessons. Missionaries from Mexico City visited Miguel to help him with his studies. In 1948 a North American missionary-linguist from the Summer Institute of Linguistics settled in San Nicolás with the aim of translating *The Bible* into the native language. Miguel was his closest informant. The missionary remained there with his family for two decades. After he left, the tale of his visit evolved into a local myth. One version states that he was sent by the United States President to bring peace to the village.

There was division in the village over Protestant ideas. To convince others that the old beliefs had no value, Miguel burned the his family's saint images.[8] Other converts followed by burning their family images or by giving them to children to play with; thereby they showed that they were not afraid of any supernatural punishment they might receive for carrying out these sacrilegious acts. As misfortune did not befall the burners, faith in the new religion was strengthened. Although the traditionalists were offended by the burning, they could not persuade the Mexican government to intervene because Article 24 of the Mexican Constitution prohibits the government from involving itself in religious matters. In the 1950s, a *Bible* study group was formed. In 1962, the jailing of the recalcitrant *cargo* nominees stopped, and the Judge was elected democratically from then on. The elders lost their power.

By 1990, ninety-three percent of the families in San Nicolás were Protestant. Most of them were members of a Pentecostal church. A more conservative Protestant church, the Church of God of the Seventh Day, had been established in 1965 by people who objected to moral laxness among the Pentecostals. The few remaining Catholic families maintained the *fiesta* of the patron saint, San Nicolás, and supported it with a collection of money amongst themselves. There were no individual *cargo* holders. The

Catholics by then were calling themselves "brothers," as the Protestants did, and they were studying *The Bible* as well.

Santa Mónica

Santa Monica was the second village to turn Protestant. The *cargo* system in Santa Mónica varied somewhat from the *cargo* system in San Nicolás. There were five village saints, each of which was served by a separate *mayordomía* consisting of one Godfather, one First *Mayordomo*, and four Second *Mayordomos*. In a public meeting, a man was heard only if he had completed at least one *cargo*. Otherwise, his opinion was considered unworthy. On completing a career of *cargos*, which may have involved half a dozen *mayordomo*-ships and at least one godfathership, a man became an elder of the village. The elders made the uncodified laws for the village. They decided difficult civil cases beyond the authority of the Judge. They determined the structure of the religious *cargos*, and they appointed new *cargo* holders each year. As a man, aided by his wife and family, completed the higher *cargos*, he was increasingly recognized by the elders.

In the 1960s the young men of Santa Mónica began to grumble about having to spend money on religious rituals. In 1968 some talked of eliminating the *cargos* and of taking up a collection from the entire village to support the *fiestas*. The power to make this decision was in the hands of the elders. Elders discussed the issue at a meeting in 1968. They admitted that it was difficult for the *mayordomos* to make ends meet. However, they concluded that the *fiestas* were held in a spirit of good faith and that there should be joy in contributing to a happy *fiesta*. One elder said that the rituals were expensive but that the saints helped the people, so people should care for the saints. Furthermore he cautioned that if the village saints were neglected, misfortune might befall the village. The general consensus of the elders, who had themselves attained their statuses by participating in the *cargo* system, was that the men of the pueblo should continue to take on the religious *cargos* and to make the necessary sacrifices. The elders concluded that the financial burdens could be eased by appointing more *mayordomos*.

In 1969 one man, Patricio, read *The Bible* and made up his own mind about the value of these rituals. In 1971 another man, Martín, returned to the village after resolving a feud that had forced him to leave. During his exile he had been converted to Pentecostal Protestantism. In 1972 Martín began to preach Pentecostal religion in the village. The two men founded a *Bible* study group and rapidly gathered adherents to the new faith. With no choice offered them by the elders, younger men who did not want to become involved in the expensive *cargo* system joined the new Protestants, who, after consulting *The Bible*, declared that the *cargo* rituals were sinful idolatry. Protestants from neighboring San Nicolás helped the new group to grow and to organize a Pentecostal church.

The last *mayordomo* in Santa Mónica served in 1977. After that, the elders made no effort to maintain the system. The images of the village saints were moved to a small dark room in the church where they are now ignored. After the village ceased to name *mayordomos* and celebrate the *cargo* rituals, the continuing alliance of families with the Pentecostal Church was halted by a new Catholic movement that also rejected the *cargo* system. Aided by the municipal priest and some Catholic missionaries, the new Catholic group reinstated some of the old village rituals. However, the expenses of the rituals are now paid by equal contributions from the entire Catholic group. In 1990 the village was divided approximately in half between the Pentecostal Protestants and the new Catholics.

In 1987, the Pentecostals softened somewhat toward the old village rituals. They joined the new Catholics in a Christmas *Posada* ritual. They even put up *piñatas* in their church. This "idolatry" and other backsliding behavior gave impetus to a second, *Biblically*-pure, Protestant movement sponsored by The Church of God of the Seventh Day. By 1990 they had attracted eight out of the 183 families in the village.

San Pablo El Grande

The village of San Pablo also has five village saints, San Pedro, San Pablo, the Virgin of Guadalupe, and two Christ images. The *cargo* system there was still operating in 1990. To be the *mayordomo* of San Pablo, the patron saint of the village, was the highest honor. His image was located in the center of the main altar of the village church and flanked by the Virgin of Guadalupe on the right and San Pedro on the left. The two Christ images of lesser prestige stood on separate altars at either side of the sanctuary.

The San Pablo *cargo* system was changing in 1990, but it had not collapsed. The Protestants in San Pablo, were few, but the threat of a Protestant revolt against the *cargo* system was strong. In response, the elders had made *cargo* service voluntary. If no volunteer came forward to take a particular cargo, the rituals were performed by an appointee of the Judge and supported by a contribution from all the Catholic families. Thus no one was forced into costly *cargo* service as they had been in the other two villages.

In 1990, the First *Mayordomo* of San Pablo was only 31 years old. He was young man who had earned money while working outside the village. One of the Second *Mayordomos* was a bit older, but the others were younger. The musicians playing the sacred traditional music were only teenagers. The young wives went right up to the altar and worked beside their *mayordomo* husbands. This rather assertive female behavior was never seen several decades before when their mothers stayed respectfully behind the altar rail and passed the offerings over the rail to their *cargo*-holding husbands.

The San Pablo *cargo* system is resisting the impact of Protestantism by making its rituals less onerous and ritual service completely voluntary. Thus it is capturing the younger members of the community who are enjoying the rituals. The new theology that supports this change holds that the traditional *fiestas* should be enjoyable and that the saints should be happy. The images are brought out of the church to see the *fiesta* fireworks. The new *cargo* theology emphasizing the enjoyment of the *fiestas* is a challenge to the Pentecostals who are regarded as too stuffy.

Discussion

A *cargo* system blocks economic activity appropriate to capitalism by insisting that wealth be redistributed in exchange for political power. It then creates a power hierarchy that becomes an obstacle to the personal and familial use of wealth.

The value of a *cargo* system fades as new opportunities of investing personal wealth appear. The supernatural power of the saints is questioned. The authority of the elders is undermined. Protestant doctrine supports this change. It states that people have the freedom to worship as *The Bible* directs them. They can reject the elders. They can reject *cargo* service. They can deny the power of the saints. Protestantism is not the only way of rejecting a *cargo* system on theological grounds, but it is one of the more mature and successful ways. For example, O'Connor shows that Protestantism in northern Mexico did better in this regard than native millenarianism (1979).

The development of a lower class under capitalism requires special social institutions. Protestantism in Latin America is facilitating the spread of wealth to a lower class. Protestantism is still connected to capitalism, but now it is connected to the lower classes not the middle classes. Latin American peasants want to funnel wealth into raising their standard of living so that they can enter new labor markets. Evangelical Protestantism in peasant areas of Latin America is simply what Protestantism has always been, a theological reaction against religiously sanctioned authorities. Weber was correct in noting that religious hierarchies of authority can block economic change and that Protestantism overthrows them in theological terms.

Notes

1. Acknowledgments. The author gratefully acknowledges the support of a Fulbright American Republics Research Grant, and the help supplied by the following persons: Roberto Garrido of the Instituto Nacional Indigenista, Mexico Prof. Ramiro Cajero José, Profa. Aurora Aguilar Jáimez, Prof. Bonifacio Téllez, and Profa. Rosalba Manilla Santos of the Secretaría de Educación Pública, Mexico.

2. Pentecostalism is the most common form of Latin American Protestantism today (Martin 1990). Bastian (1992b:548) claims that Martin (1990) and Stoll (1990) are wrong in portraying Pentecostalism as a sweeping ideological reform. Bastian proposes that it is merely an adaptation to changes imposed on the lower classes by the elites.

3. These figures are calculated from Tables 627 and 3324 of Wilkie, Lorey, and Ochoa (1988) using exponential interpolation for populations.

4. The mountains cut people off from very easy access to Mexico City. It takes about four hours on a bus to reach the city. This makes daily commuting impossible, but allows weekly commuting. Many poor Indian peasants take advantage of the better paying jobs in the city.

5. *Die protestantische Ethik un der Geist de Kapitalismus* first published in 1904 and then reprinted as the first essay in *Gesammelte Aufsätze zur Religionssoziologie* (Parsons 1958). For the translations see Weber (1958).

6. "Die protestantischen Sekten und der Geist des Kapitalismus" another essay in Volume 1 of *Gesammelte Aufsätze zur Religionssoziologie*. For the translation see Weber (1946).

7. A *municipio* is a territorial division of the state, in this case the State of Hidalgo.

8. The images in the village church were not the only saints' image in the village. Each family usually had one or more images on a household altar. Images were also kept in small family-owned oratories.

Chapter 8

Structural Adjustment Program (SAP) and the Professionalization of Theology: The Re-Emergence of Ritual Consultancy Services in Nigeria

Olugbemi Moloye

Introduction

Culture change is a phenomenon that is basic to all societies and the study of change in culture is the study of the means by which human beings develop cultural adaptations to changing circumstances (Beals, Hoijer and Beals, 1977). Cultural adaptation is an attempt to find solutions to the problems of society. Often times newly devised solutions, bring in its wake other problems which also demand further solutions. The present state of the Nigerian economy has brought to the country a variety of situations never before experienced by Nigerians. In light of the nation's poor economic performances, the general consensus was that the nation's economic policies can no longer be conducted as if it were in the days when Nigeria was awash with petro-dollar. While the country has embarked upon radical measures to restructure the economy as urged by International Agencies, the sociological fallout has been devastating to the Nigerian society. The present desperate situation nostalgically evokes memories of the 1970's when the Nigerian currency was almost twice the value of the U.S. dollar. Today the value of the Nigerian currency is a shadow of its former self as one Nigerian *naira* is barely the value of a U.S. dime. The economic downturn nonetheless has precipitated the best and the worst of human ingenuity as the will to survive has catalyzed various means of survival. The flamboyant and sumptuous lifestyle which dominated the Nigerian cultural landscape some two decades ago has been replaced by near pauperization.

It is stating the obvious to assert that the world economies which took a nosedive into recession in the 1980s badly affected African economies historically tied to Euro-American markets. Nigeria in particular, as other members of the Oil Producing and Exporting Countries (OPEC), with large populations, has been badly hurt as many development projects programmed during the oil boom of the 1970s, had to be drastically downsized if not entirely abandoned. It is no secret that the Nigerian Government since the early 1980s has had her share of economic difficulties largely borne out of mismanagement, profligacy and malfeasance by the nation's politico-military elites.

Drastic measures taken to correct these difficulties have led to excruciating belt-tightening devices with devastating social and economic consequences. On the economic side, the downsizing of economic expectations has led to inflation, currency devaluation and serious foreign debt and balance of payments difficulties. Consequently, the Nigerian government has imposed the Structural Adjustment Program (SAP) with the sole purpose of attacking "Nigeria's excessive dependence of the economy on one commodity, chronic lack of self-reliant growth and development, serious balance of payments disequilibrium, government (and) stagflation" (Phillips, 1987). While the program has been praised for its comprehensive breath and radical determination, the human effect has been devastating. The objectives of the program, among other things, is intended to change the economic orientation of the country which has been historically dominated by investments in the public sector. In addition, SAP is designed also to improve efficiency and intensify efforts leading to growth potential in the private sector.

It must be pointed out that SAP has created more enemies than friends as it left in its wake devastating negative social costs on the welfare and the quality of lives of Nigerians, most in particular, its effects on Africa's most enduring social institution, the family. To many Nigerian families, SAP means mass poverty, declining quality of life, rising unemployment, retrenchment, social disorganization and the marginalization of the middle-class. But it is remarkable to note that of all the by-products of SAP, evangelical proselytization and religious consultancy services operated by sweet-talking charismatic leaders remain one of the outstanding social consequences of SAP. The irony is that a significant number of the new "religious" leaders are made up of retrenched government employees, (thanks to SAP) job seekers and rural migrants into the urban community who have come in search of gainful employment. In harmony with precedents, the main objective of the new breed of evangelical merchants is to cash in on victims of social dislocations and the bleak economic hopelessness through evangelical consultancy services and merchandising.

The phenomenal growth of depression evangelization has precedents as through human history, the world has often witnessed a variety of movements designed to whip up emotion during periods of economic difficulties, social malaise and psychological dislocation of the masses. It is remarkable that these evangelical consultancy services are predicated on the syncretization of Judeo-Christian ecumenical doctrine with Yoruba traditional religion. The fact that the new effort involves a bit of traditional religion and a bit of Christianity has given evangelical consultancy services a resounding credibility in the eyes of adherents. The role of religious divination in the times of social hopelessness is well documented in non-Western societies (Malefijt, 1968).

Survey of Theoretical Comments

A survey of the literature indicates that a rise in independent churches is a phenomenon usually associated with social crisis in many societies. Wallace (1966) for example, in his landmark study of the Handsome Lake movement, developed the theory of revitalization movements and the cyclical nature of social and individual development and change. He contends that the frequent occurrence of reformative religious movements in disorganized societies is a conscious effort by their members to reconstruct more satisfying cultural contexts. As a result, "revitalization is accomplished through the construction of dogma, myth and ritual which are internally coherent as well as true descriptions of a world system and which, thus, will serve as guides to efficient action (Wallace, 1966). Revitalization movement therefore serves as an integrative force bringing together through religion the society's distraught, disillusioned who are searching for salvation and escape. The process of spiritual rebirth of the individual prophetic dreamer serves a healthy and therapeutic function.

A number of studies about revitalization movements in Africa, have tended to associate such movements to protests against colonialism (Balandier, 1965; Lanternai, 1963; Ranger,1968). Lanternai (1963) for example, had suggested that independent churches arose because Africans' experience with colonialism had alienated them from their land which they depended upon for agriculture.

If Lanternai's thesis were true in some parts of Africa where settler colonialism was practiced, this is hardly applicable to Ghana where the study was actually conducted because Ghana did not have a history of settler colonialism. Other studies have also emphasized that there is the need to understand Africa's religious movements from the point of view of social and psychological tensions and not necessarily a manifestation of political antagonisms to European colonization and the imposition of its social and religious values.   These writers have suggested that the rapid "modernization" which took place after decolonization lead to some dislocation in African's social and psychological stability, hence the rise of Independent religious movements as safety valves (Wyllie, 1980; Okite, 1981)

Rasper (1968) has argued initially that the rise of independent churches in Africa was a mid-way stage between early armed resistance and the emergence of modern nationalist parties. Later, he contended that there was no natural flow from this type of argument as he realized that under rare and special circumstances do rural discontent manifest in religious movements (Rasper 1986b). Similarly, Buijtenhjs (1984) has argued that nationalism and religious independence were more or less simultaneous rather than sequential and that there were few connections between them.

It is also the contention of another school of social change that "ritual patterns develop in response to emotional anxiety and cognitive frustration in a situation of uncertainty." This appears to account for the proliferation of spiritual consultancy services in Nigeria as religion has come to represent the panacea to the present economic hardship.

The present study however views the emergence of Independent Christian religion in Nigeria from a different perspective. The study contends that Independent Christian Churches in Nigeria emerged as a rejection of the inflexibility of colonial Christian religion and its failure to incorporate "Africanness" to its mode of worship as preached by European missionaries in the early part of the 20th century. This paper will not provide a detailed history of Christianity in Nigeria because this has been eloquently described elsewhere (Ayandele 1966; Ajayi, 1965). However, a short history of Independent Christian Churches in Yorubaland is relevant at this juncture as it is pertinent to the central objective of the present paper.

Independent Churches in Yorubaland

In the early part of the 20th century, a number of Independent African Churches seceded from the existing Christian Churches headed by European Missionaries. These early Churches included the Church Missionary Society (CMS), the Roman Catholic Mission (RCM) and the Baptist Church to mention the major ones. The administrators of these early missionary churches viewed the independent churches as "rebels" and vicariously tagged them as "unorthodox" and "separatist" churches. The textural heart of the present study is an inquiry into why Africans chose to secede from the colonial missionary Christian church.

The independent churches in colonial Nigeria resented the political and ecclesiastical domination of Christian doctrine by Europeans in the early stages of Christendom. In fact, the policy of European domination of Christendom in West Africa led one, Mr. Webster, a European missionary, who arrogantly claimed that "the issues (i.e. the European domination of Christendom) were the same from Sierra Leone to the Cameroon." The European domination of the church politically and ecclesiastically was no hidden agenda as they demonstrated no small resentment for any display of Africanism in the church. Among the categories of Africanisms considered nauseating and repulsive by Europeans were the introduction of African music, languages, arts, dresses and religion into the Church. In fact as far as the Europeans were concerned, there was nothing in the African cultural tradition worth considered religion. Never mind that these indigenous religious elements, much hated by Europeans, constitute the source of spiritual strength for the Africans before and after contact with the Europeans. Similarly, African resentment of European treatment of "things" African was not unexpected. The controversy finally reached a crescendo in 1888 when a Native Baptist church was established. Similar secessionist movements erupted in other denominations because Africans could no longer tolerate abuse, humiliation and the European domination of Christendom as well as their interpretation of reality.

In the Methodist Church for example, secession was spearheaded by one W. Blyden, an African-American, who came from Sierra Leone to address an inter-denominational congregation in 1891 on the issue of European domination of Christendom. The protest of Blyden culminated in the formation of a body founded to implement the center piece of his advocacy under the chairmanship of one James Johnson, who himself, was an advocate of Africanism in religious practices. It was hoped that the implementation of Blyden's idea would not only wipe out European domination but also unite Africans for the salvation of the continent and against the policies pursued by the European mission (Webster, 1964). The African had also hoped that those indigenous African elements, such as the mode of worship, dress and language, which the Europeans had despised, would be incorporated in order to enhance the relevance of Christianity in the lives of Africans. The plan however was aborted for reasons which included financial constraint and the fear that the African laity might be excommunicated by European missionaries. Although Blyden's idea was never translated into reality at the regional level, it was nonetheless implemented at the local levels.

In Lagos for example, the members of the Anglican and Methodist Churches who had craved political and ecclesiastical independence from the Missionary church were empowered by Blyden's advocacy. It led to the formation of the United Native African Church which was guided with the singular purpose of africanizing Christianity. According to Webster, the United Native African church had three main goals. These were "the evangelization of the continent, the cleansing of foreign forms, and the amelioration of the race." However the United Native Church (UNC) failed to consummate the political and ecclesiastical independence which they had sought as a complete indigenization of the church failed to materialize. Nonetheless the failure of the UNC to indigenize did not terminate the dream to establish an independent African church as it finally culminated in the establishment of a new "African Church. "

In fact the establishment of the "African Church" became inevitable in view of the way Bishop James Johnson, an African pastor in the Anglican Church was treated. Bishop Johnson was an uncompromising African nationalist and a tenacious advocate of indigenous pastorate. In 1899, Reverend James Johnson was consecrated as an assistant Bishop and then transferred to the Niger Delta of Western Equatorial Africa, a post outside Lagos. For practical reasons he could not resume his services at the pastorate because the Church Missionary Society (CMS) had not completed his traveling arrangements to the Niger Delta. An appeal was made on his behalf by both the parishioners and the CMS Church Committee headed by another African Bishop, (Bishop Oluwole) that he be allowed to stay in his Lagos office pending the completion of his traveling arrangements. It must be pointed out that Bishop Oluwole was opposed to the indigenization advocacy of Bishop Johnson, hence the rejection of the appeal. In the meantime, Bishop Johnson decided to pay a visit to his future station, at the Niger Delta to see things for himself. While returning from the trip, he discovered that both his sister and his personal effects had been thrown out of the vicarage into the rain.

The parishioners were enraged by the type of treatment meted out to Bishop Johnson but had hoped that Bishop Thugwell, the European Bishop, would overrule the decision of Bishop Oluwole and that of the committee he headed. Unfortunately that was not to be. Bishop Thugwell agreed with the decision taken by Bishop Oluwole and in fact, he (Bishop Thugwell) went to the extent of asking Africans to break away if they so desired. On October 13 1901, the parishioners decided to call the bluff of Bishop Thugwell and they heeded his advise. The parishioners seceded from the Anglican Church with no less than six hundred sympathizers from other churches in Lagos.

As any other young organization, the break-away faction was not without teething problems. However, the independent church went through the first year of creation with steady progress as more branches were established outside Lagos. It was indeed the opening of a new chapter in the history of Christendom in Nigeria as it led to a barrage of Christian denominations which today litter the Nigerian religious landscape.

The most important achievement in the establishment of independent churches was the indigenization of the Christian religion. The missionary religion had frowned upon the African family structure of polygyny which was considered inconsistent with membership of the Christian religion. The Lambeth Conference of Anglican Bishops in 1888 had declared without regards to the nature of African social organization that "baptized converts who took a second wife must be excommunicated: polygamists should not be accepted; and wives of polygamists might be baptized under certain conditions" (Stephen, 1962). It is obvious that the position taken by the missionary religion was hostile to indigenous African social institutions. It ineluctably became a major catalyst which facilitated the establishment of indigenous Christian institutions since the missionary religion had failed, as it were, the spiritual needs of Africans.

The inability of the Christian religion to replace the traditional religion is noteworthy as the Africans who go to church on Sundays often times devote the remaining days of the week to worshiping traditional deities. Resort to traditional religion during life crises such as crop failure, pestilence, famine, birth, marriage, sickness and death, is *sine qua non* among Africans and it is during these crises that the missionary religion proved to be most irrelevant in the lives of the African. To a casual observer, the ecumenical and liturgical contents of the independent African churches were in no way different from those practiced by the missionary religion. This may appear true on the surface as they both use a common hymn and prayer books, however the incorporation of healing by prayer and faith; the tolerance of polygyny; the use of prophecy and visions; the practice of ritual sacrifice and the use of drumming and dancing in most of the independent churches are legacies of traditional mode of worship. All these are in perfect harmony with the African indigenous religious world view.

It is important at this stage to give a brief account of Yoruba traditional religion as it is pertinent to its present use by the new breed of religious merchants.

The Yoruba Traditional Religion

A number of anthropological studies have indicated that "religion is at the root of African culture and is the determining principle of African life" (Opoku, 1975). The Yoruba are no less religious than other African culture groups. The indigenous belief system was so well organized and entrenched in Yoruba society before the surreptitious and often times belligerent imposition of missionary religions of Islam and Christianity. A number of studies have characterized the "indigenous Yoruba religion as polytheism."

This assertion is inferred from the Yoruba mythology which claims the existence of four hundred and one "Orisas" i.e. Deities in Yorubaland. However, the Yorubas perceive the Orisas who are similar to the Roman Catholic saints, as lesser gods through whom communication to the Almighty is effectuated. In other words the Yoruba do not see the "Orisas" as the Almighty as inadequately portrayed in Euro-American literature. In his discussion of Yoruba religion, Fadipe (1970) for example, asserted that the Orisas are "objects of worship" through whom the Yoruba commune with God. The absolute belief the Yoruba have in God is indicated by the names given to their children and the way God is described as "Olorun" (Owner of heaven). The belief that He should be contacted through emissaries such as ancestors or other spiritual mediums rather than by ordinary beings is in harmony with the Yoruba cultural practice of approaching elderly people with reverence through a third person. This is also a characteristic reminiscent of the relationship between a Yoruba father and his child whose mother plays the role of an emissary. Incidentally a good number of Euro-American observers have argued that the practice of Africans worshiping through spiritual mediums, indicates the belief that the Almighty God is just too far-away, hence it should not be disturbed. This is certainly an erroneous Eurocentric reading of the African world view.

The spirits of these "gods" which are intrinsic to the sacred "objects" are perceived to be capable of tackling problems insurmountable by ordinary mortals, hence the consultation with them during difficult times. The evocation of deity spirit during difficult times is perfectly in harmony with the Yoruba religious world view which puts emphasis on action and result *now* rather than advocate the theodicy of escape or despair. In times of crisis, it is believed that the singing, dancing, and the offering of sacrifices must be pleasing to the gods which must ineluctably promote the alleviation of human suffering, deprivation and injustice *now* rather than later. The Yoruba perception of this world's reality and importance is not denied hence the obligation to seek ameliorative redress when things go bad. This is a practice perceived to be in no way different from the way the believers of Roman Catholicism and Islam call on Biblical and Koranic apostles and saints during difficult times.

The Yoruba boast of 401 deities, the majority of whom are of local importance making their observance a community affair most in particular during times of "rites of intensification." Consultation with the ancestors is generally an individualized religious activity, however, the 401 religious deities in Yorubaland were once ancestors who had attained deification making their observance universally valid among more than the 30 million Yorubas in Nigeria and in diaspora. Ancestors are generally perceived to live in a spiritual existence. They are also considered to be in possession of special powers form God which they can use on lesser beings (i.e. the living). These ancestors are regarded to function as guardians to their offsprings on earth, hence the importance of periodic appeasement in order to pre-empt their wrath; the institutionalization of ancestor commemoration is a *fait accompli*.

Ancestors who had attained universal deification beyond family levels were acknowledged heroes in Yoruba mythology. Worship of such deities is oftentimes identified with objects of worship such as iron for "Ogun" and river for "Oya" deities respectively. However, "Ifa" otherwise known as the "Orisa" of palm-nut divination occupies a special category in the Yoruba pantheons. In view of its reputation as a means of communication between man and the other "gods", it usually directs those who consult with it to pay their respects to other Orisa.

The importance of Ifa divination in Yoruba religious philosophy is so pervasive that historically it is consulted for every important event and on every fifth day and sacrifices are made too. Such events range from what the future holds for a new born baby to the prospects of a marriage about to be contracted. In fact the pre-eminent status of "Ifa" in Yoruba religious pantheon is so well established that some other important Orisas request their devotees to inquire from Ifa when to observe their annual celebrations and the pattern such celebrations should take. Upon consultation, the *Babalawo* i.e. the Ifa priest, offers his recommendations in form of sacrifices to be offered as appeasements to Esu i.e. the trickster deity, whom the Yoruba believe is eternally mischievous, lest he thwart the plans of humans. According to Fadipe, "every time a sacrifice is made, Esu must have its share" (Fadipe, 1970).

Priesthood in indigenous Yoruba religion often times runs in the family. While Ifa priesthood is also a family affair, anyone with the necessary skill and brain power could be apprenticed to an Ifa priest. Proficiency in Ifa verses requires a high skill of memory works owing to the large number of possible combinations of draws of the palm nuts or "Opele." The prospective Ifa priest must undertake an intensive training lasting several years under a practicing *Babalawo*.

One unique characteristic of all the Orisas is their ability to peep into the future of their congregation through their devotees. The Orisas are not only treated as mere fortune tellers whose work does not end with the disclosure of what fate has in store, they often times arrogate to themselves the ability to influence the future course of events. Regardless of the outcome of prophecies, sacrifices are nonetheless requested so that what has been predicted may stay on course. This is a practice that a good number of the Independent Christian Churches have now adopted as dancing, drumming and ritual sacrifices , a staple of traditional African religion, are perceived to play a major role in the amelioration of human hardship. It implies that every response ends with a sacrifice be it bad or good as Esu, the trickster deity, must be propitiated at all times because he is a permanent feature in the Yoruba cosmology.

Liturgical Convergence of the Yoruba and Independent Christian Religion

The foundation of independent churches led to a liturgical revolution in the history of Christendom in Nigeria. In the early days of Missionary religion, clapping and drumming were alien to their mode of worship. The use of "Igbin" drums in independent churches were familiar to worshipers of Orunmila; so was the use of "Bata drums" to Sango worshipers while the "Dundun drums" were no strange objects to any Yoruba who had the privilege of attending any occasions of ancestral worship. The use of these cultural objects in the independent churches escalated membership. Dancing, clapping and the drumming of familiar tunes are daily rituals in traditional religion used by the independent churches and often times members who are in attendance become ecstatic; a condition that is reminiscent of traditional religion.

As in traditional religion, prophecy is a factual component of the independent churches. Church members regard the ability to prophesy as a rare gift by God as it can only be administered by "select" members called "Iranse" i.e. "the Messenger." The parallel in Yoruba religion, of course, are the priests and priestesses of deities who have been specially selected by the Orisas as their "messengers" or "Iranse." In some instances, priests and priestesses are believed to possess the power to pray and be consulted while at the same time foretell the future. To the Yoruba, who has recently become a Christian, he has no problems relating to the independent churches where prophesying, dancing and clapping are part of the recipe of worship. To him, it is like consulting with a *Babalawo* or the Sango priest, who is capable of warding off "bad luck" or transforming failure into success through divination and propitiation to the gods. Similarly the independent churches perform purification rites through prayers, fasting and alms giving (i.e. "Ipese") to church members who are less privileged.

Glossolalia is a Greek word which implies the ability to speak in tongues. This is a common occurrence in the independent churches which is reminiscent of the event on "Pentecost Day." Glossolalia is also a common feature among Sango or Osun deity followers in Yorubaland. For example, it is the belief among members of the "Christ Apostolic Church" sect, that water has a potent therapeutic power which is capable of curing barrenness and lunacy. Such a belief is familiar to the followers of Osun deity who through songs extol the therapeutic virtues of water:

Seleru Agbo,
Agbara Agbo,
Losun fi'n wo 'mo re,
ki Dokita o to de.

Meaning:

From the concoction of spring water
the goddess of Osun cures her children
before the arrival of Cosmopolitan medicine.

The use of certain objects in the independent churches for propitiatory purposes are carry-over from indigenous Yoruba religion. The use of kolanut, sugar cane, bitter cola etc. during the naming ceremonies of a new child by the Cherubim and Seraphim sect for example, is a re-enactment of the indigenous religious practices. Beyond the similarity of symbols and objects, there is also the dress pattern and designs with specific colors used by both the Cherubim and Seraphim and the Celestial Church sects. White flowing gowns are usually worn by both sexes in the Celestial and the Cherubim and Seraphim churches; red dresses are also common among other sects. In Yoruba traditional religion, the followers of Sango deity wear dresses of red colors while the followers of Obatala and Osun deities wear dresses made out of white cloths.

Ritual sacrifice known as "ebo" is an expedient component of Yoruba traditional religion. Sacrifices are carried to intersections to appease the gods and other invisible principalities. This is a common practice among members of the Celestial Church where members are often implored to take offerings of eggs and palm oil in a small earthenware to intersections to appease and control "Esu" known as the "Lucifer" in the Celestial Church. Most importantly, polygyny is not prohibited by the independent churches unlike the missionary religion which considered polygyny an abomination. And of course, the indigenous African religion recognizes the reality of polygyny in a society whose livelihood was based on agrarianism.

Nigerian Economy and Spiritual Consultancy

It is germane at this juncture to examine how the present economic hardship in Nigeria has facilitated the explosion of spiritual consultancy. The twin problems of unemployment and social dislocation have historically intensified the articulation of religious fanaticism and millenarianism; the present economic difficulties in Nigeria are in harmony with those criteria. They have indeed facilitated the marginalization of the civil servants and ineluctably led to their retrenchment. This is in harmony with the IMF/World Bank prescription of SAP which mandates devaluation-expenditure reduction, liberalization, fiscal and monetary control aimed at engendering supply-led economic growth. The social effect of SAP has been devastating as its implementation mandates the Government to reduce its labor force. Such reduction implies the forced retirement of thousands of civil service workers most of whom are resident in the big administrative centers. Having enjoyed the benefits of government patronage for a number of years, forced retirement in their estimation is tantamount to social and psychological death in a society where employment in government service is historically regarded with awe. In fact, among the Yoruba, it is almost a taboo to return untriumphantly to one's birthplace after years of sojourn in the administrative cosmopolitan centers without the mythical golden fleece. The propensity to stay put in the administrative centers rather than contravene the cultural taboo after retrenchment has precipitated the explosion of evangelical consultancy services in urban Nigeria. The purveyors of evangelical merchandising find easy prey among those who have become economically defeated and socially disconnected as a result of SAP by using indigenous religious symbols. As a result, the explosion in membership and joyous participation in ritual practices, such as dancing, singing and the offering of sacrifices, indicates the consummation of members' expectations and wishes. This is in line with the fact that the use of such symbols and practices by evangelists add credibility to their trade in the eyes of believers who perceive synergetic relationship between the use of such symbols and the amelioration of social, economic and personal crises as in traditional religion. The explosive increase in membership in recent times attest to the satisfaction and fulfillment members derive from their participation as the Yorubas are not known for religious dogmatism, hence the pervasiveness of religious syncretism in the lives of the Yorubas.

In conclusion, the indigenization of the Christian religion in Yorubaland has fueled the rank and file of Christian believers. The Christian religion has not only become more meaningful to the Yoruba as a result of indigenization, the spicing of Christianity with the flavors of indigenous Yoruba religion has indeed facilitated their identification with Christianity. Through human history, the use of familiar religious symbols have served humanity well in times of social, economic and spiritual crises. And with the current economic crisis and social malaise in Nigeria, the indigenization of Christianity through the use of essential symbols and practices of the indigenous African religion has done no less a purpose among the Yoruba.

Chapter 9

African Polygamy and Its Theological Lessons for America

Philip Kilbride

The Problem: An Anthropological-Theological Perspective

In this chapter, I will argue that "inculturation theology" in African religious thought provides valuable insights for those concerned about the problematic national family situation and associated values in the United States and among African Americans, in particular. Many family life professionals, theologians, academicians, and others, have lamented the present state of family life in the United States, particularly as an alarmingly high rate of divorce has frequently negatively impacted on women and children (see Kilbride 1994). While children are the ones often suffering the most by family disruption, their concerns all too often remain secondary to those of their parents, and the children's cries are heard only as a distant echo by a nation dulled by the pursuit of personal gratification and material greed. One wonders why in the midst of such obvious spiritual bankruptcy most churches seem on the whole disengaged from virtually all family issues, excepting (sometimes fanatical) concern for the rights of the unborn, usually clothed in a frequently thoughtless defense of the two parent household rigidly, narrowly called "family values."

As a Roman Catholic, one especially wonders why American Catholic theology is so culturally narrow and ethnocentric, particularly given its great potential as a universal church with ready access to the spiritual and cultural legacy of the entire human experience. Sadly, although America is the most "multicultural nation" on the face of the globe and although the Catholic Church ever since Vatican II has had a mandate to relate Church dogma to cultural values, American Catholicism remains of little relevance to numerous Catholics from various minority populations. This is so because official Church theology has been unable or unwilling to generate a consistent culturally relative frame of reference particularly if this means providing a comparative cultural critique of "middle-class," national, cultural, practices in the majority population even though such cultural practices are comparatively devoid of real meaning spiritual or otherwise according to most of its members.

The purpose of this chapter is to offer a reflection on how a "culturalized theology" might just be useful to us at this moment of spiritual crisis in our national secular and religious experience. My intention is to contribute to dialogue which begins with the premise that American social life will profit by an invigorated church engagement, but that before such spiritalized social life can be meaningful for most Americans, churches themselves must rethink outdated theological positions so as to become more receptive to a truly diverse community. My concern here is "culturally extreme" in the American context but if one can not accept polygamy on cultural and theological grounds nevertheless, a case for plural marriage, from the "cultural point of view" will serve as a bridge head such that the reader might "loosen up" on less culturally foreign ideas, such as current official Catholic dogma which precludes freedom for women to become priests, condoms to be used for the prevention of AIDS, or for sexual intercourse to be enjoyable between spouses even though procreation is precluded. Most American Catholics, nowadays, find these beliefs to be well within an acceptable cultural point of view which has come to consider gender roles and sexual practices within a changing frame of reference.

As an anthropologist, I have chosen to emulate the position taken in a previous generation by Margaret Mead when she chose a cultural perspective to stake out her stand against a once prevailing "absolutist" ideology; one which held that divorce was inherently wrong and that a "2 parent nuclear family for life" value must, without exception, be spiritually and legally sanctioned (Mead 1949). Presently, our prevailing ethos in court and pulpit still overwhelming holds "absolutist" tendencies although unrestricted divorce has largely joined the heterosexual, nuclear family and monogamy as a "mandatory" norm expected by adults irrespective of situational contrasts even, I restate, at the expense of the needs and feelings of children implicated in many divorces. Mead labored to impose a cultural-informed family ideology while not intending to elevate "alternatives" to cultural absolutes, as in the case of divorce. As an anthropologist, I will argue also on behalf of pluralism and situational understanding, particularly where the interests of children can be shown to be enhanced by such a view.

Despite the scholarly opinion that Jesus of Nazareth was, unusual for His day among public teachers, a great lover of children (Sommerville1990: 5), experts largely agree that America's children are overall at great risk although Christian values are widely subscribed to. Children as a category are now not only the nation's poorest population in economic terms, but recent studies have shown overall that women and children have suffered terribly from the current, excessively high American divorce rate. For example, a striking downward economic spiral for women after divorce has contributed to a sharp rise in mother-children, homeless families in our nation's cities and suburbs. Children from single parent families, fueled by the high divorce rate, are over-represented in child populations of drug abusers, school dropouts and suicide victims (Whitehead 1993). Moreover, we are moving, primarily because of divorce, into an extended family context that has not yet been defined and given cultural recognition; namely, that of the blended family. In *The Wife-In-Law Trap*, Ann Cryster (1990) sets out some of her thoughts, findings, and experiences about the wife-in-law who is a key figure in the blended families that have emerged. Wives-in-law are women who are connected to each other, most often unwillingly, because they have been married to the same man. Frequently, this is a relationship between adversaries in the forward of the book. Mary Ellen Durham provides some demographics on this topic. There are currently over 14 million wives-in-law in the United States and the projected growth of this group is 1-1/2 million a year. Furthermore, one of every two children will experience the wife-in-law relationship at some point during childhood, and tens of millions of extended family members will be effected as well.

There appeared in *The Philadelphia Inquirer* (December 9, 1992), a story by Sandy Bauers called "Seasonal Adjustments" which described stresses associated with holiday routines and blended families. Bauers stated, "For children of divorced parents, the holiday routine may include two batches of presents. It also may include a tug of war between their mother and father." These parents reported a great deal of trouble, anxiety and upset over such things as the intrusion of stepchildren into their new marriage, sadness if a husband decides he doesn't want a second family, complaints over the others parenting skills, concern about details of visitation rights, and worry about the emotional price that their children must pay.

Similarly, Cryster (1990: 67) concluded:

> Children from former marriages often walk a difficult road. They not only have to deal with their mother's bitterness toward the new step family; they must also relate to a step-mother and step-siblings who may not be ready or willing to accept them.

The pain experienced would arguably be minimized if the relationship were legalized or made normative through some kind of a culturally legitimate marital concept, particularly *from the child's point of view*.

The present chapter will focus attention on the African American family where family disruption has been especially acute. Andrew Billingsley (1993), in a landmark study, emphasizes the concept of "strengths" and "adaptation" in the African American family tradition. He notes, for example, that "The allegiance to family is still so strong that on any given day the overwhelming majority of African American people will be found living in families of one type or another. In 1990, for example, 70% of the 10.5 million African American households were family households with persons related by blood, marriage, or adoption. Contrary to popular belief, this is about the same as the proportion of Whites who live in families (1993:37)." Nevertheless, due to unfavorable economic forces, migration , racism, and a decline of available Black men for nuclear family roles, there has been a striking decline in nuclear families. Billingsley reports that in 1890, 80% of Black families with children were headed by two parents. Moreover, he continues that "as late as 1960 when educated Black men could still hold good paying blue collar jobs in the industrial sector, 78% of all Black families with children were headed by married couples...(1993:36)." This figure has, however, dropped to 39% by 1990.

The African American man has been hit especially hard by the contemporary forces of economic deprivation and racism. Nathan and Julia Hare (1989: 26) have edited a   well-documented, informative book that deals with gender issues in the Black community: *Crisis in Black Sexual Politics*. The Hares report that one University of Chicago study predicted that at present rates, by the year 2000, "seventy percent of Black males will be either unemployed, in jail, on dope, or dead; with obvious consequences for their women, children and for society in general)." In a chapter entitled, "The Making of the Black Male Shortage--and Its Implications for the Black Family," the Hares acknowledge that Black males are at a disadvantage economically in providing for their families. They state that as much as 42% of all people incarcerated are Black males. An impoverished wife and children often were left behind by these men. About three out of ten Black males are unemployed. If one counts only Black youth, the figure rises to 48%; still others have given up the search for work entirely. Even worse, the Hares (1989) report that in one chance out of twenty, young Black males may die before reaching the age of 21. For those who do make it to between 20 and 35 years of age, the leading cause of death is homicide. Black males increasingly appear to be an "endangered species" (Harte and Hare 1989: 25).

Demographic patterns in America demonstrate the reality underlying the observation that Black women are increasingly either unwilling to marry or, when willing, frequently experience a shortage of available Black men. In 1975, 90% of Black women had married by the age of 40. By 1985, this figure had fallen to 81%, and by 1990, to 75%. Among White women at age 40, the marriage rate over these years was steady and over 90%. These statistics from an article in *The Philadelphia Inquirer* entitled, "Black Women Found Less Likely to Marry" by Tim Bovee (December 9, 1992, p. A3), show that at age 40, one in four Black women has never married as compared with one in ten White women.

In *Plural Marriage for Our Times: A Reinvented Option* (Kilbride 1994), I suggest that our thinking about solutions to America's current family crisis might well involve considering "plural marriage," for example, as an alternative arrangement that might serve to offset divorce in some situations. It might also make fathers accessible when males are not generally available. Sanctioning plural marriage in situations where it is already practiced (e.g. among Fundamentalist Mormons) would legitimize the parents and children in these unions. What I am suggesting then is greater choice in the form and structure of marriage in the United States.

In this chapter, I will focus my analysis so as to support those who critique theological discourse because it is my conviction that it is imperative to redirect Judeo-Christian theological ethics away from its commitment to philosophical "absolutism" in the direction of a "constructionist" position.[1]

Such a theological move would readily open up the doors to those now estranged who might subsequently enjoy an improved opportunity for "spiritual" renewal. In short, plural marriage may in some circumstances not only work well for children, but in some of these circumstances might, if approved by church and synagogues, serve to discard cloaks of secrecy where such practices already exist informally. It might also serve to unburden estranged individuals who might otherwise avail themselves of options to join (or rejoin) religious communities now closed to them. The winds of pluralism, I might add, if fanned by plural marriage, can only help the current general move against "absolutism" now being waged across the country by gays and lesbians who increasingly seek not only legal but also spiritual recognition of their conjugal aspirations.

Although I have discussed theological and historical-cultural issues in regards to plural marriage in general elsewhere (Kilbride 1994), here I will focus only on the African American family situation. In doing so, my objective is to illustrate what might be called an "anthropological, theological" perspective, one that I hope might be evidenced by more anthropologists choosing to reflect on theology from their disciplinary perspectives. Theologians already do refer routinely to anthropological materials, an example of which will be presented shortly.

First, let us open for discussion the question as to whether or not Judeo-Christian theology can justifiably oppose plural marriage on absolutist grounds *within* the "Judeo-Roman-European" cultural context that frames theological opposition to its practice. There is good reason to reject absolutism even in this cultural context. There is even stronger reason to reject an anti-polygamy Christian theology in the African cultural traditions where it has become a modern pastoral problem. African "inculturation" theological debate will accordingly be discussed below precisely because the African American cultural tradition is itself a historic extension of the African one now commonly recognized by most scholars (see Halloway 1990; Herskovits 1958; Billingsley 1993; Sudarkasa 1982; Young 1986). Moreover, as we have seen, there is a demographic male shortage crisis which itself may impose plurality on the community. For this reason, there is already an ongoing debate in the African American community on man-sharing.

Man-Sharing: An Ethnographic Interview

While researching the topic of plural marriage, I encountered an announcement in *The Philadelphia Inquirer* (January 27, 1993) which appeared under a personal briefing column and was headed "Polygamy or What?" The question posed was whether or not polygamy was a practical alternative for African American women who were having problems finding a mate. This issue was to be discussed that night as part of an agenda entitled, "Man-Sharing--African American Male/Female Relationships in the Nineties." This panel discussion hosted by the Delaware Valley Association of Black Psychologists was to be held at Temple University in Philadelphia, Pennsylvania. A $5.00 donation was requested, and the wider public was invited. It was with much curiosity then that I attended this man-sharing discussion which had about 100 people present, seemingly equally divided by gender. Although advertised in a major city newspaper as open to the public, the audience appeared to be mainly professionals in their thirties and forties and, with the exception of myself, entirely Black. The composition of the audience could indicate that there was very little interest in the topic of polygamy outside the Black community or, perhaps on second thought, that some people may not have wanted to be seen in public at a meeting of this sort given the stigma associated with polygamy in our culture. There appeared to be few university students in the audience, even though the meeting was being held on a university campus. Perhaps the expectation of monogamy is overwhelmingly prevalent among this younger, educated group. Indeed, very few people who do wind up in a polygamous relationship expect to do this at the outset.

The panel which was made up of professionals associated in one way or another with the topic of man-sharing, included a counselor from a neighboring university, two licensed psychologists, and a university archivist who was familiar with the literature of polygamy. Also participating were two male panelists and two female ones. A very lively moderator and several officers of the Association of Black Psychologists made opening and closing remarks. The first speaker, an animated, young woman whose views we will consider in some detail momentarily, stated that many of her women friends have had the experience of sharing a man at one time or another. When the audience was asked about their experience in this matter, all but four people indicated that they knew someone who was currently sharing a man. This observation lends credence to the fairly widespread practice of man-sharing, or polygamy, as suspected by Scott (1989) from his academic study.

In this meeting, overall the women tended to be opposed to man-sharing or some associated terms while the men were, on the whole, approving of it. Due to the often heated nature of the questioning, the moderator took male and female questions alternately. Nevertheless, widespread applause came from both men and women when a woman said that we needed to learn from Africa, where polygamy was responsibly practiced. One man offered what I consider to be the crux of the issue when he stated that the moral level of society overall needed to be raised; polygamy itself would not improve male behavior without an improvement in morality. In her closing remarks, the president of the association said that she herself was not ready to endorse or oppose polygamy herself, although after having lived in Nigeria, it made her identity as an African American more salient. She suggested that African Americans need to continually explore their African roots, particularly the reverence for God.

In attending the above meeting I met a particularly articulate person who agreed to speak to me at length about man-sharing from both personal observationals and familiarity with the available literature. While not especially favorable to the institution, she seemed willing to consider man-sharing as a possibility under certain circumstances. Ms. Julie Mallory-Church, one of the panelists, in a very lively and informative later meeting, shared with me some invaluable information on man-sharing in the Black community. Many people known to her were or had been involved in a man-sharing relationship. When I asked her whether she knew personally of any successful man-sharing relationships, she pointed out that the term, "successful," itself, is relative and that we must consider first what needs are being met by the relationship before we can evaluate it in terms of success. Furthermore, she doubts that all needs are successfully met even in monogamy. She cautions also that if one did not have a good self image, it would be difficult to call any kind of relationship successful, be it monogamous or man-sharing.

One problem Mallory-Church has observed in man-sharing situations is the reduced self-esteem of the woman involved. She noted that women "in favor" of man-sharing were generally women involved with someone else's husband. These were not short-term relationships. One benefit of man-sharing was that women need not worry about the authority of husbands, thus giving them freedom from the difficulties that sometimes come up in monogamous relationships where husbands and wives have to relate to each other on a daily basis. One understanding in the relationships with which she was familiar was that if something "better" (i.e. single) came along, the woman was free to pursue that. Julie, therefore, skeptically raises the question that if the women are as much in favor of man-sharing as they say that they are, then why search for something else. Their positive evaluation of man-sharing seems to be conditional, "unless there is something better." She also wonders if they would be in favor of "their" man or husband being involved in a relationship with another woman. Very much at the heart of this "shared" relationship is the issue of power which came up over and over again in our discussion. For instance, women involved in a man-sharing situation with a married man have little control over when they see their man. In this regard, Mallory-Church notes that a lot of her friends in this situation feel left out and lonely on holidays, in particular, since more often than not the man spends them with his other family. Concerning money, she gave the example of a woman who is involved in man-sharing with a wealthy married man. When he goes on business trips, say to the Caribbean Islands, he doesn't take his wife but he takes her friend. This friend has a car phone which he pays for, presents for her daughter, etc. He, thus, serves the role of provider. She obtains financial gain without the responsibility of sharing money which ideally occurs in a monogamous marriage.

A major problem of man-sharing in Mallory-Church's view, is the secrecy involved. She knows of only one case in which the women have openly agreed to sharing the same man. She believes that the issue of secrecy is very important in that it goes with the issue of trust, something especially important these days because of AIDS. There is a power issue involved here because the wife is never consulted in these matters. To be successful, man-sharing must be agreed upon by the wife and done openly rather than in secrecy as it now operates. At present, the "other woman" is involved in a kind of conspiracy, since she usually does know about the wife. To make matters worse, everyone else in the community, except the wife, may know about her also. The elimination of secrecy would serve to balance the power between the first and second woman involved, thus elevating the status of the first wife. In sum, she views secrecy as leading to the exploitation of women.

On the matter of jealousy, she admitted that it is a problem for the wife who, when she discovers the existence of the other woman, often goes out and gets another man for revenge. The mistress usually isn't jealous of the wife, but she would be jealous if another woman entered the man-sharing relationship. Julie finds this situation perplexing, although she knows of some cases of man-sharing that have gone on for many years. In one case, the other woman is now thinking about marrying another person, but Julie considers this to be unlikely. Asked whether she could conceive of any alternatives to man-sharing other than polygamy, she stated that she believes that polygamy is only one way to meet sexual needs. We also need to have sexual alternatives such as lesbians, turning to younger or older men, or outside of race relations.

In addition, she believes that celibacy is a viable option. In any case, these arrangements should be considered as choices not as circumstances forced on a person. The problem now, as she sees it, is that many women are forced to live without a man not by choice but by circumstances. It is her belief that women would have more choices if they were desocialized out of thinking about themselves as not important in terms of their own pleasure and positive experiences. At the same time, not only should women stop worrying so much about pleasing others, they must also stop thinking that they are less of a woman if they don't have a man in their lives. Overall, women are made to feel that they don't have much of a choice whereas they should and do have a choice.

When I turned our conversation to a consideration of children, Julie pointed out that children also have little input into the system of man-sharing as now practiced. It is only the man who is entirely in the know, possessing "the whole story" followed by his mistress. Wives and children "only suspect." She knows of one case in which she thought that the wife did not know when, in fact, she did. In this case, the man is fearful that his wife will tell their children. She knows of another case where a man has, in fact, raised the other woman's three sons. While this is seemingly a good outcome, Julie wonders whether his own children might not have suffered as a result. We don't actually know the effect on children or how much they suspect or really know.

Examples given by college students she counsels concern "strange" women who turn up on family trips as father's secretary, but who they later discover are mistresses; when parental divorces occur at college age as such secrets are unveiled these children feel betrayed. They sometimes not only get angry at the father for having betrayed them, but also at the mother for having put up with it. On reflection then, Julie concluded that secrecy seems to be a problem not only for the adults involved but also for the children. I asked if she thought that breaking down the secrecy would help reduce the workload, especially for working women experiencing the "double shift?" Julie said that she knew of a situation in which one woman baby-sat for the other woman's children although there was still some secrecy. In her view, however, men often play women off against each other for their own advantage and aren't always interested in fostering situations of cooperation.

I asked her whether she thought there was a male/female difference in tolerance for man-sharing and whether or not she thought that man-sharing would reduce male promiscuity. She responded that the issue wasn't so much whether polygamy would reduce promiscuity, but one of why fidelity itself is so valued. The issue is not how many women does a man have or how many men does a woman have; what is at issue between the couple is one of honesty or dishonesty rather than fidelity itself. How honesty is handled would be another element in the assessment of success raised earlier in our discussion. She, furthermore, reminds us that the term man-sharing itself has a gender bias and should be eliminated. Her preference would be for the term mate-sharing if there is to be any sharing at all. This would eliminate the implication of the term man-sharing that the man is the valued commodity in the equation; the word sharing is a misnomer because, in fact, there is no sharing due to secrecy. Unless one takes away the secrecy, it should be noted that one woman has not agreed to share at all.

Additionally, Mallory-Church believes that we need to destigmatize the very concept of man-sharing before we can give support to those fathers made available to single mothers with the approval of their spouses. One situation she knows personally involves an "outside child" who, now that he is an adult, is accepted more so, particularly at certain functions such as funerals and weddings. He still, however, is not fully accepted. She would like to see a situation where this "outside child" would have been more fully integrated into family life. One needs to destigmatize the "outside child" so that he can use the father's name and inherit property; that is to say, we must destigmatize for the sake of the children.

Inculturation Theology

Taking into account the overall "maladaptive" condition of family life in the United States, my objective is to bring about a re-thought theological posture, one that would welcome cultural pluralism and, even in some cases, encourage plural marriage. Central to a rethought theology would be what is known as inculturation theology in Africa, a subject to which we will now turn.

In Africa and elsewhere, the term "inculturation" is broadly used in reference to current attempts there to reformulate Christian doctrine into the culture patterns of any given society. Crollius (1986: 43) defines inculturation as follows:

Recapitulating, we can describe the process of inculturation in the following way: *the inculturation of the Church is the integration of the Christian experience of a local Church into the culture of its people in such a way that this experience not only expresses itself in elements of this culture, but becomes*

*a force that animates, orients and innovates this culture so as to create a new
unity and communion, not only within the culture in question but also as an
enrichment of the Church universal.*

Inculturation in Africa is a necessary response by international Christian
churches in light of the existence of more than 9,000 independent or
"breakaway" churches which have broken away from the mission churches
since the last century. Nevertheless, some of those pastors and theologians
who choose to remain within the missionary church umbrella, may view
inculturation differently. Frank Salamone (1991: 86), for example, working
in Nigeria, observed that Christians there sometimes prefer a religion that is
"different" and perhaps "better" than merely "pagan" beliefs such that, "They
ask, 'Why do you wish to give us a version of Christianity so different from
that practiced in your own country'?" While inculturation discussion broadly
embrace such customs as traditional religious rituals, ancestor beliefs,
healing practices, and burial customs, the question of polygyny remains,
perhaps, the most pressing, current pastoral and theological topic.

In a provocative book on the church and marriage in Kenya, Bishop Henry
Okullu (1990) (Church of the Province of Kenya, Anglican-derived)
observes that he has become painfully aware that polygyny is the single
largest pastoral problem in western Kenya. Although details vary, both
Catholic and Protestant denominations, in Kenya and throughout Africa,
currently stigmatize polygynous marriage. Routinely, for example, a
polygynist man must send away all but one wife if he is to be accepted for
Holy Communion, Baptism, etc. Children of additional wives are considered
illegitimate and not acceptable for Baptism. Some churches accept
polygynists provided all sexual relations are terminated with all but one wife;
this couple is then eligible to be married. Bishop Okullu decries this state of
affairs, one which keeps many people out of church. While he favors
monogamy as the Christian ideal, he believes that monogamists are often
defensive and unforgiving in their attitudes. He believes polygyny has much
to recommend it, such as, limiting divorce and negative consequences for
children.

Father Michael C. Kirwen (1974) has questioned current Roman Catholic
teachings on African marriage. In his own work he considers the levirate as
practiced among some societies in Kenya and Tanzania. In this custom, a
widow is still considered married even though her husband has died; she is
literally a wife of a lineage. For this reason, her brother-in-law, honoring a
commitment to family values, cohabits and provides for her as a substitute
for his dead brother. Kirwen notes that this custom would make little sense

in a European society where "individuals" marry and where strong family lineages are not the basis for social organization. For this reason, European-derived Catholic policy is maladaptive in its opposition to the levirate in Africa. Such a policy has not "incarnated" itself to local custom. He believes that this failure is a grave pastoral problem, an unending source of anxiety and frustration to both clergy and laity alike.

Father Kirwen also has provided an excellent critique of 19th century, neo-scholastic theology whose canons were the basis for the pre-Vatican II "manualist" ("textbook" and "culture free") theology taught to missionaries of his generation. Such marriage canons were "foundationalist" (or absolutist) in assumption, and thus thought to be suitable for all cultures although, in fact, they were European in assumption. Marriage in this European view is between two people, legally *independent* of their families. In manualism, no other model for marriage is mentioned or even hinted at. Ironically, the post-Vatican II revolution set in motion by Pope John XXII has not yet taken hold. In fact, His Holiness wrote "the church...does not identify herself with any particular culture, not even with the Occidental culture to which her history is so closely bound" (Kirwen 1974: 20).

Father Eugene Hillman (1975), among others, has called for a reconsideration of polygamy in Christian Africa. He makes his case by observing that polygamy is practiced widely in the Hebrew Bible and that it is not explicitly condemned in the *New Testament*. Both of these arguments frequently have been made by African parishioners themselves. The Council of Trent which made polygamy anathema in the 16th century did not consider the situation of non-western cultures; therefore, on the "constructionist" view of theology, Trent Dogma should not be taken as an "absolutist" dogma. Given the many reasons why polygamy is functional in Africa, Hillman thinks that it should be rethought theologically. Hillman, himself, suggests that the Lutheran Church in Liberia provides a good model where persons who already practice polygamy in good faith should not be prevented from participating in the sacramental life of the church. In a manualist vein, however, he cautions that once becoming Christians through Baptism, no more polygamous marriages should be allowed.

Rt. Rev. Dr. David Gitari, C.P.K. (1985), in a comparative study of polygamy, has reviewed Anglican attempts to address the polygamy question. He finds international conferences wholly inadequate, that is, when the question is even considered. Even African-derived canons are concerned primarily with how to "discipline" the polygamist rather than on how to care for him pastorally. He thinks this shows that African theological thought has been overly Westernized. In a view similar to my own (see Kilbride 1994),

Rt. Rev. Gitari writes that polygamy as ideally practiced is, in the abstract, "more Christian" than divorce and remarriage as seen from the vantage point of the abandoned wives and especially their children. However, like myself, he would not oppose divorce (or annulment) in principle either. In conclusion, Rt. Rev. Gitari recommended to a C.P.K. synod that while the church teaches monogamy, it must be sensitive to the widespread practice of polygamy. Importantly, while generally requiring that Christians who become polygamists be excluded from Holy Communion, it is imperative to consider special factors on a case by case basis.

Presently, however, the weight of African "mainstream" theological opinion is, in the main, for the prohibition of polygamy. For instance, Hillman's rethinking of polygamy was critiqued in a follow up study entitled, *Monogamy Reconsidered* (W. Blum 1989). That polygamy can evoke harsh negative affect in the inculturation community is seen in the opinion of Lamin Sanneh (1968: 237) who writes:

> One other matter that relates to indigenization is polygamy. Because it is an emotional issue, invested with high stakes by the patriot, it has been used as the touchstone of genuine indigenization... There is nothing inherently African about the institution of plural marriages, nor can it be said to be a universal rule applied in all societies. We need also to avoid the danger of describing it in such a way that it is made to embody all the ideals of the African past. There was much abuse in the system, and its benefits were not always the unmitigated boon claimed. Its modern proponents, who are mostly men, risk alienating a whole community of women from the social and education pressures which may tend towards a more just world. In any case it seems inconceivable that in such a vital area as marriage and family life the church should stand aside or else come into the picture only to make an opportunistic endorsement of an arrangement that panders to the male ego.

The inculturation debate in Africa is relevant for current theological, constructionist-oriented discourse in America. Perhaps the most immediate benefactors from an African theological reflection would be those African American churches where it seems parishioners and clerics alike will be increasingly confronted with the "man-sharing" debate. However, given the great diversity in these churches (see Blackwell 1991), including Black, interracial Catholic and Protestant, etc, it is not possible now to ascertain which churches are most affected by the issue. It is my belief that, first and foremost, what is needed are social and economic policies to ameliorate the racism and poverty which is at the heart of the present crisis in Black gender relations described earlier. Meanwhile, what is hopefully the short run, and in light of minimal evidence for racial and economic reform, African

American theology might well reasonable confront the man-sharing issue; perhaps, this can best be done somewhat along the lines of the inculturation issue in Africa. This is reasonable given that, in actuality, polygamy is informally practiced among some African Americans for economic reasons and most likely for cultural reasons also (see Scott 1989; Herskovits 1958). A. Billingsley (1993), for example, believes that a number of African family patterns have persisted in America, although in somewhat diluted from. Among such patterns is the primacy given to the extended family and consanguineal ("blood") relatives over the nuclear family. There is a strong value placed on children and respect for the "elders." He concludes that a "distinctive and often misunderstood feature of African family patterns was the acceptance of polygamous marriages... From all indications, polygamous marriages were as functional as monogamous ones" (Billingsley 1993:95).

An African American theological reflection on African theology, apart from polygamy, is not, of course, novel. Young (1986), for example, considers the notion of whether or not Black and African theologies are "siblings or distant cousins." There are sharp differences to be sure. Black theology is primarily concerned with the consequences of life in a racist society, a response that has produced, among other things, a rich *Old Testament*-based salvation and other worldly theology, in comparison to Africa where "cultural questions" (inculturation) as opposed to political problems predominate. In spite of some theologians who believe that Black and African theologies have little in common, Young identifies common ground in mutual experiences of poverty and a strong sense of community. Significantly, he believes that "African theologies of indigenization" have much to offer African Americans, although he does not mention polygamy.

Within Roman Catholic circles African American religious and laity alike often express feelings of cultural and racial alienation. Preston Williams (1990: 315), for instance, observes that "the needs of African Americans receive little attention...racial incidents... are not seen as being in part related to the failure of Catholic teaching or practice and the absence of African American Catholic clergy and lay leaders, but rather to black immorality or government programs farming blacks." Williams continues that the United States Catholic church still largely resembles a European "monolith" and that reconciliation of White and Black Americans will necessitate incorporation of elements of Black culture into the national life of the Church. A good example of reconciliation is provided by a Cardinal Ritter issue of the magazine *America*, in which Black religious provide testimony on the question of their minority racial and cultural status in the Church. Bishop W.D. Gregory (1991: 414), for example states" We are holistic in the sense that we don't see a Jansenistic difference between body and soul." For this reason Black ministers are often politicians and excellent jazz musicians and singers frequently come from the churches, and the Bishop continues that there is in Black life and spirituality an emphasis on communitarian values. While Bishop Gregory has remained in the Church while at the same time speaking out for liturgical reform, others such as Bishop George Stallings have led their followers away from the Roman Catholic Church for more conducive services where liturgical practices are more in synch with African American cultural practices.

Conclusion

The present chapter following Robert Egan (1992: 13) accepts that "theology can be understood as a disciplined way of thinking and talking about the practice of our religious faith - asking questions about it and trying to answer them in the context of our own time and culture." Roman Catholic theological reflection can only gain cultural insight as it is currently undergoes a process of "laicization" wherein "theologians" are no longer confined, as in the recent past, to the "specialist " laboring in seminary and monastery to pass on largely European values thought to be entirely spiritual or independent to culture (Egan 1992). Lay theologians for instance including university professors, men, women, non Catholics, non Europeans, as well as celibate priests are all welcome in the emerging scholarly theologic field, seen to be an academic discipline. Although, of course, it is still the case that not all theologians are "official" spokespersons for the Roman Catholic Church's dogmatic mission. Hopefully, however, the official curial dogmatic theology will be somehow moved from its sometimes archaic, culturally ethnocentric, positions on family values and reproductive ethics, by increased attention, if not acceptance of viewpoints expressed by its "loyal" opposition, including those in the lay ranks.

A "lay" cultural theology arising from the side of anthropology would seem to have much to offer theological pluralism. For example, Crollius (1986:36) has observed that the concept of inculturation has many characteristics of the process of "acculturation," long studied in the cultural change literature of anthropology where acceptance, rejection, and modification of cultural traits and institutions in particular societies is well documented in contact situations. In a thoughtful piece in the *American Anthropologist*, Michael Angrosino (1994) offers several models derived from anthropology which he believes describe how "inculturation" concerns do or should proceed within the Roman Catholic faith. In what he calls the conservative approach, for example, immutable doctrine is upheld at the expense of any major tinkering with ritualistic forms so as to uphold the sanctity of the Latin rite. In contrast, he believes Liberals freely innovate in ritual practices and beliefs based on a pluralistic vision of society, very much along the lines of the polygamy debates discussed above. In the largely unexplored "radical" approach favored by Angrosino (1994: 830) as seemingly "most attuned to anthropological thinking," the Gospel message must be purged of classism, sexism, racism and all beliefs that are seen as "essentialist" rejection of tradition in favor of whatever flows from the popular religion of the people as seen by him to be empowered. While it is clear that many Christian "essentials" are merely cultural outcomes, particularly from powerful European sources, it seems to me that the liberals might well ask if the radicals would not hold that "universal love" even of enemies might not be somehow "essentially" Christian whatever the culture? Angrosino (1994: 827), however, makes an excellent point when he observes that inculturation "tends to divorce ritual from its social context." It is one thing, for example, to inculturate marriage rituals variously involving veils, rings, drums, etc., but having no concept of the social structure that actually gives organizational meaning to marriage in a given society, may be self-defeating in the long run. One could apply to polygamy Angrosino's distinction between ritual as commonly understood in inculturation thought and social structure as not understood. It would certainly require considerable reflection in order to deduce what theological principles might intersect with such aspects of social structural principles of descent, inheritance, and post marital residence rules, as these are differentially related to monogamy and plural marriage. For instance, how might co-wives who reside together "share" child care (and even procreation functions) for their family as a moral obligation?

Finally, other standard practices of anthropology also would be useful rapprochements with theology apart from the culture concept which is the "cornerstone" of the discipline (c.f. Langness 1975). Comparison of cultures, as here attempted between Africa and the United States, is standard in anthropology. Reliance on ethnography and the personal interview, as here reported for the man-sharing debate, is also common anthropological method. To get the "insider's" view, ethnography in African communities where plural marriage rules are likely to be more relaxed, and likewise in churches in the United States where new marriage practices are evolving would provide insightful and practical information for future study and discussion of the plural marriage issue. Importantly, a cultural theology might be most useful for awakening anthropology from its (often unconscious) acceptance of atheistic theory as its current "absolutist," fundamental, theoretical paradigm in a discipline where pluralism and relativism are standard. Religious belief and practice, anthropologically, are now seen largely as "false consciousness," "group worship," "displaced aggression," "symbolic action," etc. (c.f. Shweder 1991). There would be much to gain should anthropology, itself, become spiritually pluralistic and embrace some of the theologically-influenced literature concerning culture which does not rule out the existence of God and spiritual phenomena as "really real."

Notes

1. *Absolutism* or *Foundationalism* is the belief that reality and knowledge exist apart from, or prior to, cultural construction (e.g. as natural law). *Constructionism* is the view that social practices and beliefs are socially constructed, that is, culturally interpreted or influenced.

Chapter 10

Adoring the Father: Religion and Charisma in an American Polygamous Community[1]

William Jankowiak and Emilie Allen

"A father's ghost is the one we can never shake." A son's comment in Ibsen's *The Ghost.*

Introduction

There are few modern cultures where religious meaning is derived entirely from its theological tenets and where religious dogma is forcefully applied uniformly. Most cultures find themselves adjusting to other psychological needs, cultural values, and social and personal interests. Religious meanings, like all cultural meanings, invariably reflect the interplay between official creed and other structural and psychocultural factors. This interplay accounts, in large measure, for the institutionalization of father adoration or reverence in the Fundamentalist Mormon cosmology.

In this chapter we will explore the origins, persistence, and meaning of a social and familial institution we will call father adoration or father reverence. It is our contention that father adoration is a psychocultural configuration that arises from four separate yet intertwined components: 1) a theology that endows men with a supernatural essence that commands the regeneration of a religious organization primarily, but not exclusively, through copious reproduction; 2) a closed-corporate, theological community that confers its greatest esteem on men in leadership positions as members of the church's priesthood council or on men who are independently wealthy; 3) a polygamous family system organized around a husband/father, who is the primary focal point, at least at the symbolic level, and, who unites the often competing female-centered natal family units; and, 4) an American cultural ethos that values emotional familial involvement over a detached, albeit respectful, role performance. Together, these forces introduced new factors into the fundamentalist cosmology which, over time, became incorporated as a new, albeit sacred aspect, of the community's world view. Within this world-view, fathers are the most valued social category.

We intend to explore how these components not only foster the formation of father adoration but, also, account, in large part, for the variation found within that formation. Specifically, we will examine father adoration as it manifests itself most powerfully: a fondly-remembered, deeply troubling, and socially salient experience of adulthood. The institution of father adoration is a product of numerous factors that are, in themselves, suggestive but when they cohere, as they do in Angel Park, they form a seminal family form (2). The data presented in this chapter were collected between 1993 and 1995, during a seventeen month study of a Fundamentalist Mormon polygamous community we will call Angel Park.

Angel Park: The Religious Community

Angel Park is a sectarian religious community that forms one of five polygamous communities found in the western United States, Canada, and northern Mexico. Each of these communities is separately governed and maintains only nominal, if any, contact with one another. The population of Angel Park, located in the western United States, is approximately 9,000, including 687 families ranging greatly in size from four to six-eighty family members, accounting, in all, for less than one tenth of the 21,000 to 50,000 Americans (depending on which source one uses) who follow a polygamous life style (Kilbride 1994; Quin 1991).

On the whole, Angel Park is a town which from, at first appearance, looks like a rather quaint and ordinary community. Like other small American rural communities, all of its main roads (seven in all) are paved, whereas its side streets are not. It has one grocery store, a health food store, a post office, a police station, a volunteer fire department, two elementary schools, two junior high schools, one high school, three private home schools, and one religious school (first through twelfth grade), one dentist (who is non-Mormon), two gas stations, a small motel, several auto shops, a milk plant, a large mortgage company, three restaurants (two for locals; the other more upscale, for tourists on their way through the Southwest), and a petting zoo. The houses and mobile trailers range in size from 32,000 square feet to around 1100 square feet, with many in various stages of completion or renovation. Because of its location, Angel Park's economy cannot support all of its residents. Most men work in the construction industry while other men and women work in a variety of other kind of jobs (e.g., accountants, janitors, masseuses, caretakers, teachers, nurses, mechanics, and long-distance truck drivers) *outside* the community.

Given the uniqueness of the community's family system, it is easy to overlook the commonalities that Fundamentalist Mormons share with mainstream American culture. Forged out of the 19th century American frontier experience, Fundamentalist Mormonism embraces many American middle class values: a basic frugality of means, emphasis on controlling one's destiny, a striving of upward mobility and a belief in personal autonomy.

Although many residents of Angel Park feel certain that aspects of the mainstream culture are immoral (e.g., cigarettes, drugs (but not alcohol or caffeine consumption), MTV, R-rated movies, and so forth), most residents occasionally participate in the American consumption ethic even while simultaneously voicing their disapproval of that ethic. Several polygynous families have even appeared on various talk shows to defend their religiously based life style from stereotypical and shallow attacks. Thus contemporary fundamentalists are, not like the Amish, who sweepingly disapprove of, and strive to withdraw from, contemporary American culture. For the fundamentalist, life is to be enjoyed and that enjoyment includes many of its sensual pleasures coffee-drinking, alcohol consumption, and feasting at local all you can eat buffets). Common dinner topics range from religious issues, the merits of secular philosophy, the entertainment value of Jurassic Park to President Clinton's seemingly uneasy marriage and its reflection of changes in American culture, and what herbs are best for preventing sickness.

Angel Park is not isolationist by choice or inclination. Fundamentalist Mormons never rejected American society as much as they feared provoking its wrath. As a middle-aged man puts it, "We follow the law of the land except when it contradicts with God's law of plural marriage." Nonetheless, for most of its 80 year existence, the community has repeatedly encountered social harassment and political persecution. Whatever physical and psychological withdrawal fundamentalism has made has been for its own self-preservation.

From 1882 on, federal and state governments sought to disenfranchise the Mormons in Utah. As a result, many polygynists went into hiding, fleeing into remote areas of Utah, Idaho, Arizona, and into Mexico. By 1897, almost 200 Mormons were sent to prison for practicing polygyny (Bohannan 1985:81). However, despite the arrests and the often vocal opposition from Americans outside the community, several church leaders, including some of the founders of the Angel Park community, came to believe that the 1890 Manifesto which declared that polygamy was a sin and, thus, prohibited to any devout Mormon was invalid, and against God's will. During the 1930's, a small groups of "true" or "fundamentalist" Mormons rejected the 1890 Manifesto and sought to establish new intentional communities which would provide encouragement, support, and protection for those who wanted to practice their religion in its entirely, which meant the formation of a polygamous family system.

Thus began an ongoing antagonistic and sometimes bitter conflict between Mormon Fundamentalists, the mainstream Mormon church, and state and federal governments. From the 1930's until the 1950's, Angel Park was the site of numerous governmental raids, the last and largest taking place in 1953, which resulted in the arrest of 39 men and 86 women and their 263 children. The children were placed in foster homes for up to two years (Bradley 1993:110; Von Wagner 1991). An unintended consequence of the raids was to "strengthen everyone's conviction and dedication to maintain their life-style. Outside pressure had in effect turned everyone into a community of believers" (Bradley 1993:110).

Since the late 1960's there has emerged a greater tolerance, albeit a reluctant one, between the State and the polygamous community. Although the State remains adamant in its insistence that polygamy is illegal, it has tacitly adopted a 'live and let live' attitude toward Angel Park. Given contemporary American mainstream culture's tolerance toward cohabitation, alternative child rearing practices, and other related social experiments in family living, the polygamist community is culturally and politically tolerated - a position that has been reinforced by the 1987 Supreme Court ruling which found that children could not be taken from their mother solely on the basis of living in a polygamous household. The Court ruled that documentation of child abuse and not unorthodox family form, was the primary basis for police intervention (Quin 1992). Today some community members are openly proud that, after decades of persecution, their religiously inspired way of life has finally received legal protection.

Angel Park is an intentional community where practitioners live, or expect to live, in a plural family. Unlike l9th century Mormonism, where an estimated 10 to 20 percent of the families were polygamous (Foster 1991), more than thirty percent of the families in Angel Park are polygamous. Often individuals who do not plan to create a plural family leave the community. This practice ensures that the community is constantly replenishing itself with those who are committed to living "the principle" (i.e., plural marriage). Recent disagreements within the community have resulted, however, in Angel Park splitting into two rival religious communities or wards (e.g., first and second ward). With the exception of different notions of political succession within the church organization, both wards are, by and large, remarkably similar in their cultural and theological orientation. In this and every other way, Angel Park has remained, throughout its history, both demographically and culturally, a male-centered theologically governed, family-oriented religious community.

Mormon Theology~ Christianity and Honoring Thy Father

Mormonism, or the Church of Jesus Christ of Latter Day Saints (LDS), emerged out of the American frontier experience which shaped, and continues to shape, its interpretation of Christian doctrines. Its theology is grounded in the teachings of three books: *The Bible, The Book of Mormon*, and *The Doctrine and Covenants*. The latter two books are prescribed as holy scripture, the words of God revealed directly to Joseph Smith (Musser 1944).

These revelations and doctrines contributed to the formation and growth of a distinctly new kind of American religious canon. Although Mormonism is derived from a Judeo-Christian cultural heritage, it is not a typical Christian denomination. rather, as Jan Shipps (1985) points out, its reinterpretation of many of Christianity's most basic axioms produced a strikingly novel synthesis which, she insists, generated a new American religion.

With the exception of plural marriage, there are several non-negotiable tenets forming the core of Mormon theology. One such tenet holds that God is a polygamous man who loves all his children but confers on men, and not women, an elevated spiritual essence which insures that "righteous" living men will obtain a higher spiritual standing. Women's standing, on the other hand, is determined by their performance in the highly valued complimentary roles of wife and mother. Men, on the other hand, occupy leadership positions in their families, on the church council, as well as having the potential, in the next life, to become a godhead with dominion over all their descendants.[3] Within this cosmological framework the father is charged with the duty to constantly expand his kingdom by entering into the institution of plural marriage (Musser 1944).

A second tenet holds that an individual's celestial rank is determined by the performance in this life of virtuous deeds. It is important to point out that a man's celestial rank is not determined by the number of wives he has or the number of children he reproduces. It is determined primarily, by a person's ability to live righteously, correctly, according to God's will, with the highest virtue reserved to those who enter into a plural family. In contrast, women achieve salvation primarily by becoming a sister-wife (I.e., a co-wife) in a celestial or plural family. Because the family unit extends beyond the grave into an eternal world, whereby the marriage contract "seals" a man and woman together "for time and eternity" in the Heavenly Kingdom, it is in a woman's "best interest to advance her husband's interests which meant that she should bear a large number of children" (Bohannan 1985:81), while also striving to uphold her husband's behavior, especially in front of his children.

Accordingly, Fundamentalist Mormons, more than those of its contemporary mainstream, hold that a central purposes of this life is to prepare for the coming of the Celestial Kingdom, a belief that supports the fundamentalists' conviction that they are God's chosen people born to live "the fullness of the Gospel" and, thus, create God's ideal - the polygamous family (Baur 1988). This conviction lies at the heart of Angel Park's communitarian impulse to create a socially-unified and spiritually-harmonious united order. Significantly, the creation of this new order depended upon the contribution of fathers.

Honoring of Fathers and Competing with Fathers

Social standing in every American town is organized around race, wealth, religious membership, and ethical conduct. This is certainly true in Angel Park, a small town which is governed by a religious elite who is "called by God," in a rank order of succession, to the office of the Brethren or the priesthood council.[4] It constitutes, as such, a sacred chartered dedicated to creating a social environment conducive to supporting the polygamous family system.

To achieve this ideal, Angel Park was formally incorporated into a religious trust in order to provide social and economic assistance to its members.[5] The ideal was to create a supportive environment which would enable one to transcend his or her more base human nature and become, in the process, a more tolerant and loving person and, thus, spiritually worthy to enter into the kingdom of God. Within this religiously-inspired framework, men, as fathers, occupy an important place. Not only are they the religious specialist in their family, the final arbiter of all spiritual and ethical conflicts, but also the high priests of the entire community.

The history of any group is often shaped through the stories it tells itself. None are as powerful as the historical testimonials that people tell one another in gatherings of public remembrance. In Angel Park , these testimonials invariably focus on their father's heroic deeds and accomplishments which ultimately advanced or improved the community. These testimonials, devotional in tune and presentation, honor the deceased father's memory through the selection of hagiographic accounts that ritualistically praise the fathers' actions, while, at the same time, overlook their shortcomings.

The hagiographies are remarkably alike in their content. They typically tell as story of a just and honorable man whose steadfastness to his religious convictions, often in the face of personal financial loss and hardship, demonstrate his commitment to cherished community ideals or participation in important community activities These activities included the building of some structures, often a drainage ditch, the operation of a much needed saw mill, the creation of a mortgage company which would employ residents, make large contributions to the community's legal defense, or strive to uphold the United Order.

The public testimonials are customarily received as wonderful tales of loving devotion.[6] The devotional tone can be heard in a mid-twenties woman's remembrance of the role her deceased father played in her life. Delivered during a church service, she stressed how "my father always explained the importance and meaning of the Gospel to his family." "Although," she added, "he was strict and diligent in his work, he was also a concerned and loving parent who always worked with his children so they never got in trouble." She concluded by saying how she loved to "see him in the morning pour milk into his coffee and that even today every time she makes coffee the smell reminds me of his wonderful presence." This palpable visionary presence of the father is not uncommon.

The love of the father is found, too, in the remarks of a woman in her mid-thirties who recalled that, as a young girl, she would go on walks with her father who never failed to explain the importance of the living God's law (i.e., polygamy). She declared, with an emotional timbre in her voice, that through "his kindness and love, I am a better person." A teenaged, unmarried woman whose father had passed away when she was eight years-old, remembered her father as a sensitive man who "I appreciated for his kindness and commitment to the family." She added that "he will always be an inspiration to me." Father adoration is also often expressed outside of church. A man is his forties said at his family's Sunday dinner, where the entire family eats together, to his wives and children, that his father always stressed the importance of eating, at the very least, one meal a week together as a family. "Dad always said," he added (with tears in his eyes), "the family that eats together stays together." He dwelled on his father's enlightenment and how he, too, as a father, wanted to continue what was, for him, a memorable family tradition.

The honoring of the father as either an important founder of the community, or the founder of a family line, is reinforced by Angel Park's private school requirement that every graduating senior must write a report about either his or her family history or the history of a significant community founder. In this context, the community founder defined as anyone who made a significant contribution to Angel Park's growth and development. Such a man is regarded as a kind of father to the whole community and, in a way, everyone's father. Significantly, women, as mothers or wives, are seldom the subject of these student essays. Nor are they ever commemorated during church service.[7] Hagiographies, in Angel Park, are reserved only for fathers.

These examples do not mean that mothers are less loved or regarded as unimportant in Angel Park. Adults are quick to acknowledge their mother's contribution (discussed below). Appreciation of the mother is more private though not necessarily less emotionally intense. In the public arena, however, fundamentalists prefer to speak entirely in the idiom of father adoration and seldom in terms of mother adoration. Typically, after the father has "passed to the other side," he is commemorated by the placement of his photo in a prominent place in the family living room. A deceased mother's photo, however, is usually smaller or, if it is the same size, is placed under his, or, inconspicuously, on an adjacent wall. The placement of the photos of the deceased constitute the highest form of remembrance and the declaration of filial affection. In this sense, there is a restricted form of ancestor reverence in Angel Park, with almost exclusive focus on one's father.

Familism: Competing with a Father's Reputation

Although Fundamentalist Mormon theology and church leadership actively discourage familial ranking (i.e., the ranking of families into a hierarchy of relative social worth) it nevertheless flourishes in Angel Park. Its social repercussions encourage a kind of clannishness whereby individuals seek to advance their own reputation and, indirectly, their family's status through economic achievement and superior moral performance. Although an individual's actions are felt to be either an aspect of family inheritance or something unique to one's own personality, status competition often involves the advancing, or smearing, of a father's reputation. It is not surprising that children, but not necessarily adults, often believe their relative social standing depends upon advancing or criticizing one another's accomplishments. There is nothing novel in this pan-human propensity.

What is illustrative is the fact that gentle and not so gentle "digs" are couched in a father-centered discourse, which often is nothing more than an exercise in status-leveling or status assertion. Such inter-family competition takes place in a variety of settings: 'song duels' between children of rival families, general peer group teasing, and public criticism and ridicule of another's behavior.

One popular form, in the song duel, takes place only between children and never, as in the case of the Eskimo song duel, between adults. As an example, a eight year-old girl encounters two seven year-old half-sisters from rival religious factions, and immediately sings: "Your family is too simple, just too simple..." The seven year olds just as quickly repeat the song fragment but substituting the eight years old's family name in place of their own. Claims and counter-claims are flung backward for the peer group.

Teasing always involves mockery in the name of one's father, another child's supposed family-centered personality traits that the family, and its figurehead, the father are implicated in the defect can be seen in the interaction of children playing a game of playground basketball. When one boy repeatedly kicked the ball, some children ridiculed his physical clumsiness as "typical of all the Jacksons." In a reversal of father adoration, the Jackson's father is belittled, for he's the source of the clumsiness. Father mockery is inevitable in a community where his adoration is crucial. If the father is mocked, he can also be praised. Positive attributes are seen as a trait typical of a certain family. For example, when a particularly gifted musician performed at her school reception, she was warmly applauded with many in attendance noting in appreciation that "all the Boyds are gifted musicians, just like their father." When one wants to raise up in awe or mock, the image of the father is invoked as an indication of strong feelings either way.

Unlike children's status competitions which take place in semi-public arena and are directed at a specific person, adults prefer to voice their negative evaluations in private settings amongst family members and close friends. These evaluations invariably take the form of teasing put-downs such as the so-and so "family puts on airs" or "they think they are so special," in order to uphold, on one hand, a community ethos of fellowship while, also defending, if not advancing, one's own family reputation. There is, thus, in Angel Park a kind of balance of power involving mockery of fathers and adoration of them as a way of preserving the historical continuity of status. Mockery is one way of keeping certain fathers in their place within the local social hierarchy.

Adult family rivalry often involves the embellishment of one's father's accomplishments through the manipulation of historical facts. Before the religious split in the community, a man, who arrived in the community during the sixties instructed his children, who performed, in a school play about the history of the community, a scene that glorified his communal contributions (many of which never happened), while neglecting to mention other men who played a more pivotal historical role. Immediately after the performance, other family members returned home and retold to one another the special exploits of their father in building up Angel Park. Of course, status competition or the manipulation of local history in communities and cultures all across America, but in Angel Park these are invariably expressed in the name of honoring or dishonoring someone's father.

Not every embellished historical account is made to advance a father's accomplishments. Some accounts are invoked to defend what the family considers to be slanderous charges made against their father and, indirectly, themselves. A family's low status can be altered with pervasive historical revisionism. In 1930's, for example, one man was charged by police for sexual indecency. Fifty years later, his middle-aged daughter habitually explains to anyone who will listen how her father was framed and thus was never sexually immoral. In this way adults try to maximize their father's memory in order to advance or maintain their position in a social hierarchy that is only partially shaped by principles derived from its fundamentalist theology. In essence, because father adoration is so strong and pervasive a phenomenon in Angel Park, the historically-based status of one's family has a long and durable shelf-life.

The Charismatic Father: Imaging the Polygamous Family

The polygamous family's social organization is derived, in part, from theological axioms which uphold men as the religious specialist and authority in the family and, in part, from the social dynamics of polygamous family life which make men, as husbands and fathers, the pivotal axis by which wives and children organize attention and internalize family identity. From an organizational perspective, intense and persistent familial attention is on the father, as the ultimate adjudicator of family affairs. For children of a plural marriage the notion of familism and thus belongingness stems from an image of the all-powerful father who is the biological, social and religious pater to his children. In a very practical way, the plural family is held together as much by an image of sharing a common bond as it is with actual memories of interacting with one's father (who embodies the common bond at its highest). It is a bond that needs the active involvement, participation and affirmation of fathers, co-wives and mothers.

American psychologists have long noted that, for American children of both sexes, the mother is the most important figure" (Sered 1994:57). Because families tend to be organized, in the daily give and take of life, around the mother, there is a general tendency, especially among white American middle-class families, toward developing greater emotional ties between mothers and children than between fathers and children. Sered (1994) points out that matrifocal units often arise within patrilineal social organizations. In Angel Park this American tendency toward matrifocality is undermined by the cultural emphasis on the spiritual and administrative authority of the father, while giving equal attention to the husband-wife and the mother-child relationship.

Unlike other polygamous societies, Mormon polygamous couples expect to develop strong intense emotional relationships with each other. Such strong husband-wife relationships may undermine a woman's ability to challenge her husband's authority. It is the desire for romantic intimacy that intensifies a woman's identification with the role of wife/lover in addition to that of mother - an orientation that stands in sharp contrast to the mainstream matrifocal ideal where the image of motherhood holds the greater emotional and cultural salience. In Angel Park a woman's primary emotional and psychological identity often swings between that of wife and mother. This split dampens the pull toward de facto matrifocal units. In a sense a woman's role is to balance and humanize the desires of marginal intimacy with the needs of her children. To lean too far in either direction would undermine the whole delicately weave structure in the polygamous family life.

Because co-wives are often in competition for their husband's attention, they contribute to the idealization process by focusing their children's attention on their father: They are focused on him for attention, so, in a turn, should their children. He becomes the symbolic link between himself, the family, and the community. As mothers, co-wives instruct their children to love and cherish their father and strive to fulfill his expectations.[8] This effort, along with the child's own desire to bond with his father, enhances the father's stature and esteem.

Zablocki (1980) reminds us that charismatic leaders have to constantly prove that they are worthy of the special grace extended to them. He adds that "tangible failures in the external domain have a way of increasing rather than decreasing [a father's] charismatic legitimacy" (1980:323). Left to themselves, the ideological dreams and day to day organizational realties soon go separate ways (Zablocki 1980:326). The community of Angel Park recognizes the tendency to fragment and strives to achieve consensus by stressing obedience to higher ideals, as does any close-knit culture or religious group. In the case of the polygamists, scriptural authority enhances a father's authority by conferring the priesthood on men alone. A priest can withhold blessings and, thus, delay a son from going before the priesthood council to request a wife. At the family level, the father's authority is reinforced whenever he leads the family in Sunday school service (usually conducted in his home), participates in arranging the marriage of his children, leads the family in its daily prayers, disburses the family's income, and reveals his religious dreams to his wives and children.

The experience of visions and dreams are the most vivid evidence of a person's ability to interact with the spirit world. By imparting such religious visions and their meaning to his children and wives, a father's authority is unmistakably affirmed. It is understood that personal visions are of profound religious significance and must be taken very seriously. To this end polygamists seek to understand God's will through the aid of visions and dreams. Prayer, visionary dreams, and one's own inner promptings are evaluated in an attempt to understand God's will processes not unlike the approach taken by American puritans to spiritual values and conflicts. The validity of dreams as a vehicle of truth are so strong in the fundamentalist religion that they are often the critical guide in making important decisions. A middle-aged man, for example, told his family about an angel who instructed him that his oldest son would live the fullness of the gospel (i.e., would stay in the community and form a plural family). In another dream a father told of his son's ability to support the family and sustain the family unity. Still another father reminded his wives of a vision he had when he was a young man, which signalled that he would live a short life but very fulfilling. This dream affirmed his religious righteousness and the need to follow his instructions, cherishing his time with them. Such dreams circulate within the family and, at times, into the community, serving to uphold the father's authority (directly supported by God) and to make him not only a moral force but a charismatic presence within the family.

In every moral community there is identification of the self with the leader. If "identification is the process of developing bonds to an object and altering one's actions because of these attachments" (Ross 1993:58), then the peculiar inter-dynamics of the American Mormon polygamous family likewise contribute to transforming the father from an important, albeit respected parent, into an all powerful charismatic figure whose memory is privately cherished and socially adored. Since the father is given God's will, he is the voice of spiritual idealism: as vehicle, he must be heeded. In doing so he imposes the conditions for transcendence which is derived, in part, from social organization and, in part, from emotional identification with father, the man. This image may or may not be at odds with a son or daughter's actual experience and thus remembrance of their father. Even when it is, however, the power of father adoration is so strong that it can erase the discrepancies.

Love, Ambivalence, and Hostility: Resolving the Father

The internal dynamics of polygamous family life contributes to the production of charismatic awe felt towards the father. It is an adoration that will continue throughout most people's lives. It is, however, an adoration tempered by the actual quality of the childhood and teenage relationship with the father. For those whose father passed away when they were children, there is only an unqualified adoration for the father. However, for those who had long term interaction with their father, their memories are less clouded with idealization based on fantasy and more grounded in actual reality. The reality forces or compels many sons and daughters to assimilate the cultural ideal to their own more personal encounter which may be less than perfect. Before exploring the darker side of father-child interaction, we want to look at the children's perspective, especially those whose father died when they were too young to have many meaningful or memorable interactions.

A common theme, a consistent lament, in Angel Park is the yearning of children for a closer relationship with their deceased father. A fourteen year old boy, for example, whose father had passed away six years earlier, when asked about the importance of a father, said that "a father is so important for a boy. He will give you guidance, leadership, and direction. I regret I didn't have a closer relationship with my Dad, before he passed to the other side." The intensity of such idealization is revealed in the following event. An eleven year-old girl was walking up a mountain path when she spontaneously exclaimed "I remember going up here with Dad. It was so wonderful." She turns to her mother and asks. "Mom, did I go up here with Dad? The mom nods, and the girl says: "Yes! I remember it was so wonderful."

Another example of how yearnings for closer intimacy contribute to generating an idealized posture toward one's father can be seen in a twenty-five year old married woman's efforts to come to terms with her biological father who abandoned her mother and left the community when she was a toddler only to return when she was a teenager. She refused to accept her step-father as her father but rather maintained a detached and resentful posture toward him. Toward her biological father, however, she maintained a positive, albeit fantasy grounded, relationship. Although now in her late twenties and with seven children, she calls her biological father twice a week "just to talk about things with the man I adore." One's ego identification is based, in part, on recognizing one's biological roots and, in part, on rendering homage, regardless of biology, to whoever is the patriarchical family head. In this instance, however, she refused to accept her step father and preferred to dwell on an idealized image of her biological father who would some day return and be worthy of her love.

The above idealizations are as much about fantasy as they are about reality. As psychological projections they are a familiar theme in mainstream America society. What is unusual about these accounts from Angel Park is the tendency to recall only enjoyable or blissful childhood experiences involving one's father.

Although Fundamentalist Mormons want nothing more than to honor and admire their fathers, often as not, despite their best efforts, it is a qualified honor. It is, nonetheless, the depth and the persistence of the desire to do so that indicates the hold of father adoration as an institution. Because the father's actual involvement with his family ranges from intimate involvement to outright indifference, it is not surprising that there is a deep underlying ambivalence toward one's father who, as a valued social symbol, is the focal point of family organization and identity. In effect, the father is the key metaphor that links the church and self together into a unified cultural system.

There are two often competing images of the father in Angel Park. The cherished and revered public image (discussed above) is often modified, in private conversation, by a more guarded and obviously ambivalent attitude which ranges from clear fondness to smoldering resentment and outright rejection. Given the community's social dynamics and the core tenets of its religious creed, most are uncomfortable in acknowledging their ambivalence, and prefer instead to praise their deceased father's memory. However, the actual reality of their father-child interaction as often as not gets into the way.

The quality of one's feelings toward one's father depends on the degree of the father's involvement in his child's life. If the father passed away when his children were young, as we have shown above, there is a tendency to internalize their father as a revered and valued symbol. Here the idealization is personal in tone and substance. It is a fantasy but it is still valued. For those who maintained a long-term interaction with a father who was an active parent, but emotionally aloof, the idealization process is seldom complete.

We found that, if the father had a warm relationship with his children, there is no contradiction between the father's public image and the child's actual remembrance (as an adult) of their interaction. However, if the father-child relationship was grounded in what a child believed was an abusive relationship, then that adult daughter or son's attitude could veer from absolute adoration to smoldering resentment. If one felt anger toward one's father and still lived in the community of Angel Park, that anger would be reconciled with that the cultural ideal of the father as the central person. The reconciliation often takes place in three ways: absolute devotion, guarded adoration, and rejection. Guarded adoration, by far the most common attitude toward the father, is characterized by maintaining a clear distinction between the accomplishments of the father, the cultural and family symbol, and the qualities of the father as a man. For example, sons of a prominent family repeatedly praised their father's accomplishments and what he meant to them. But in private they acknowledged their lack of real closeness and the emotional gap it left in their lives.

Significantly, brothers, more than sisters, admitted a fear of their father and, even, at times, a deep resentment. One brother recalled that he admired deeply his father but often wondered if he loved him. He noted that, personally, he had no difficulty in distinguishing between his father as a cultural symbol from his actions as a man. Such an ability to compartmentalize is not shared by most of his nineteen other brothers who feared the consequences and were anxious of the implications of a failure to completely honor their father's memory. The brother further observed that "My brothers are afraid that if they acknowledge the more personal aspects of his [father] character they might completely hate him. They do not want to look or acknowledge that he was also a man. They can only handle him as my honored father. They think they have to adore him in every way or not at all.'t For them there could never be guarded adoration, only an absolute one.

An example of guarded adoration can be heard in one middle aged woman's reminiscence that she "wasn't that close to my dad. The only reason I want to write my father's life history is do it before someone else does and then read it at our church service." For her, it is celebrating the father's public image and publicly proclaiming that holds the greater interest.

Another attitude is total rejection. When a son or daughter rejects, especially in conversation, his or her father it usually means that they no longer participate in the community's social life. By rejecting the father as a critical cultural symbol, the individual effectively severs his ties to the wider cultural and religious order. He or she can now leave the community, which they invariably do. Rejection of the father entails a kind of self exile from Angel Park - so deep is the necessity of father adoration that when rejections occurs the child will often bitterly curse his or her father.

It is important to point out that in every polygamous culture there is a shortage of women. Angel Park is no different. Most sons must leave the community to search for a wife who, more often than not, refuses to convert to the religion and move back to the community. In these instances, the son leaves the community to find a wife and not because of a strained relationship with his parents, living or dead; whereas rejection of the father usually means rejecting the religion; rejecting the religion or its community, does not necessarily mean it will result in the rejection of the father.

The various attitudes toward the father hide a deep seated ambivalence and emotional volatility which can fuel his idealization as bearer of family pride and identity. We believe that ambivalent anger toward the father actually contributes to the institutionalization of father adoration in Angel Park primarily by rechanneling the guilt that accompanies the rejection. The characteristic ambivalence does not satisfactorily reconcile the father-son relationship and, as such, constitutes an emotional reservoir for the unresolved emotions that shape the style in which father adoration is manifested in ceremonial and ordinary life in Angel Park.

In contrast, mothers are seen as an emotional constant: warm, nurturing and intimate. They embody strength and continuity and are seldom perceived to be a force to contend with. Seldom feared or rejected, they are the emotional, but not symbolic, glue that holds the polygamous family together. More importantly, there is not the difficult and sometimes troubling expectations and pressure of adoration or reverence. It is not a culturally proscribed response. The bifurcation of the father into two parts, the symbol and the man, is one means that men and women in Angel Park use to manage what is, for many, a ghost they can never shake.

Conclusion

The emergence of father adoration arises in part from theological centrality of the father in the Fundamentalist Mormon religious system as well as from the peculiar social dynamics of the polygamous family household. It is the social dynamics, and not just an endemic form of child rearing practice that generates this phenomenon.

We have sought to explore the interplay between the psychocultural dynamics of the polygamous family and its male-centered theology and how it transforms the father into a revered cultural, if not personal, symbol.

Although fundamentalist theology discourages familial ranking, the dynamics of living in a close corporate community, especially one organized around a patriarchal theology, encourages the development of an intense sense of familism that is crystallized in the adoration of the father.

It is the transformation of the father, but not the mother, into an venerable, powerful, and loving memory that distinguishes the contemporary Fundamentalist Mormon community from the mainstream Mormon church as well as from the numerous Christian denominations. In periodically gathering together in the name of the father, the family, and the community celebrate their cultural heritage as well as renew their dedication to the creation and maintenance of what it believes to be the Heavenly Father's ideal family unit - the polygamous family.

Notes

1. The data that forms much of this research is part of a larger ongoing research project that began in 1992. The work is partially supported by a mini-grant from the Nevada National Endowment for the Humanities and a UNLV Research Grants and Fellowships Award. We would like to thank Jim Bell, Martha Knack, Barry Hewlett, Thomas Paladino and Gray Palmer for their encouragement, suggestions, and comments.

2. Polygyny has been studied primarily from a structural perspective which seeks to understand its evolution as a form of adaptation to certain ecological restraints. With the notable exceptions of Young (1954) and Bohannan (1984), analysis of an individual's experiences in a polygamous household is, for the most part, overlooked.

3. A patriarch is the head of a family holding the right to rule its members with unquestioned authority. Technically, a patriarch is a member of the upper or Melchizedek priesthood who has been appointed within the church ward (or stake) to pronounce blessings upon those members who call upon him.

4. An unintended consequence of this system of political succession is to increase the difficulty of creating and sustaining a family-based religious dynasty. In the entire history of the Mormon church, there have been only two examples where a previous council member's son, but not his grandson, was also called to the priesthood council. So too in Angel Park's history. Because appointment to the priesthood council provides a council member with important resources of power which range between perceptions of being blessed with superior religious purity to the ability to grant important and valued material benefits (such as arranging marriages, bestowing house lots or homes, and granting small loans to the faithful).

5. Until the 1985 religious split, Angel Park was unified in its commitment to create a more benevolent collective order. The principal was the incorporation into a religious trust which facilitated the (distribution of food supplies, practical assistance in home, and, most importantly, access to land). An unintended consequences was to confer on the leaders of the trust an enormous fund of power. Historically, the trust

provided the church leadership with the means to reward its followers while evicting those who failed to conform. Because families merely lease their land and do not own it, the church leadership is able to evict "undesirable" members from their homes by terminating their lease. However, the recent religious split has generated additional problems for the members who want to leave the church but retain control of their homes which they built with their own money. In the past, expulsion was reserved only for the marginally deviant; today it is being used to evict the entire membership of the rival religious faction. The disagreement has become a legal matter that has been tied up in the state courts for more than five years.

6. If private criticism is motivated by a zero-sum prestigious economy, then public adoration of the father is perceived to be based on an ever expanding sphere of possibilities. In a way, parental or noble love is a bottom less substance that is potentially available to everyone. It is never seen as a zero-sum commodity: the more I have the less you can get. Its potential is vast and it is open to everyone.

7. Among children the primary identification is on father's role; however, amongst adults, especially women, the mother's contribution is also acknowledged. Thus Mother's Day, as in mainstream culture, is more important than Father's Day.

8. Women are the custodians of family memory. They preserve and nurture in their children important cultural values. Nothing reflects the dual role - of family memory and cultural values that women play than remarriage when they must manage their bond with their children while reaffirming their loyalties to their new husband while not abandoning their former husband. The division is a classic American experience. They continue to honor their deceased husband's memory, in the name of her children or his children while, simultaneously, placing a photograph of the new husband into the intimate space of her bedroom. In this way women strive to balance twin demands. Again, we see that women must mediate competing or co-existing duties.

Chapter 11

Natural Modeling in Lacandon Maya Mythology

R. Jon McGee

Introduction

In the religions of Mesoamerican peoples the expression of fundamental sacred concepts has been based on models derived from the natural world for almost three millennia. In particular, geographical features, animals from the local environment, and astronomical phenomena have provided inspiration for religious concepts and ritual practice. Among various Maya peoples this pattern is commonly expressed in the sacred implements, ritual structures, or costumes of religious specialists.

The Lacandon, are the last of the non-Christian Maya in Mexico. However, despite their traditional religion and detailed knowledge of their forest environment, few ritual symbols based on natural models exist. To the contrary, it was discovered that the natural symbols in Lacandon religion are not found in the materials associated with ritual, but rather in their mythology. In particular, the swidden cycle of agriculture on which their livelihood depends is recreated in a Lacandon myth recounting one of the creations and destructions of the world. The analysis presented here focuses on this myth as a metaphor for the swidden cycle on which the Lacandon base their lllllivelihoods.

Natural Modeling in Maya Religion

The expression of religious concepts through symbols taken from nature has been found throughout history in most, if not all, Mesoamerican aboriginal cultures. During the Formative-Period (1500- 400 B.C.) for example, the Mesoamerican peoples conceived of the cosmos as layered, with a watery underworld, earth, and sky. In Olmec art for instance, the surface of the earth was represented as a crocodile or turtle floating on the surface of a primeval ocean. The famous La Venta sarcophagus, which depicts this concept of alligator as earth (see Figure 1) is one example of this form of symbolism (Reilly 1987 and 1990).

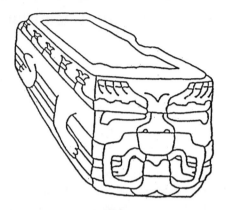

Figure 1. Alligator sarcophagus from La Venta (from Reilly 1990).

The Maya of the Classic Period (250-900 A.D.) followed the pattern of natural symbolism developed by the Olmec. The natural world of the Maya was recreated on a fantastic scale in monumental constructions at sites such as Palenque and Chichen Itza. Ancient Maya rulers constructed pyramids; which were conceptualized as artificial mountains. Called *witz* "mountain" these structures were built to house the divine rulers after death, when they assumed their place among the gods. Similarly, mountains are sacred sites for many Maya peoples today. Among the Lacandon for example, mountains are believed to be homes of various gods.

Buildings did not just represent geological features for the ancient Maya. Site planning could also recreate cosmology. Sky, earth, and underworld, as well as the Maya's sophisticated knowledge of astronomy, are all represented in sacred architecture. At Chichen Itza, for example, the Castillo, one of the principal pyramids at the site, is a solar calendar, marking the equinoxes and solstices. On the evenings of the spring and fall equinox the setting sun makes a pattern of shadows down the giant serpent balustrade of the pyramid's main staircase. This pattern of light and shadow creates the illusion that a huge serpent is descending from the top of the pyramid. Following the serpent's path one crosses the plaza that represented the primordial ocean, and follows the *sac be* or ritual road. This path leads to the site's sacrificial *cenote*, which Chichen's ancient inhabitants believed to be a portal to the underworld (Freidel et. al. 1993). In this way, structures at Chichen Itza represented the three-layered cosmos.

The ancient Maya also derived mythological symbols from the natural world. Accounts of the creation of the cosmos are described on Stela C from Quirigua, and the Tablet of the Cross at Palenque. The inscription on Stela C tells us that the center of the cosmos, the "Three-Stone-Place" (three stars in the constellation of Orion) was set on August 13, 3114 B.C. The Palenque tablet repeats a similar account but provides additional details. According to the Tablet of the Cross, 542 days after the creation of the Three-Stone-Place, or February 5, 3112 B.C., the god Hu-Nal-Ye or First Father, entered the sky and raised a world tree. The erection of this tree, a sacred ceiba tree, formed the axis mundi of the cosmos and separated the underworld, earth, and sky (Schele 1993). This symbol is beautifully illustrated at the Classic Period site of Palenque. At Palenque this World Tree was depicted as a cross, at the center of the panel in the Temple of the Cross (see Figure 2).

Figure 2. Interior panel of the Temple of the Cross (from Schele 1990).

Figure 3. An illustration from the Dresden Codex. A ceiba tree growing from the chest of a sacrificial victim. (from Villacorta and Villacorta 1933)

Thus the cross and ceiba tree were used interchangeably in ancient Maya art to represent the *axis mundi* of the cosmos. A later representation of the ceiba tree as *axis mundi* is found in the *Dresden Codex*, written in the eleventh century A.D., where it is pictured rising out of the chest of a sacrificial victim (see Figure 3).

Contemporary Maya continue to use many of these symbols. Like the Lacandon, the Maya of Zinacantan, believe *vitz* "mountains" are still homes of the gods. The world tree/cross symbol is also common. Sacred places in Zinacantan are marked by shrines with blue/green crosses. These crosses are called *yax che* "green tree." *Yax che'* is also the modern Maya word for ceiba tree, and these cross shrines still mark the center of the cosmos. In Zinacantan, this is the *mixik balamil* or "navel of the world" (Vogt 1976).

In the Yucatan, ritual processions are also modeled on a natural process, the sun's apparent movement across the sky (Sosa 1989). Since the Formative Period, Maya peoples have conceived of the cosmos as a layered quadrilateral, and measured the change of seasons by the movement of the sun. This preoccupation with the sun is still found among many Maya groups. In the Yucatan, *hmen* or shaman, identify the corners of their quadrilateral cosmos as the rising and setting points of the sun on the summer and winter solstices. During traditional and Catholic rites, Yucatec worshipers process in a counterclockwise direction around church compounds. This is a horizontal imitation of the movement of *Hahal Dios*, the combined sun/Christ, through the sky. Counterclockwise is the appropriate direction because in the Maya view of the cosmos the rising sun faces us, and *Hahal Dios* moves to his right as he climbs into the sky and looks down on his people (Sosa 1989). Gossen (1974) describes similar ritual behavior among the Chamula in the Highlands of Chiapas.

Natural Modeling Among The Lacandon Maya?

The Lacandon are the last of the non-Christian Maya Indians in Mexico. Largely because of their historical isolation in the forests of southeastern Chiapas and northwestern Guatemala, these swidden farmers succeeded in maintaining a traditional belief system that incorporates many aspects of pre-Hispanic Maya beliefs and ritual. In previous work, I extensively documented pre-Hispanic religious survivals still in practice among the Lacandon living in the community of Najá. These include the use of pre-Hispanic ritual implements in Lacandon rites (McGee 1987), drinking of the sacred beverage *balché* (McGee 1988), and the continuation, in symbolic form, of ancient Maya human sacrificial practices (McGee 1990). Additionally, some of the relationships between ancient Maya astronomy and contemporary Lacandon star lore are only now being investigated (McGee and Reilly 1994).

Despite striking parallels to ancient Maya ritual practices, religious symbols based on the natural world are lacking in Lacandon religion. Many ancient Maya buildings were oriented for marking the movements of the sun or observing the course of Venus in the sky. The *yatoch k'uh* "god house," the place for virtually all Lacandon ritual activity, is not used as an architectural marker for the solstices, equinoxes, or any movements of Venus. God houses are traditionally oriented to the east. However, this is because the Classic-Period site of Yaxchilan, which Lacandon believe to be the home of their gods, is located directly east of Najá (McGee 1990). I have found no evidence that the Lacandon take any interest in the timing of the equinoxes or solstices. They certainly make no attempt to measure these solar events directly.

Like the ancient Maya, many Lacandon believe that caves are passages to the underworld. Also, I was shown local geological features, typically hills and large rocks, in which deities of the rain and forest are thought to live.

However, none of these are represented in Lacandon ritual symbols or architecture.

Like other Maya groups, the Lacandon think a ceiba tree was the primeval *axis mundi*, separating the layers of the cosmos and providing a path between earth and sky. In Lacandon belief this was a specific tree, located at the Classic Period site of Palenque, in the courtyard of a structure called the Palace. Palenque is sacred to the Lacandon because they believe it is the place where the gods created human beings. But the tree is no longer standing in the Palace and the gods have since moved and built new homes at Yaxchilan. Consequently, Palenque is not a focus of Lacandon ritual action although it is the location in which are set several of their myths. Probably because Palenque no longer has ritual importance, I failed to conclusively identify any crosses, trees or other symbols for the axis mundi in Lacandon rites. The possible exception to this is during the *mekchul* rite.

The *mekchul* is a rite of passage into adulthood performed when young Lacandon enter adolescence. During the *mekchul* the initiate's legs are squeezed around the timber supporting the northwest corner of the god house as they are ritually instructed to learn how to climb a tree to avoid dangerous animals (McGee 1990:102). Although this is practical advice, the northwest corner post of the god house is the post aligned in the direction of Palenque, about 70 miles northwest of Najá.

Environmental Awareness in Lacandon Life

Like their contemporary descendants, the ancient Maya were farmers. The ancient Maya consulted an elaborate calendar, and followed the course of the sun and Venus throughout the year in order to know the appropriate times for the burning of fields and planting crops. At the Classic Period site of Copan, for example, the appearance of Venus as the evening star heralded the onset of the rainy season (Aveni 1992: 111-112). However, the Lacandon keep no calendar and pay little attention to the movements of the sun or Venus. Possessing a detailed knowledge of the plants in the forest, they correlate their seasons and agricultural schedule with the leafing out or blooming of various primary forest trees. The period during which these trees flower is called the "foot" of the crop, and crops are planted during these foot periods (Nations and Nigh 1980). For example, when mahogany trees start to put out new leaves it is the season *u yokol ya'ax k'in* the "emergence of the spring." Corn is planted in the following season, *na ya'ax k'in*, "mother of the spring," which begins when the mahogany trees bloom. One should complete corn planting by the time the mahogany trees loose their blossoms, an event which also marks the ending of *nah ya'ax k'in* and the beginning of the next month *mani ya'ax k'in* the "passing of the spring."

In addition to their knowledge of the surrounding forest, the Lacandon practice one of the most productive forms of swidden agriculture in the world. Harvests average about 2.8 metric tons of shelled corn per hectare (Nations and Nigh 1980). One reason Lacandon swidden practices are so productive is that they attempt to recreate rather than replace the structure of the natural forest. Outstanding features of the primary forest are the layering of ground plants and tree canopy, the variety of life forms in the environment, and their wide geographical dispersal. Lacandon swidden gardens or *milpas*, reflect these same patterns.

A Lacandon *milpa* is a layered micro system. Root crops such as taro and manioc are planted. Above these plants, beans, squash, tomatoes, onions, and a variety of other vegetables are cultivated. Corn is planted in between these crops, and produces its ears 5 to 10 feet above the ground, while trees such as oranges, tangerines, and bananas bear their fruit above all the other crops. Similar to the diversity of life in the surrounding forest, the Lacandon also cultivate a large variety of crops, between 30-50 different types of plants depending on the family. This practice insures that Lacandon families have access to a varied menu of fresh vegetable foods all year around. Finally, Lacandon farmers plant their crops at random, scattering different plants throughout a *milpa*. This practice imitates the dispersal of non-cultivated life forms through the forest and may help to prevent crop loss due to insect infestation.

The *Milpa* Cycle in Lacandon Mythology

The relationship between Lacandon agriculture and mythology is not readily apparent. I worked with the Lacandon almost ten years before I made the connection, and another four years before I understood its significance. Believing that the Lacandon must practice some form of natural modeling in their religious activities, and having exhausted most other ritual possibilities, I turned my attention to Lacandon myths. The Lacandon call their myths *tsikbal* or "talk." When asked to describe what they call these stories in Spanish, Lacandon told me *historia* "history." In this respect, Lacandon narrative traditions clearly parallel the linguistic taxonomies outlined for other Mayan languages such as the genre of "ancient narrative" that Gossen (1974) identifies among the Chamula and the category *ik'ti'al* "history" that Maxwell (1990) describes for Chuj Maya.

The Lacandon term *ṭsikbal* typically refers to conversation, but in reference to myth telling it describes a characteristic genre of Lacandon discourse that is different from everyday conversation. In this type of narrative, actions recounted in a myth are believed to be historical in the modern Western sense of the word, but the narrator makes it clear that he is not describing his personal experiences. A myth is typically introduced by the phrase *Paytan* "In the beginning," or *Baik u tsikbal-tal* "This is what they say." Further, ritual speech is different than ordinary speech. One of the most obvious characteristics of Lacandon myth telling is that they are recited in semantic couplets and triplets. The myths are thus similar in structure to many ancient Maya hieroglyphic inscriptions.

Mythic narratives are set in the area where contemporary Lacandon reside and typically occur in an earlier period of creation. There is a tremendous body of oral material recounting the cycles of creation and destruction of the world, the creation of life and origin of death, and detailed accounts of the actions of individual characters who lived during these long ago times. In this respect, Lacandon myths are similar to Western mythic traditions. For example, the ancestral character *Nukuch Winik* "Ancient Person" descended into the underworld to witness the journey of souls to judgment and the afterlife.

The story presented here is a portion of a larger collection of sound and videotaped material recounting the cycle of creation and destructions of the world, the creation of the gods and human beings, an ancestor's journey through the underworld where he sees the trials a soul undergoes after death, and marries the god of death's daughter. I first recorded this myth in January 1985 in the Lacandon village of Najá. I had the opportunity to record and transcribe a more complete version of the story in February of 1995. The speaker was sitting at a table in his kitchen after the evening meal. Also present were his two wives and several children. The taping session was precipitated by my introductory questions about the different creations and destructions of the world.

The Maya believe that the world has been through a series of creations and destructions. This myth is the Lacandon account of the first destruction of the world. The principal characters are: *Hachäkyum*, "Our True Lord," the Lacandon creator deity; *Chäk Ik Al*, "Red Wind Lord," the personification of hurricanes; and *Äk'inchob* "Corn Kernel Priest" the guardian of Lacandon *milpas*. In the myth *Hachäkyum* orders *Chäk Ik Al* to destroy the world. *Chäk Ik Al* carries out the order, but not before *Äk'inchob* saves humans by sheltering them in a dugout canoe. Although this action may remind one of the *Old Testament* story of Noah and the Ark, the Lacandon myth does not contain any moral lessons. The Maya gods are capricious. They create and destroy for their own reasons, not to reward or punish humans for their behavior.

The following account is my transcription of the story recorded in February 1995. I have resisted the impulse to put the story in Western narrative form. Rather, I have written the myth more or less as it was told. My addition to the narrative is its division into numbered episodes to serve as reference points for the discussion which follows the myth.

1. In the beginning, it is said that the ancestors saw Chäk Ik Al.
The gods first sent Chäk Ik Al.
There were few people and they did not die.
People die now.
The gods do not protect us.
But long ago there was a dugout canoe, a great straight canoe.
There the people were sheltered. They were protected.
The first people didn't all die.
They were sheltered in the dugout canoe made by the god.[2]
A giant straight canoe.
The god took all of us.
He placed us all there.
Äk'inchob covered us all.
That's right, he took everyone.
Snakes, animals everyone was sheltered.
People like the Lacandon were sheltered in the first destruction.
People of the spider monkey *onen*, the peccary *onen*, and jaguar *onen* all were sheltered.[3]
The deer *onen*, the currasow *onen*, everyone was sheltered.
Äk'inchob took and sheltered them all in the dugout canoe.
Äk'inchob protected two people from each onen, one man and one woman.
He sheltered everyone, even foreigners like you.
He took all the animals, all the howler monkeys, all the snakes, all the game.
He took everything and placed them in the giant canoe.
The jaguars came and the ants, everything in the forest.
He took them all.
He enclosed them all in the giant dugout canoe.
Äk'inchob guarded them all, because that is what Hachäkyum commanded.
This is what Hachäkyum said to Äk'inchob, "Go and guard those on earth. Go gather them all because Chäk Ik Al is coming. There is a flood coming."
That is what Hachäkyum said.[4]
Bay.[5]

2. Äk'inchob gathered the people. "Good, I have gathered them."
Now the sun left the sky.[6]

The Red Wind Lord thundered.
The poor people not in the canoe all died.
They did not understand why.
Chäk Ik Al was very happy.
The rain came and he thundered again.
He stood erect and thundered.
The ancestors, those Äk'inchob protected in the forest did not understand the thunder.
Chäk Ik Al raised up and his wind swept everything away.
Those left on earth ran to their god houses to pray but there was nothing there.
Trees were torn out of the ground and thrown far away.
No one heard the prayers of those who were abandoned.
That is what is said.
You could not hear their voices because of the roaring wind.
The great wind.

3. Then he who had arrived left.
There were no trees.
All had been torn from the ground and thrown far away.
There were no homes
All the homes were blown straight into the sky.
No trees, nothing.
The trees were blown far away.
They were thrown from here almost to Ocosingo and fell everywhere.
They were thrown up into the sky.
Then the trees fell.
Nothing was left.
There were no people, no children.
Everything was burned.
All were killed.

4. One person went to where the ancestors were protected.
He did not know why they were sheltered.
He hugged a tree trunk to protect himself from the wind.
The trunk of a tree called äkäm which was one of the pillars of his god house.
He hugged the pillar but no one passed by to save him.
No one saw his face. Not even his wife.
That is what they say.

5. Then the wind stopped.
What did he hear? A terrible rain.
The water rose quickly around him.
The water rose too high for the ancestor to hold on to the god house pillar, but he saw a tree floating by.
"Here I go."

An alligator was swimming around.
He watched the log approaching.
The ancestor jumped and threw his arms around the tree and climbed into the branches.
He climbed into the tree.
But the water continued to rise.
The alligator grabbed him.
That was the end.
The alligator ate him.

6. The water rose almost to the sky.
In five days, in six days it covered everything.
The dugout canoe floated at the top of the sky.
It floated at the top of the sky.
Everything was finished.
That what they say here.
All the people were gone.
For one year everything was a swamp.
The water did not recede.
Then it went down a little.
Not after one year but in two years it receded.
The water slowly receded.
It was better.
But the ancestors did not leave the canoe.
The gods had not cleared things.
Everything was there protected in the canoe.
There were animals.
There were snakes.
Everything was protected in the canoe.

7. Then they saw the sun rise.
They saw it arrive.
After one month of sun all the water was gone.
There was no water, only the sun in the sky.
After one month of sun the sky cleared.
The sky cleared and when the sun came out everything was burned for one month.
Everything burned.
The gods burned everything.
They lit the forest and burned it.
The trees there all burned.
That is what they say.
Then the forest finished burning.
Then the earth finished burning.
Then it was all burned again.

Bay.

8. [Before the flood] Äk'inchob gathered fruit from all the trees.[7]
8t was all taken.
All the blooms and fruit were taken from the trees.
Äk'inchob picked everything.
That what is said now.
Äk'inchob picked them all. [He used those seeds to replant the forest.]
He picked the fruit from all the trees.
There was forest.
Another forest grew.
After one month there was a new forest.
Everything emerged when the sun came back.
That was the end of the destruction.
That is what they say.

9. In the canoe where the people were protected, all were alive.
Their houses had been destroyed.
But the people arrived where there were trees and houses.[8]
No trees were burned.
The living people had been protected by the god.
The gods' houses were there.
They came out of the canoe and sat down.
They left the dugout and went to these houses.
"The sky is clear now. I am going to pray to the gods."
Everyone else was dead and there was nothing left of them.
There was no forest, no mountains, no houses, everything was completely flat.
Only those alive went to the gods' houses.
The surviving people all left.
They went to the gods' houses [Yaxchilan].
Bay.

10. There was food.
All the animals emerged from the canoe.
There were bananas.
All the animals emerged from the dugout canoe.
They finished emerging from the canoe.
All the game left.
All the game animals emerged from the canoe.
The giant canoe where the ancestors were sheltered.
The canoe was abandoned in the east.
It was thrown straight into the middle of the sky.
Straight into the sky it went.
It was cast away.
It was abandoned in the east.

The canoe was united with the middle of the eastern sky.
Joined to the eastern horizon.
The joining was created.
From here it was passed to its joining with the sky.
That is what they say.
It was united with Kakoch's sky.[9]
It passed there. It passed there.
Long ago, very long ago it was passed into the sky.
I do not know. That is what is said.
The story of the ancient ones.
That is what they say.
Joined in the middle of Kakoch's sky.
There is an ocean in the east now.
Now in the east where we were sheltered.

11. It is said that there was maize.
Maize covered the earth.
They gave tobacco as offerings in thanks for the maize.
The gods gave maize for everyone to eat.
First came the great trees.
In only one month there were trees for the ancestors to clear for *milpas*.
In three months the ancestors cut their *milpas*.
There were huge plants.
They cleared new *milpas* and sowed their food.
First there was corn for the ancestors' food.
Now they would not die from hunger.
If there was only a little left they could shell more corn.
The corn on one ear could feed many people.
They shelled half an ear of corn and they had a lot.
They had corn for atole, tortillas, everything.
They had food for all time.
Now I am finished.

Discussion

The parallels with the story of Noah and the Ark are obvious to anyone familiar with the *Old Testament*. Nevertheless, there is compelling evidence that this myth is pre-Hispanic in origin rather than borrowed from Christianity, and that events in the myth are based on natural phenomena within the Lacandons' local environment. I have previously analyzed this myth as the folk-historical account of a hurricane (McGee 1989). The god *Chäk Ik Al* "Red Wind Lord" is associated with the east, the direction from which hurricanes in the Caribbean strike the Maya area. He tears all the trees in the forst out of the ground and hurls them to Ocosingo, a town in the

Figure 4. A carved bone from Tikal. The maize lord being paddled to the Three-Stone-Place (from Freidel and Schele 1993).

highlands of Chiapas. *Chäk Ik Al* is also given the title of *bulha'kilutalk'in* "flood water from the east" which precisely describes his function. After the howling winds he innundates the earth with a flooding rain. Additionally, descriptions of hurricanes are found in Yucatec Maya books written not long after the conquest. In the *Chilam Balam* of Tizimin, for example, the hurricane, is called *noh chac ikal* (Edmonson 1982:131).

The evidence indicates that *Chäk Ik Al* is the mythological embodiment of a hurricane. This explains the winds and flooding. But what are we to make of the giant dugout canoe in which life is sheltered during the destruction? It is impossible to conclusively demonstrate that Äk'inchob's canoe is not a Lacandon adaptation of the story of Noah's Ark. However, depictions of cosmic canoes are not uncommon in Classic-Period Maya art and have been identified as depictions of episodes in Maya creation mythology (see Figure 4).

In the Classic Period account of creation, the maize lord First Father, is paddled through the sky in a canoe to the three-stone-place where he creates the universe (Wertime and Schuster 1993). This canoe scene is depicted on pottery as well as carved on bones found in Burial 116 at the site of Tikal in Guatemala (Freidel et. al. 1993: 90-93). These lines of evidence lead to the conclusion that the Lacandon myth is not borrowed from Christian tradition. Events in the myth take the form that they do because they are modeled on the natural environment in which the Lacandon live, and several of its elements are of pre-Hispanic origin.

The hurricane lord's arrival, the canoe, and the world's destruction are realistically described in the first five episodes of the myth. But the myth's most important links to the natural world are found in episodes 7, 8, and 11. In episode 6, over the course of a month, the sun dries out the earth. Next, all the debris felled by *Chäk Ik Al* is burned. But *Äk'inchob* has saved the fruits and seeds of all plants, and he reseeds the forest. After the forest has regrown the animals leave the great canoe. In one month the survivors are clearing the forest for their *milpas* and growing giant corn. The ears of corn are so big that one ear feeds several people. And so life returns to normal and the earth is repopulated.

Episodes 7, 8, and 11 are a reenactment of the Lacandons' cycle of slash and burn horticulture. Only it is the earth which has been cut, dried, burned, and planted, not just a *milpa*. In the myth, the ancestral Lacandon are required to undergo the process which they impose on the environment every spring. The Lacandon jungle averages about 100 inches of rain a year. A Lacandon farmer begins to fell the growth on his *milpa* site in January and February at the conclusion of the rainy season, finishing by early March. After waiting about a month (the time between flood and fire in the myth) to let the cut brush dry, the *milpa* is set on fire and the accumulated brush and trees are burned. In the myth, the storm's survivors wait one month before leaving the canoe. Similarly, Lacandon farmers wait a month or so before planting their most important crop--corn. Interestingly, to prevent soil erosion in the interim period between burning a field and planting corn, farmers plant fast growing tree and root crops such as papaya, bananas and chayote. Correspondingly, in episode 8 of the myth, *Äk'inchob* replants the forest in the month after the burning of the world while humans wait to leave the canoe.

Conclusion

The parallels between the story of *Chäk Ik Al* and the Lacandons' *milpa* cycle are strikingly exact. For every event in the myth there is a corresponding real-life stage in the *milpa* cycle. Rituals and religious implements of Maya peoples have been based on the natural world for millenia. In the case of the Lacandon, one of their most important myths provides a model of the cycle of swidden horticulture, the process upon which they base their lives. Other elements of the myth such as *Chäk Ik Al* and the giant canoe in the eastern sky add tantalizing glimpses of their ancient past.

Notes

1. *Acknowledgements.* This work was made possible, in part, by grants from the Wenner Gren Society for Anthropological Research and the Office of Research and Sponsored Programs, Southwest Texas State University. I gratefully acknowledge Professor Linda Schele and Dr. Kent Reilly for their permission to use Figures 1, 2, and 4.

2. The repetition of lines is a fundamental feature of Lacandon prayers and myth performances. It is one of several poetic devices that help a performer remember the stories, some of which last up to an hour.

3. An *onen* is an animal name that identifies one's patrilineage. The Lacandon use them as a surname, for instance Chan K'in Ma'ax "Chan K'in Spider Monkey." Up until the early part of this century the Lacandon were probably *onen* endogamous, but depopulation led to a breakdown of the custom.

4. When a myth-teller takes the god's role and speaks in the first person it is a signal that what is being said is important and everyone should pay attention.

5. *Bay* literally means "ok." In a Lacandon myth it signifies a change of scene or time period.

6. The change from past to present tense is not a grammatical mistake. A Lacandon myth teller's switch to the present tense, like speaking as a god, is a sign that listeners should pay attention.

7. Another feature of Lacandon storytelling is that stories are not told in strict chronological order. The fruit and seed gathering episode actually occurs earlier in the story before the flooding and burning.

8. In Lacandon belief the canoe came to rest at the site of Yaxchilan, a Classic Period Maya city that is directly east of Najá. The Lacandon believe that the ruins of Yaxchilan are where their gods currently reside.

9. The Lacandon believe in a multi-level cosmos. Kakoch is the ultimate creator deity, who made the earth and the plumeria flower out of which the other gods, such as *Hachäkyum* and *Äk'inchob* were born. He lives in one of the most remote layers of the cosmos and is uninterested in human affairs.

Chapter 12

"Back Home in Indiana:" The Semiotics of Pilgrimage and Belief In Honor of an American Icon

James F. Hopgood

Each September thousands of people visit the small Indiana town of Fairmount on "Museum Days," a festival manifestly held to honor several "famous sons." Attending the numerous festivities are tourists, people from the region, reporters, car buffs, and the curious. Also present are the "Deaners," the devoted disciples of James Dean and Fairmount's most famous son. I examine the festival with particular attention to the Deaners as pilgrims, the associated semiotics, along with discussion of the Deaners as an incipient religious movement with a nascent theology. Participation and observation of Deaner activities, together with analyses of interviews and testimonials by Deaners provide insights into their quest for meaning, self-identity, and renewal.

Introduction

My research in Fairmount and on the "Deaners" began in 1989 and is oriented towards (1) interpreting James Dean as a charismatic leader and a modern American analogue to a traditional folk saint and (2) the interpretation of the Deaners as a formative or incipient movement with clear similarities to more mature and ostensibly religious movements (Hopgood 1991, 1993, 1994, 1995). The specific purpose of this paper, however, is to extend analysis to (3) the area of semiotics associated with the Deaners, or more specifically, the meanings sought, experienced, created, or renewed in the pilgrimage to Fairmount. Background material on Dean, the genesis of the Dean image, and the Deaners as an incipient religious movement with an incipient theology are covered for contextualization of the semiotic analysis.

The focus of this paper on semiotics is a logical progression in the research I have been conducting with quasi-religious charismatic movements and specifically with the Deaners. Deaners is the term I use to refer to a cadre of devoted followers of James Dean, the American actor who died in 1955 at the age of 24. I was drawn to frame this project when I realized that I was treading sacred ground on my first visit to Fairmount. Fairmount seemed imbued with "heavy," sacred meaning coexisting with the everyday secular world. Like most pilgrimage sites, a round of sacred places associated with the honored person is understood and easily discoverable by simple inquiry. During that first visit to Fairmount I picked up an expressly prepared visitor's map of Fairmount. The map located the major places associated with Dean when he lived there: his uncle and aunt's farm where he grew up following his mother's death, the high school he attended, the motorcycle shop he frequented, the Church he attended, his grave, a memorial erected for him in the cemetery, the local historical museum with the "James Dean Room," the new gallery dedicated to him, and a dozen other places. This ordinary looking secular map turned into a guide to special (or sacred) places and sites.

Fairmount attracts thousands of visitors yearly, with the greatest numbers appearing on certain special, sacred days. The most important being Dean's birthday, the day of his death, and during "Museum Days." On any day, however, visitors and pilgrims will be found visiting Dean's grave, the museum and gallery, and other special places. In fact, many Deaners prefer less chaotic times for their visits. I must also point out that Fairmount, though the most important, is not the only pilgrimage site associated with Dean and many Deaners are committed to visiting all of this places, ranging from New York to Los Angeles.

James Dean

Who was James Dean? Today many people will remember Dean as a movie actor of the 1950's. Some may remember one or more of his three major film roles. Only the first, *East of Eden*, was in release at the time of his death on September 30, 1955. For other people, Dean may only be linked to Marilyn Monroe and other American "icons" representative or symbolic of a near-mythical 1950's. Deaners, however, find in James Dean an array of meanings well beyond the simple facts of his life and accomplishments.

James Byron Dean was born in Marion, Indiana, on February 8, 1931, to Winton and Mildred (neé Wilson) Dean. He was an only child. His father,

Winton, was a dental technician at the local Veterans Administration Hospital. When the future Hollywood star was five years old, his father was transferred to Santa Monica, California, and four years later his mother died. The young Dean was given over to Marcus and Ortense Winslow (Winton's sister and brother-in-law) to be raised with their children and on their farm just outside the small town of Fairmount, Indiana.

For the next nine years young James Dean flourished under a variety of influences emanating from life on the Winslow farm, the Fairmount schools and the ambiance of a small, rural Quaker community. Among those who significantly influenced Dean was Adeline Nall, his high school speech and drama teacher, and the Reverend James DeWeerd, a pastor at the local Wesleyan Church. According to his teachers and classmates, he was very interested in the arts, including theater and drawing and painting. He also excelled in high school sports such as basketball and baseball, overcoming a deficiency in height and size. This trait of surmounting "average" attribute is later employed in the "boy next door" image of Dean.

Dean acquired his first motorcycle when he was fifteen or sixteen years of age. He became well known in the community for his love of riding the motorcycle at breakneck speeds on local country roads. His love of motorcycles and speed became a defining attribute of the Dean image later in life.

Following graduation from Fairmount High, Dean moved to California and, for a very brief time, lived with his father and step-mother. He tried pre-law briefly at Santa Monica Junior College and University of California, Los Angeles, partly to please his father. However, acting still interested him and he soon began seeking roles, including school plays. Near the end of 1950, Dean acquired an agent and appeared in a Pepsi-Cola commercial. The next year he appeared in an episode of *Family Theatre*, a religious television program, in which he played John the Apostle. This small role spawned the first Dean fan club organized by female students of the Immaculate Heart High School in Los Angles, called the *Immaculate Heart James Dean Appreciation Society*. This was a small, but significant manifestation of the adulation that would follow.

Dean studied with actor James Whitmore in his Hollywood acting school for a while and was introduced to "Method Acting." In 1951 he took Whitmore's advice and moved to New York. Dean was dissatisfied with his progress, Hollywood's artificiality, and with the bit parts he was getting in films. He believed he could better develop his talents in New York. There, with the aid of director friend Rogers Brackett, who had befriended and aided Dean in Hollywood, he obtained an agent and received bit parts in television shows. Eventually he landed a major part in *See the Jaguar* (1952), his first Broadway play. The play was not a success, but it was a major breakthrough for James Dean and more and better roles followed. He was 21 years old.

A major goal of young, aspiring actors to stage and screen in the 1950's was to study at the Actors Studio, regarded by many as the best acting school in the country. There they would study "The Method" style of acting under Lee Strasberg. Auditions were very competitive and very few applicants were successful in their bids to study there. In 1952, Dean auditioned, and out of more than 100 other applicants, was one of fifteen accepted. Dean's association with the Actors Studio was a major boost to his career.

More television roles followed in which Dean was often casted as a disturbed or misunderstood youth. In 1954 he appeared in a major role in *The Immoralist*, at the time a highly controversial play in its treatment of homosexuality. The play opened on Broadway on February 8 with Dean receiving excellent reviews for his performance. On the 23rd, Dean gave his final performance in the play. His abrupt departure was for Hollywood and an assured role in a film of *East of Eden* for Warner Bros. Based on John Steinbeck's novel and to be directed by Elia Kazan, another Actors Studio alumnus, this film would secure Dean's place in film history and in the hearts of millions of movie goers.

Before *Eden* was released, Hollywood hype was announcing that James Dean was a star. In fact, Dean was already at work on more television roles and was being courted for the lead in a film called *Rebel Without a Cause*, a role he accepted shortly before *East of Eden*'s premiere in March, 1955. *Eden* received excellent reviews from the critics, with Dean and his performance being generally lauded.

Dean had actually become a "hot property" in Hollywood and his third and final film, *Giant*, was in production before he finished his work in *Rebel*. Finishing *Rebel* in May, 1955, he spent a weekend indulging one of his other loves racing his Porsche, an activity seemingly suited to his fast-pace life. He then joined the cast and crew of *Giant* on location in Marfa, Texas, in June. Then back to Hollywood in July where work on *Giant* continued in the studio. Dean finished his work on the film on September 17. Days later he took delivery of a new Porsche 550 Spyder in great anticipation of the forthcoming races. He had the car prepared for the race with the assigned number of "130" painted on the car and his own motto, "Little Bastard," painted on the car's rear.

On September 30, on his way to the races in Salinas, California, and driving the new Spyder, Dean was killed in a two car accident near Cholame. He was 24 years old.

Genesis of the Dean Image/Icon and Deaner Theology

Developments following James Dean's death were not foreseen by members of Dean's family, the people of Fairmount, Warner Bros., or the media, generally. One of the first signs that something unusual was in the making was the turnout for his funeral in Fairmount eight days later. An estimated three thousand people attended. The substantial outpourings of anguish, mystery, and speculation combined with anticipation of future revelations produced what newspaper and movie magazine writers, among others, came to label a "cult." The "cult of James Dean" was born in the public imagination. The intricacies of the development of Dean's public image can not be fully explored here, nevertheless certain aspects are clearly important to the analysis of his significance to the Deaners in particular, and fans, generally. In part, the continued good reviews of Dean's work in the two unreleased films during 1955 and 1956 continued to add to his growing fame and image, and since *Giant* did not receive general release until November, 1956, anticipation heightened and interest increased for his third and final performance. Though mostly a phenomenon that appealed to the young of America, people of all ages and other nationalities also were drawn to Dean's screen and rapidly evolving legendary persona (see, for example, Truffaut 1978: 296-299). Dean's appeal at that juncture was not cross-cultural; nevertheless, he was admired and acclaimed throughout Europe and Japan. The stage was set for further image elaboration and exploitation by the film industry, among others.

Deaner Theology

Speculation about the details of Dean's personal life have been a favorite topic of friends, media, fans, and Deaners since his untimely death. It remains so today. Given the ambiguity of much of the information, the details of his private life remain a rich field for speculation and personal projection. For Deaners, the life and roles of James Dean are blended into a mythic unity. Dean is loved and admired as much for his future promise as for his accomplishments. The known facts of his life are enhanced and blended with the less established material of his private life. Deaners find in him hope for the discovery and development of their abilities.

The belief system of the Deaners *qua* Deaners, their theology, is not formally codified. As an emergent religious manifestation, the theology of the Deaners is likewise emergent, yet one grounded in a broader American "civil religion." Theology, in its usual western Judeo-Christian expression, is text based. That is, there are sacred texts from which mortals attempt to speak rationally of the divine. Theology, as the result of the substantial intellectualization and professionalization of the study of sacred texts in the West, is not a necessary component of religion. Following Walter Adams' liberal conception of theology (this volume), I follow with a liberal understanding of "texts."

Deaner texts consist of images of Dean (in movies, television performances, photos, drawings, paintings, and sculptures), locations, artifacts, and memorabilia associated with Dean, biographies and hagiographies (including film, video, and staged versions), other published media, and Dean quotes, writings, and art works. The Deaner epistemology, if you will, is the study Dean's special persona as revealed through these texts. And, as with the reading of sacred texts in other contexts, there are contradictions in the interpretations.

The emergent Deaner theology is in flux around a core of common understandings and generally accepted truths regarding Dean, his life, accomplishments, and potential. James Dean, person and icon, is associated or identified with a series of values and ideals characteristically, though not uniquely, American: creativity in the arts, courage and daring, eternal youth and beauty, rebellion against authority, individualism and "lone wolfism," self-seeking introspection, and the "common person" (see Figure 5). From the combination of Dean's lauded talents and creativity, with such qualities as the "boy next door" and "from a small town," a powerful all-American image and ideal emerges.

Figure 5. Suggestive List of Deaner Beliefs, Sentiments and Values

♦   *Individualism*: (cf. "expressive individualism" in Bellah, et al 1985: 32-35; 333-334)
♦   *Rebel*: Non-conformity valued
♦   *Creativity*: Develop one's artistic talents
♦   *Finding Oneself through Dean*: Self-realization
♦   *Struggle to Overcome Disadvantages*: Personal and environmental
♦   *Determination to Succeed*: Belief in one's own abilities
♦   *Heroic bravery*: Finding one's limits
♦   *Optimism*
♦   *Liberalism, Egalitarianism, and Tolerance*: Social, political, sexual
♦   *"Common Man" Motif*: Humble origin venerated
♦   *Comradeship and Empathy with other Deaners*
♦   *Small-town/rural Personalism*
♦   *"Real" Dean in one or more of his roles as source of understanding and model of ideal behavior*
♦   *Dean as continuing therapeutic source*

[* Sources: Correspondence (58 letters; 1989-90) and the *We Remember Dean International Newsletter* (1988-90)]

The view of Dean as potential, often phrased in terms of "if only he had lived he would have accomplished so much.... ." is common among Deaners. They refer to his wide range of interests, not only in acting, but in directing, filming, photography, writing, painting, sculpting, dance, music, auto racing, bull fighting, and so on. This view is a strong source of personal inspiration for Deaners to achieve in their own way, as he would have done. Dean is the guide in a Deaner's search for his/her own special talents and gifts.

Dean's appeal today in terms of "nostalgia" for the "good of old days of the 1950's" can be demonstrated, as well. However, for many Deaners, this nostalgia is not the only or central element in their devotion of Dean, and for some Deaners, it plays no role at all. The 1950's may have an appeal apart from the actual 1950's, that is, an intrinsic appeal of a kind of "golden age." But, when this appeal is expressed today by a teenager who only just "discovered" James Dean, clearly it can not be nostalgia. The 1950's are discovered via Dean in that case. The inter-/cross-generational aspect of Dean's appeal continues to sustain the Deaner movement, as demonstrated by continuing flow of young people to Fairmount from around the globe in search of Dean.

Deaners: an "Iconic" Movement

Who are the Deaners? I can not supply complete demographics, however a thumb-nail sketch will be helpful. Most come from the United States, but many come from other countries, including Canada, Mexico, England, Germany, Spain, Switzerland, France, South Africa, Japan, Australia, Malaysia, and the Philippines. Deaners are all ages and genders. The youngest Deaner I have interviewed was nine and the oldest in his sixties. There are many teenagers and young adults who regularly participate in Dean-related activities in Fairmount and elsewhere. Another large block are adults in their thirties and forties. Economic and occupational statuses can not be specified in any detail. My impressions are of a considerable range of income groups and occupations being represented, although most would fall into the working- to lower-middle class and the blue and white collar occupations.

Overall, I estimate approximately 3,000 Deaners worldwide. Many, but not all, are members of the *We Remember Dean International* club. In terms of American ethnicity, most Deaners are Anglo-American, with an occasional person of Italian descent or Jewish identity. I have seen only a few African-American and Latino participants in Fairmount. Most Deaners are from the Midwest, East, and far West. Southerners and Southwesterners are fewer in number. My research on the Deaners as a movement has focused on movement dynamics and characteristics; comparisons with religious movements, including folk saints, and exploration of the semiotics of Deaner pilgrimage (e.g., Hopgood 1991, 1994, 1995). I have lately settled on the term "iconic" to describe this type of movement. It is a movement that is dedicated to, and continues to receive inspiration from, the words and acts of a charismatic person; through the person's example, creations, desires, and aspirations. Its roots are secular since Dean was not a religious leader, nor even outwardly religious. Lack of an existing suitable term for this kind of movement brought me to this somewhat peculiar term. It shares characteristics with Robert Bellah's "lifestyle enclave" (Bellah, et al. 1985: 71-75) as well as having ingredients of Bellah's "expressive individualism" (1985: 32-35). There are also obvious similarities to the notion of a person as "sacred symbol" representing a kind of "collective charisma" a la Durkheim (1915; and via Lindholm 1990: 27-34; cf. Hopgood 1991).

In the iconic movement there are strong similarities with charismatic religious movements generally, although the iconic movement is ostensibly, a secular cluster of social processes devoted to a charismatic person. Such an assemblage of processes maybe a more or less organized expression of popular or folk culture, as is the case with the Deaners. In certain other cases, however, it may be argued that the iconic movement is a charismatic movement of a formatively religious variety. This, I think, is the case with the Deaners.

However, the "concreteness" of this Durkheimian derived approach does not exhaust the issues involved and the exploration of associated semiotics are helpful in distilling the brew of movement significance to its participants. For example, on the issue of the transformative process: How do ordinary things become "sacred" things? In this connection, if beliefs, ideas, and thought generally, are regarded as behavior and, therefore, real and potentially having effect, and affect, then the problem is partly solved. This provides a general premise for framing or allowing for the change or transformation of apparently secular and mundane things into sacred ones.

Fairmount's Museum Days and Deaner Pilgrimage

I will introduce the festival and then move on to an analysis of the semiotics associated with the Deaners. The festival itself is called the "Fairmount Museum Days" or just "Museum Days," and held in the small Indiana town of around 3,000. The festival is sponsored by the Fairmount Historical Museum. Begun in 1975, it is always held the last full weekend in September, and manifestly to celebrate the "famous sons" of Fairmount - living and dead. But, above all else it is James Dean who is honored and many visitors think the events are entirely for Dean. The phrase "Jimmy Dean Days" in place of "Museum Days" is often heard in conversation. It is no coincidence that the last weekend of September was selected for the festival, because Dean died on September 30th, 1955. Long a separate activity, fans, friends, and family also hold a separate memorial service for Dean and always on the 30th. In fact, fans and devotees of the late actor began making annual pilgrimages to Fairmount beginning with the very first memorial service in 1955 (although the first service was on October 3rd). The genesis of the Museum Days festival twenty-five years later is in those pilgrimages and with those first pilgrims.

The scheduled activities for Museum Days start on Friday and continue through Sunday afternoon. Main street is closed off to allow for the carnival rides and concessions. There are a number of activities held each year: the

James Dean Memorial Rod Run (a pre-1970 car and custom show), crowning of a "Museum Days" Queen, the Annual James Dean Memorial 10K Run, a children's pet parade, a kiddie tractor pull, James Dean Rock Lasso Contest, the Grand Parade, a "Garfield" cat photo contest, best of the 50's dance contest, the James Dean Look-a-like Contest, James Dean Bicycle Tour, screening of Dean's films, assorted entertainment (like high school bands, barbershop quartet, and other live entertainment), and a golf tournament. The James Dean Memorial Service may or may not occur during Museum Days, but in any case will be held on September 30th. During Museum Days, the James Dean Gallery and the Fairmount Historical Museum are open all day and into the night. Attendance in Fairmount during Museum Days is estimated at 20,000 - 30,000.

Dean's image is everywhere, yet not literally everywhere. His image in various forms is sold at the gallery, the museum, in stalls, on the street, at the car show, and so on. Some people are wearing him on their jackets, ties, and tee-shirts, while others are dressed like him. Dean seems to be everywhere. Yet, curiously, he is largely absent from the grand parade. No floats feature him and no look-alikes are featured in the parade. I did not see any formal acknowledgment of him in the parades of 1990 and 91. I did see his photo attached to a side window of a '49 Merc like the one he drove in *Rebel Without a Cause*.

Discussion

Perhaps the parading of Dean's image, or even giving him an obviously predominant place, in the grand parade is too reminiscent of a Catholic practice of carrying the images of saints in processions for the Protestant sensibilities of the larger community. It is significant to note that the memorial service for Dean is always held on the 30th regardless of what day of the week that happens to be and the "Museum Days" festival is always the last full weekend in September. This means that the most "sacred" activity undertaken, the memorial service, is often separated from the "secular" Museum Days activities by as much as a week, although some years the memorial service is close to Museum Days. It is important to note, so far at least, commercialization has not altered the practice of holding the memorial service on the anniversary date of Dean's death.

The festival consist of many separate "performances" played-out conterminously. There is overlap, of course, but the agendas of the casual visitor will be quite different from the long term Deaner, or any serious Dean fan. There are many levels and dimensions to this that can not be adequately covered here. Briefly, I want to note that there is an interesting combination of activities commemorating Dean with activities celebrating America. The festival is held on a weekend in traditional Protestant American fashion, in deference to the work ethic and in the autumn (like a harvest festival). The grand parade looks like a thousand other parades throughout the U.S. with beauty queens, high school bands, clowns, politicians, Shriners, military color guards, trucks, tractors, floats of many kinds, scouts, and the ultimate American symbol - the automobile in its multifarious forms. The broader social and economic issues involved are yet to be systematically studied. Nevertheless, there are some obvious and interesting issues, such as the local and regional economic effects. Not only Fairmount, but the nearby towns of Marion, Gas City, Anderson, and others benefit greatly from Fairmount's Museum Days. Fairmount, for example, has no hotels or motels, although a few "bed and breakfast" type arrangements are available. These in no way meet the demand. The nearest motels are in Marion and Anderson, each being about 30 miles away, and reservations during Museum Days must be made a year in advance. The car shows in Fairmount and nearby Gas City during Museum Days are, in themselves, a major draw for thousands of people.

Another indication of the impact is indicated by the retail sales by the James Dean Gallery (Hausknecht and Casper 1991: 610 -612). In 1989, its second year of operation, retail sales are reported at $13,500, plus admission charges of $2 per person with approximately 6,000 recorded admissions. Similar data are not available for the Fairmount Historical Museum and, in any case, admission is free with a request for a donation at the entrance. The Fairmount Historical Museum reported 8,329 visitors during 1994, but again, during Museum Days when long lines of people stretch around the block, no effort is made to maintain good records.

One clear reason for the continuing success of the festival is that Fairmount still looks like a small, typical Midwestern town of the not so distant past. In fact, Fairmount still looks much like it did when photographed by Dennis Stock during his visit there with Dean in 1955 (Stock 1978). I find this enduring, unchanging quality of Fairmount to be of utmost importance to many Deaners and fans: Fairmount itself is symbolic of another time and creates or recreates an important setting for those seeking James Dean.

Referring to the Deaners, the pilgrimage to Fairmount is more than a mere trip to Dean's home town, it is a pilgrimage on at least two interlinked levels: (1) it is a quest for self and meaning for one's own existence and struggle through James Dean and (2) it is a tracing backwards, a struggle with the present and the future, through a search for lost roots for a present and future state. In either, it is a search for meaning, perhaps lost or past meanings, or unknown meaning, in or through this place and the critical link, James Dean. The Deaners, then, are the siblings, the sons and the daughters of James Dean, and his true descendants.

Semiotics and Pilgrimage

What follows is an exploratory analysis of the semiotics associated with Deaners pilgrimage to Fairmount and their devotion to James Dean. At this stage I rely heavily on Milton Singer's *Man's Glassy Essence* (1984; cf. Singer 1980) and Victor Turner's *The Ritual Process* (1969). I find much there to stir thought on many aspects of pilgrimage and the associated semiotics. In addition to exploring pilgrimage and its role, I will explore the interactions and relations of the devotee and follower and the object of devotion. I am interested in what passes or transpires between the two, specifically, what meanings are "received" or "created" by the devotee. The central question is the meaning of the pilgrimage for the Deaners. For present purposes, I will maintain some degree of analytical separation of reactions to the place (Fairmount) from the object (Dean) of the pilgrimage.

Transformations

I view pilgrimage in the sense of emotional or intellectual movement, or transformation, from one state or condition to another, an application clearly related to Turner's (1969: 94ff; Turner and Turner 1978: 1- 38) use of liminality. Deaners are transformed from the everyday world of the ordinary (or profane) to the extraordinary (or sacred) in Fairmount; beliefs and values are reinforced. For me this transformation was given sharp relief when speaking with a Deaner about his being in Fairmount. We were standing near Dean's grave and he said, in an utterly somber manner, that he experiences that same intense feeling only at the Vietnam War Memorial in Washington, D.C. For this Deaner, the emotional impact he feels is part of a transformation he has experienced again and again over many years on his visits to Fairmount. For him, and most Deaners, such experiences are "bundles" of complex feelings, not easily put in words.

By way of analysis, I employ six sorts of transformations connected with Deaner pilgrimage. None of these are necessarily exclusive or discreet acts or affects, nor is any ranking of relative importance possible except in the most generalized way.

Physical Transformation. One of the more obvious examples are the Dean "look-alikes." They are usually male, white, and young. I have observed only one female dressed as Dean, and she did not compete in the "look alike" contest. There are other "play-acting" activities associate with the activities in Fairmount including dressing-up in the styles of the 1950's and engaging in 50's dancing. Obviously these physical trappings can serve as a means to an emotional transformation, although they are not necessary or required for most Deaners. The dress may only provide the "trappings" for a more significant emotional process.

Temporal Transformation. Transformation back to a generalized or "mythical" past: The illusion to "the good old days" is useful in setting one's self apart from the current or ordinary into another frame and in seeking transformation through the sights, sounds, and feelings of this place and that "other time." For the serious devotee, this illusion is not necessary, though it may be helpful, and many Deaners are not the least nostalgic. Deaners need Fairmount to get close to Dean, the notion of "the good old days" of Fairmount may or may not be useful to this process.

Existential Quest. An existential quest for meaning and fulfillment is a significant if not overriding reason for seeking Dean. Deaners are on a quest for new or old truths or insights. They are seeking the "meaning of one's life" or a personal insight into what "it all means." The reference here includes vague expressions of "experiencing the place," yet in the case of the Deaners this is not the experiencing of another tourist site, of course.

Tactile Transformation/ "In Touch." Attempting to get in touch with Dean and his roots is a major reason for visiting Fairmount, during Museum Days, or any other time. One clear reason for a pilgrimage to Fairmount is to get closer to Dean in the sense of exploring those places where he was, and perhaps, still is. Besides the spots and places James Dean knew when living there, there are numerous persons who knew and remember him. Speaking with Dean's high school buddies, his teachers, members of the Winslow and Dean families, and others who knew him is an important step is getting closer to him. (and sometimes, almost an effort to get inside his skin). "What is it about Fairmount," many Deaners wonder, "that makes it so special?" Others wonder what is it about Fairmount that contributed to Dean's genesis. There may be no answers to these questions, and when there are, they vary from Deaner to Deaner. The answer may be in the qualities they find in Dean's teachers, family, and classmates. In stark contrast, some find in Fairmount the antithesis of what Dean means to them and they say, "Dean had to get away from here to survive and flourish."

Journey Completion. The reference here is to (a) a Deaner's life - as a trip, journey, or trajectory - leading to this point or juncture in one's life and destiny and (b) completion of a pilgrimage or a step in a pilgrimage. In both cases are people who have "always wanted to come to Fairmount" as well as those who are going to all pilgrimage places associated with Dean. Some visitors were touched by Dean many years ago (in some cases as early as 1955 or even before his death) and are "returning," or seeking to return, to that earlier state by making the pilgrimage. Others, however, discovered Dean only years later or recently.

Communitas. The transformation into a state of "communal" understandings: Being with others of like mind and sympathies is important for many and an important consideration in making the trip. It is an occasion to share one's latest creation (poem, photo, art, etc.) or latest "find" of Dean memorabilia. It is a time to renew old friendships and make new ones. Sharing experiences, hopes, and problems is of continuing significance for many Deaners. Many Deaners have made numerous friends on their trips to Fairmount and maintain those friendships by keeping in contact and visiting in Fairmount. Some of these friendships have existed for many years and are often strengthened by taking trips to other sites associated with Dean and visiting each other at their homes. At times, I have the strong impression the Deaners understand intuitively each other's relation to Dean without the need to say so or how. They often seem in touch with each other's feelings and souls. These characteristics are aspects of what Bellah, et al. have called a "lifestyle enclave" (1985: 71 ff.), and what Turner (1969: 96 ff.) calls *communitas*.

Another integral dimension of this quest is seeking self-identity, individuality, and community within the dominate, homogeneous culture of the United States. Most Deaners are white, with little special or strong ethnic identity beyond "American" and are perhaps seeking a form of community analogous to an ethnic group.

Codes and Decoding Semiotics Extended

Semiotic Interaction. Next I will explore those interactions between the devotee and the object of devotion, i.e., the Deaner and Dean. What transpires "between"the two? What meanings are "transmitted" and "received?" I noted above the relevance of Singer's *Man's Glassy Essence*. Specifically, I find Singer's discussion of C. S. Peirce's (1984:74 ff.) "dialogical analysis of sign action" and especially the discussion of inner and outer dialogue and related concepts useful in this discussion. Here I will concentrate on the interactions and relations of the devotee/follower and the object of devotion. I am interested in what passes or transpires between the two, specifically, what meanings are "received" or "created" by the devotee. What is the content and specific meanings of the pilgrimage for the Deaners? Upon viewing the image of Dean in the gallery and the museum, and experiencing the settings associated with him in Fairmount, what do Deaners experience? For present purposes, I am maintaining some analytical separation of reactions to the place (Fairmount) from the object (Dean) of the pilgrimage. Dean's image is "emblematic" or iconic. Within that, there is a range of meanings and codes evoked in/by the viewer. Dean's image, in other words, is laden with non-intrinsic meanings. Deaners are in interaction and in tension with Dean via his image and the setting and draw or extract from this process significance, relation, and meaning. This is place again and that takes us back to Fairmount, and other important sites. Dean is a symbol or icon and is "read" and interpreted in certain ways. The follower is in interaction or in "dialogue" with the icon. But, the nagging question is: What does a Deaner "see" and "feel" and what is it s/he responds to?

The Dean image represents to his followers a bundle of highly charged, emotive meanings of seemingly unending significance. His image evokes many messages such as legend, beauty, love, sensitivity, understanding, greatness, potential, rebellion, youth, creativity, inspiration, and other personal or individualistic messages. This "dialogue" is not limited to the interaction of a static image and viewer. It extends to other actions and arenas of interaction. This includes being where he was, adopting some his characteristics, doing what he did, reading what he read, being "like him," and perhaps most important, finding him inside oneself.   There are many codes (or symbolic elements) to which Deaners react or interact. These codes are found mainly in visual forms such as photos, drawings, paintings, and sculptures of Dean. There are also special scenes from Dean's films that include important dialogue, movement, and interaction. (In the current context, I won't be getting into the codes found in the Deaner's own creations in poem, prose narrative, painting, and so on. However, there are of equal importance and are studied by Deaners as closely as other items and products.) Some codes are simple and others complex. A simple one is represented by his glasses, with or without clip-on sunglasses. Wearing his eye glasses alone communicates the un-Hollywoodesque "like you and me" quality. Add casual clothes and you get the "boy next door." With the clip-on sunglasses added the message is "being cool." The "disarranged" hair, the "lost" look, the pensive look, the red jacket of *Rebel Without a Cause*, the cigarette - these may be simple or complex codes depending on setting. Examples of simple codes are found in certain images of Dean such as photos that communicate a casual, yet defiant stance that equals "attitude." Other photos communicate the "the little lost boy" or "lost puppy look," that equals "help me." [A recent biography of Dean, *James Dean: Little Boy Lost*, by Joe Hyams (1992) clearly alludes to that quality.] Some photos or series of photos even have acquired names such as "the crucifixion" and "the torn sweater series." Other photos, for example, are open to considerable discussion, and offer complex coding. There's a particularly well known photo of Dean taken by Dennis Stock in the same cemetery where Dean is now buried. It is complex in meaning and, in part, communicates the perennial dilemma of mankind's past and future. In a sort of looking both ways manner Dean looks first to his home or roots and second to his future. This symbolizes origins and destiny, with the present (Dean as a free soul) in the middle. Dean's decision that he "can't go home again" is indicated by his looking away from his eleven year old cousin (also in the photo) and the headstone of Cal Dean (Stock 1978: 32-33). An opposite "reading" is also possible: Dean is looking away from his destiny - death and the eventual or inevitable return to his roots. Maybe some Deaners can get earthy origins and stardom - another important theme among Deaners - out of this photo, as well. Another Stock photo taken at the farm where Dean grew-up communicates much the same message (Stock 1978: 62-63).

Another interesting complex bundle worth consideration is Dean with his Porsche sports car (or, another variation, with his motorcycle). Briefly, this is Dean as a quintessential/ consummate symbol of youthful rebellion combined with the automobile (or motorcycle), the American symbol of freedom. Together they produce a most powerful icon.

Conclusion

The interaction or dialogue I noted earlier is personal and individual. This personalistic/individualistic nature of the relationship is an overriding characteristic of Dean's followers. Deaners draw similarities and parallels from Dean to themselves - i.e.,they link themselves to him. The fact that aspects of his life, such as growing up on a farm in the rural Midwest or having self-identity problems, can be easily linked is important in the "like me" equation. Personal identification with Dean is a strong element in the process leading to his consecration and adulation (including pilgrimage). This linkage provides for further elaboration and exploration of the self as refracted again and again through the Dean icon.

I think many of the codes found in Dean may also be viewed are ambiguous and may suggest opposition, depending on the viewer, such as: establishment anti-establishment; conformist rebel; ordinary extraordinary; insider outsider, and so on. The more conservative or traditional views are expressed by family and friends ("insiders") in Fairmount and provide an interesting tension with the Deaner "outsiders." For individual Deaners this creates some confusion over the issue of "the real James Dean," yet adds to the dynamics of the quest for understanding of self through Dean. At another level, it is another example of the perennial struggle over control of an important commodity and in this case the image of an important American symbol. The struggle is over Dean as the secular, "just like you and me," being who was another American success story and Dean as the sacred being who is continuously transformed and renewed in the image of all young gods and the source of inspiration, self-understanding, and hope.

Milton Singer in *Man's Glassy Essence* provides an apt quote from W. Lloyd Warner's *The Living and the Dead: A Study of the Symbolic Life of Americans*, that is a fitting conclusion to my remarks:

> The sacred world is not just a reified symbolic expression of the realities of society, but also an expression of the ongoing life of the human animal.
> Men can fully realize all they are as members of a species and a society at the supernatural level. Here they can love and hate themselves as gods and be loved and hated by the deities they have created (Warner 1959: 488; quoted in Singer 1984: 103).

Chapter 13

Processes and Dynamics of Community Fission and Maintenance: An Ojibway Case[1]

Walter Randolph Adams

Introduction

Between 1832 and 1881, an Ojibway community in Michigan's Upper Peninsula underwent fission into two parts, each of which stabilized into a separate social entity and evolved in a different direction. This study examines a case of community division and evolution; in analyzing the processes of development and change, we emphasize two concepts. First, that evolution involves the interaction of endogenous and exogenous factors. Second, that communities are not homogeneous structures. Rather, individuals within communities will respond in ways that they believe may help them survive without fully understanding the situation to which they are responding. The combination of these two concepts can result in a situation similar to that reported in these pages.

Most community studies which analyze fissioning approach the subject from one of two perspectives. Some take a local approach, examining processes such as factionalism or ethnicity, to account for the division of the community, while giving little or no emphasis to factors outside the community. Others, emphasizing state penetration or macro-micro analysis, take a regional approach. These approaches stress the dynamics of the relationship between the community and the larger world outside while giving little consideration to the internal dynamics of the community. This study differs in that it combines both internal dynamics and external factors in its analysis.

A second area of distinction concerns the historical basis of the fission. Most studies of community division are essentially synchronic. This study, however, sees the division and its repercussions working over a half century. It also emphasizes the two centuries of events leading up to the fission as being essential elements in the complete understanding of the ethnographic conclusion.

A final area of distinction is that many ethnographic studies of divided communities have tended to focus mainly on one faction in the division. This is due in part, at least, to the exigencies of field work. The researcher must win rapport with individuals in a community to conduct field work. Gaining rapport with an individual who belongs to one faction in a divided community creates additional rapport with other members of the same faction, but creates barriers with respect to members of the opposing faction. This historical study, relying heavily on documents, is not hampered by this constraint, and focuses equally on both factions. The resulting analysis permits an understanding of the processes involved in community fission and the dynamics of social interaction resulting from different perceptions of external conditions.

Perception of external conditions is a study that necessarily requires the researcher to analyze the psychology of the individuals involved. Information on the psychology of individuals in a past period is often unavailable. This is true in this case because the majority of those documents that have survived are concerned with economic issues. Even economic data, however, suggest something about the psychology of individuals in the community, because individuals behaved in differing ways about such matters as the degree of indebtedness into which they entered with European traders who worked in the area.

Data on the extent to which individuals among the Ojibway of this community became indebted to others can be found in account books kept by traders who served that community. In some cases these documents indicate items purchased, the prices paid for goods, as well as the amount of debt incurred by their purchase. Because they contain this information, at least two scholars have argued that account books provide more than simple economic data (Jarvenpa and Brumbach 1985; Flandrin and Hyman 1986), and have used them to make cultural inferences.

Another way to view these documents is as an indicator of risk-taking. When an individual incurs a debt, s/he assumes s/he will be able to pay it back within a reasonable period of time. By making this assumption the individual is taking a risk. The willingness to take this risk is a psychological construct, not economic. Therefore, the analysis of account books provides information about the extent to which an individual is/was willing to gamble upon uncertainty.

While conducting research on the fission of this Ojibway community, I found a document indicating the debts incurred by members of the community from 1832 to 1834. This document is important for at least three reasons. First, a census indicates that 140 people lived in that community in

1832 (Schoolcraft 1958). If that was accurate, the 44 individuals named in the document represent 31.42% of the total population and a higher percentage of those deemed capable of repaying their debts. Thus, there is a statistically adequate sample upon which inferences may be made. Second, the document indicates that debts had a large range of variation: the biggest debtors had over 200 times as much debt as the smallest. Therefore, there are significant differences in the extent to which individuals were willing to incur debts.

Third, the list contains names of individuals with Ojibway names and individuals with French names, providing a measure of cultural affinity. Equally significant is the observation that individuals with French names predominate in the high debtors while individuals with Ojibway names predominate among the lowest debtors. Thus, it is a reasonable conclusion that individuals in the community differed in patterned ways not only in their indebtedness, but also in their adherence to traditional culture, or affiliated themselves with the new system embodied by the traders.

We can begin to understand this pattern by differentiating between risk takers. Entities can be divided into two groups, hierarchists and entrepreneurs, relative to their approaches to risk (Douglas and Wildavsky 1982). Hierarchists are individuals who adhere to the *status quo* while entrepreneurs are those who reach out more aggressively to the opportunities presented them by the environment. Patterns of indebtedness reflect these differences. Those who hold tightly to traditional values--unwilling to take great risks, and thus have lower debts--are hierarchists. Those willing to take greater risks (and to incur higher debts) have characteristics held by entrepreneurs. Acceptance of new values is an individual achievement. Individuals, through necessity, must approach new situations in manners consistent with their previous experience. Because no two individuals share similar experiences, approaches to new situations will necessarily be individualistic. Individualistic approaches to risk are entrepreneurial.

By contrast, the retention of traditional values requires group effort. Traditions pass from generation to generation only through group effort and change slowly because any alteration requires the tacit acceptance of the change by participants. Those groups that approach new phenomena carefully, guardedly, and with great attention to traditional values are hierarchists (Douglas and Wildavsky 1982). The hierarchist-entrepreneur dichotomy exists within communities, too, because there is never agreement on what constitutes acceptable risk in any society (Fischhoff, et al. 1981). Many authors focusing on Native American factionalism refer to the development of groups labelled as "Conservative" or "Progressive." These terms reflect the degree to which an individual adheres to traditional (Conservative) or new (Progressive) values. In some cases, such as at Old Oraibi (Sekaquaptewa 1972) and the present case, the development of Conservative and Progressive factions results in the community's fission and the development of two communities. In such cases, the two communities develop distinct cultural manifestations. This is in part because of the degree to which they are willing to adopt new ideas, and also because methods of performing a particular task becomes a symbol of membership in a particular community (Kennedy 1982). Through time, the interaction of both forces results in the divergence of the two groups. Consequently, with the passage of a greater amount of time, it may become difficult to conceptualize that the two communities were historically a single community.

By analyzing the evolution of this community over a 49 year period after its fission, and analyzing an account book's information on the indebtedness of individuals dating from the time of the schism, and knowing the community in which these individual's resided, it is possible to infer hierarchist and entrepreneurial adaptations to White encroachment. In this paper, I first present a sketch of the conditions exerted upon the community. I then focus attention on how groups living in the community responded to these pressures. The final section analyzes the foregoing in relation to account books dating from the time of the schism. Data contained in this document and knowledge of the subsequent evolution of the community permit an interpretation of the psychological orientations of members of each community in reference to risk.

External Conditions

The Ojibway migrated along with the Pottawatomi and Ottawa to Michigan only shortly before the arrival of French fur traders (see note for references).[2] Current interpretations suggest that the Ojibway, searching for fur-bearing animals (Hickerson 1973), migrated in band-sized groups into the interior of the Upper Peninsula (Danziger 1978), into Wisconsin and Minnesota (Cornell 1986), and into Manitoba (Vecsey 1983). By moving into Canada they displaced the Cree (Vecsey 1983); by moving into Wisconsin, the Fox (Mittelholtz 1957). By 1750, they also displaced the Sioux from Mille Lacs in Minnesota (Mittelholtz 1957) and initiated a long-standing hostility with them (Hickerson 1970).

The French established a trading post on the eastern side of the Keweenaw Bay, located on the southern shore of Lake Superior, in 1710 (Vecsey 1983). The North West Company established a trading post there sometime between 1780 (Peters 1983) and 1801 (Coues 1965). The American Fur Company took possession of this post after the War of 1812 (Johnson 1919). In 1832, the American Fur Company factor introduced a Canadian Methodist missionary to evangelize the Native Americans living around him (Schoenfus 1963). While the trader's `real' reason for this will never be known, a number of factors encouraged him to do so.

A religious revitalization movement took place in the United States in the late 18th and early 19th centuries (Goodykoontz 1939). Concurrently, United States - Indian policy stressed the involvement of Protestant missionary groups in assimilating Native Americans (Viola 1974; Prucha 1973). Protestant missionaries, products of their own culture, firmly believed in the values of agriculture, industrial expansion, consumption of manufactured products, and `the American way.'[3] They believed it was their duty to instruct the Native Americans in these values.

Many Protestant missionary organizations emerged to evangelize Native Americans. Each of these groups received Federal monies to support their activities. They received further support from members of those denominations who donated clothing, money, time, and other goods and skills. While their missionary activities may have been performed for altruistic reasons, the critical importance of economic expansion and the development of new markets also played a fundamental role (Adams 1988).

There was a political motive for evangelizing Native Americans, too. Although the United States had defeated the English in the War of 1812, British subjects were in the Northwest Territory until much later. Moreover, the boundary between the United States and Canada in the Northwest Territory was not clearly defined. Consequently, the United States could not control the movement of British subjects. Their presence hindered the United States' industrial expansion and economic growth, and encouraged the development of political alliances with the Native Americans. The establishment of missions among these `non-American' groups was also an attempt to woo the Native Americans from the British and provide a buffer zone between the United States and Britain.[4]

England, too, was held firmly in the grips of a religious revival and by the forces encouraging industrial expansion. The imperialist tendencies of the United States exemplified by the American Revolution; attempts to conquer Montreal and Quebec during that confrontation (Parks 1986); the War of 1812; and the expansion of United States into the Northwest Territory; and, laws restricting the movements of Britain's government to fear that the United States would not respect Canadian territorial claims. Thus, British Protestant denominations were interested in evangelizing Native Americans on both sides of the United States - Canada border for the same reasons that motivated their United States counterparts to do so.

A final motive for the promotion of Protestant missions among the Native Americans by United States Protestant denominations was the rapid expansion of Catholics into the United States throughout the nineteenth century.[5] There is no indication that British Protestant denominations were held by the same fear. A leading reason why the United States developed this concern was to promote national unity (Adams 1988). This was important because the economies of the original thirteen colonies were so different from one another (industrialism along the coastal sections of the northeast, small-scale family farming in the interior portions, and plantation farming in the southeast) made it difficult for the colonies to agree on many things. Appealing to a higher ideal, then, provided the basis for the "United" States.

Moving from the wider political and economic conditions to those closer to the area under study were additional pressures. The proximity of the region to Canada and the presence of mineral deposits underlay the United States' political and economic concerns in the region. The anti-Catholic movement had an important impact to this study. In 1835, John Jacob Astor stepped down as President of the American Fur Company and Ramsay Crooks took over. Crooks reorganized the company, such that Protestant traders moved from secondary to primary posts or upper level positions. Catholic French Canadian traders were placed in charge of posts of lesser significance or released (Adams 1988).

A final pressure exerted upon the Native American community was tangentially related to Anglo - United States relations. As the United States became more assured of its status in the world economic community, its dependence upon Native Americans as allies diminished. Between 1820 and 1832, the Supreme Court ruled in the cases of *Johnson and Graham's Lessee v McIntosh* (1823), *The Cherokee Nation v the State of Georgia* (1831), and *Samuel A. Worcester v the State of Georgia* (1832) (Washburne 1971). These decisions caused Native Americans to lose their status as sovereign nations and placed them in the position of domestic dependent nations (Boxberger 1988).

A by-product of these decisions was the demotion of Mixed-bloods.[6] While the Native Americans were desired as allies, this segment of the Native American community were often the liaison between the Whites and the Native Americans. They functioned as traders and Indian agents; in Canada they also served as Protestant missionaries; as such they were integral to U.S. government -Indian relations (Johnston March 12, 1828;

Johnston February 29, 1829). When the Indians were no longer needed as allies, Mixed-bloods lost their positions as intermediaries. Henry R. Schoolcraft, an important individual in United States - Indian relations during this period, and married to a Mixed-blood, remarked:

> ...the partially educated halfbreeds have been hitherto found the most effective and unscrupulous advocates among the bands. Too indolent and improvident to succeed in business among the shrewder whites, and having lost their relish for the hunter state, this turbulent class, generally fill the places of petty clerks and interpreters at traders' houses, or wander to and from the Indian villages, living on their bounty, preying on their prejudices, and filling their minds with discord and dissatisfaction (Schoolcraft July 15, 1840).

By 1848, Mixed-bloods were regarded as Indians, not as Whites (Richmond 1848). Their demotion from liaisons to impediments to United States policy in less than one generation had an impact on the Mixed-blood population (below).

Some of the primary external pressures exerted upon this Native American community, then, included 1) the relatively short period of time that the Ojibway were in the area prior to White encroachment; 2) Missionaries who were evangelizing Native Americans for altruistic/ economic/ social/ political ends, and the cultural baggage this entailed; 3) tensions in United States - British relations; and 4) the demotion of Mixed-bloods.

To this one must add the unmentioned, but understood importance of the decline in the fur trade during the 1830s. This opened the way for economic expansion in the Northwest Territory and brought Whites searching for copper and other minerals with which to feed the expanding east coast industries. These conditions contributed to the tense political relations between the United States and Britain. With this as background, I now focus on the Native American community in question.

The Community's Response

Because it is uncertain when the Ojibway entered the Upper Peninsula, it is not certain to what extent ignorance of the environment (relative to the knowledge possessed by indigenous groups) played a role in their rapid (Shifford nd; James 1954; Copway 1851), but selective (Bishop 1974) acceptance of European manufactured products. It is fairly certain, however, their adverse relations with those groups they had displaced had some positive impact.

Very little information is available for the community before 1832. What information is available, however, suggests the following scenario. The establishment of a permanent trading post provided Native Americans with European goods virtually year-round. In response they began to live near the trading post throughout the year. By the end of the eighteenth century, the local community had developed a hereditary chieftainship (Schoolcraft 1962).

Documents dating from the third decade of the nineteenth century do not suggest that the community was homogeneous. The community's leader switched his allegiance from the British to the United States in 1823, angering a `majority' of his followers, but no single person emerged to oppose him (Schoolcraft 1962). Later, the American Fur Company factor had adverse relations with some of the members of the community. The trader had married an Ojibway woman (Chaput 1970). This relationship, in other communities, provided economic benefits to individuals related to the woman (Armstrong 1892). One can only assume the sme occurred in the community under study, too. In 1829, documents reveal that some members of the community were unhappy with the treatment they were receiving from him (Walker December 25, 1829). There is no evidence, however, that everyone in the community shared these complaints.

The community, from external appearances, was homogeneous. The bucolic scene, however, erupted quickly and cleanly in 1832, when the trader went to Sault Ste. Marie, ostensibly to get "fire-water." He brought back a Canadian Methodist native missionary (i.e., Mixed-blood) to evangelize them instead (Hall 1856)--precisely when Temperance was a prominent social, political, economic, and religious movement (Tyrell 1979). Immediately after his arrival the Indian community fissioned into two groups, one of which established another settlement on the opposite shore of the bay (Prindle 1842).

Sometime in 1834 the trader lost his eyesight making him of little value to the Company (Crooks October 20, 1834). As part of the general reorganization in the American Fur Company occurring at this time, a French-Canadian replaced him the following autumn (Franchere October 11, 1835). Two years later, in 1837, another French Canadian, known to be a Catholic, took over the post.[7]

There is no evidence this trader gave preferential treatment to either group. However, the trader, upon request, gave instruction in Catholic doctrine to the leader of the schismatic faction, who was a direct descendant of the first hereditary chief (Rezek 1906). The trader, also at the leader's request, invited a Catholic missionary to establish a mission. The missionary arrived after the chief's death in 1843 (Ibid.).[8]

This missionary was heavily influenced by the Jesuits and, like them, attempted to protect Indians from White encroachment (Verwyst 1900). He modelled his community after the *reducción* system used in Central and South America (Verwyst 1900).[9] He purchased about 500 acres of land, which he later deeded to the Catholic Indian community. Whether by accident or design, this land contains some of the best agricultural land available in the Upper Peninsula (Veatch 1941), a feature that helped the Indians adopt a self-sufficient economy, which was one of his primary goals.

The Indians did not have to make drastic alterations in their culture to live at his mission. He allowed them to live in wigwams and practice many traditional economic activities. He did not force them to adopt agriculture, but provided instruction to those who were interested in learning the art (Jamison 1948). He also allowed them to determine their own political structure (Baraga March 22, 1849). Thus, those who chose to reside at this mission were assured of their own economic base, a life-style that approximated traditional Ojibway culture, and their own political structure. In short, although Catholicism was a departure from Conservative values, the Catholic mission allowed the Ojibway to be more conservative than did the Methodist mission.

The Methodist missionaries vehemently protested the Catholic missionary's arrival (Gray 1936; Brown December 29, 1843; Carrier February 5, 1844). They asked the Indian Agent to order the Catholic priest to leave the area (Carrier February 5, 1844; Brown December 29, 1843). In response, the Indian Agent issued an order stating that two denominations could not establish missions among the same band (Stuart April 4, 1844; Stuart April 15, 1844). Violators would not receive money from the Civilization Fund. He also ordered the government-appointed blacksmith, carpenter, and farmer to withhold services from the Catholic Indians (Stuart April 4, 1844).

The Catholic missionary, a student of law before entering the seminary (Jezernik 1968), wrote the Indian Agent that laws could not be enforced retroactively (Baraga May 20, 1844). Because he had established his mission before the edict was promulgated, he argued, the circular could not apply to him (Ibid.). Notwithstanding, available documents suggest the Catholic mission did not receive Federal funding until at least 1881. Ironically, however, these events and his own philosophical orientation, facilitated the Catholic missionary's goal and permitted those members of the community to be self-sufficient.

Whites, attracted by copper and iron deposits (and later lumber extraction), moved to the area around the Methodist mission and established a White community in 1841 (Lambert 1971). This was over 20 years before Whites established a town near the Catholic mission (Dompier 1969). Documents indicate the Methodist Indians were angry about White encroachment on reservation land (King January 7, 1865). No such documents were generated by the Catholic Indians. This suggests that although some Whites had settled on the West side of the bay, the land on which they settled was not a fundamental part of the Catholic Indian community.

The Methodist community was affected by four conditions between the late 1840s and early 1880s. First, it continually received support from the government, even during the tenure of the Catholic Indian Agent. Second, the differential distribution of Whites on reservation land had adverse impacts on them. Third, the poorer quality of the soil (Veatch 1941) encouraged members of this community to look toward the cash-and labor markets made available to them by the expanding economy occurring around them. Finally, the demotion of Mixed-bloods to an unimportant status in United States - Indian relations seems to have taken its toll on the Methodist community.

A manifestation of the differences these conditions generated within the two communities can be seen in the patterns of alcohol abuse: Alcohol consumption, long considered as an indicator of social problems, has been rampant in the Methodist community. For the past 150 years, the only deaths attributable to alcohol have come from this community. No deaths from alcohol-related causes have been reported from the Catholic mission, even though it has to report to the same governmental agencies as does the Methodist mission.

These conditions, and their own social and economic orientations, encouraged the Ojibway living at the Methodist mission to subscribe more fully to the economic and cultural styles of the Whites, and thus were heavily influenced by the economic expansion occurring in the Upper Peninsula between 1843 and 1881. They were so much a part of the cash market that one individual reported the Indians "already bring the finest Potatoes to market at Copper Harbour eighty miles in their canoes" (St. John 1846). Members of the Methodist community were also attracted to the wage-labor market. In the mid to late 1840s, the Methodist missionary stated that "Several of the Indians were employed as guides, packers, and voyageurs [for the miners] which materially affected our forces at the mission" (Pitezel 1857). On at least one occasion the government-funded school was closed because the students had followed their parents to locations where jobs were available (Lee August 1880). There is no evidence that the Catholic school closed due to lack of students (Ibid.), suggesting the parents of these students were not as attracted to the cash-labor market as were the Methodist Indians.

Another indication of the extent to which these communities differed in their is the extent to which they were dependent upon United States Government funds. As a result of land sales, the Government, in 1875, realized it owed the band $20,000. The Methodist Indians requested that their share be given to them to purchase United States Government bonds (Betts March 29, 1875) and they would use the accumulated interest (Betts March 2, 1875). The chief of the Catholic Indians, by contrast, wrote "I do not wish my young men to receive these goods if they are stolen or do not belong to us" (Assinins October 28, 1875).

Differences between the two Ojibway community, already inherent in internal community dynamics and social and philosophical orientations, were encouraged by the external pressures exerted upon them. Thus, not only was there increased presence of Whites, but increasing pressure exerted on the Methodist Indians to adopt the ways of Whites--a life-style to which they were already attracted. The Catholics, by contrast, less attracted to the White lifestyle, were subject to less intense pressures from the Whites; aided in large measure by the sensitivity to the protection of Ojibway culture by the Catholic missionary.

Analysis

Although the community fissioned immediately following the introduction of the Wesleyan Methodist missionary, available evidence suggests that the motivation for community fission was social and economic rather than ideological. That is, there is little indication that those who remained at the Methodist Mission did so because they believed in the doctrine. The same was true when the Catholic missionary established his mission about ten years later.

The literature suggests Native Americans converted to western ideologies for two reasons. First, some saw conversion as a means by which they could acquire European goods and wealth because the missionary provided a conduit through which the Ojibway could obtain material rewards (Vecsey 1983). Although this comment was made specifically to why some Ojibway accepted Catholicism in the 17th century, the same may be said about those who converted to either Methodism or Catholicism in the 19th century (Pitezel 1857). To obtain these rewards, however, Native Americans had to "convert" to the religious persuasion espoused by the missionary. It is important to note, however, that conversion does not imply wholesale acceptance of a doctrine. Indeed, it is always difficult to estimate the extent to which any individual--other than one's self-- believes in a doctrine.

Recall the negative relations between some members of the Native American community and the trader. Recall, too, that Protestant missionaries inculcated the values of White Protestant society--industrial expansion and involvement in the expanding cash-and labor-economy. Finally, recall that the missionary represented another channel through which industrial products were made available to the Native Americans.

These conditions seem to have coalesced in 1832 with the arrival of another individual who espoused these values: the Methodist missionary. This caused some members of the community to revolt because he represented an additional threat to their lifestyle. Their revolt took the form of community schism and the subsequent development of a new community. However, the schismatic group could not live without the products available to them at the trading post. Consequently, although they moved to the opposite shore, they only moved three miles away.

This interpretation is supported by a document indicating the extent to which community members were indebtedness to the local trader between 1832 and 1834. The dates covered in this document are very important because they are coeval with the development of the Methodist mission (Table 2). Consequently, it provides information about the extent to which individuals in the community were attracted to the new lifestyle at the same time that the Methodist missionary, representing an additional conduit to that lifestyle, arrived at Keweenaw Bay. While the information contained in this document does not tell us what the individuals were purchasing, it does show that approximately one-third of the community had incurred a debt to this trader. Because all but one of the names seem to belong to a male, and because it is unlikely that the trader would extend a debt to a juvenile, we are led to believe that almost every household was indebted to the trader.

Table 2. Memorandum of Outstanding Debts of Indians for the Years 1832-1834 (Source: NAM M1, Reel 54, Frame 37)

Name	Amount	Name	Amount
Aninance	$16.50	Me gee since	$21.50
Benjamin Clutier	$22.00	Le lou cheux	$1.00
Abretau Wagewas	$4.50	Quivisance	$114.00
Champaigne	$71.00	Tay ache	$51.90
Waubekaakicke	$13.50	Puck go na ga shick	$66.60
Quivisenshish	$6.00	Dee been dee	$8.50
Tagamance	$3.00	Caug waw	$15.28
Sagataugan	$13.00	Little Frenchman	$82.90
Meegeesee	$5.10	The Bell	$19.00
Young MacGillvray	$164.40	Quiway no quette	$13.00
Wa ba noo	$182.60	Pin ny shish	$24.30
Waga-cootoonis kois	$8.00	Pee way bica kay	$40.50
Joseph Laundron	$29.00	Nay gan ash	$40.40
Antoine Lendron	$26.00	Cay Kaik	$29.10
Naose key tea yea	$50.60	Match e gee shick	$28.00
Homme des Pere	$16.20	o saw gee	$21.40
Quinisahishish Ojibway	$72.90	Key che in min ney	$3.00
Young Wolf	$80.70	Ocupe wan	$115.10
manog sid	$64.20	Panseek squaw	$4.00

(Table 2 continued)

Pay-can-nouch e	$19.40	Lhomme de Been Deishi	$131.60
Wah poose	$27.30	Lhomme du Sault	$6.00
Matt way ance in a quois	$10.00	Attaya	$4.80
Miau wash	$212.10		

The information contained in this document can be reorganized to reveal a clear pattern of indebtedness. Table 3 suggests that three groups of individuals lived in the community.[10] The divisions are arbitrary, but logical in view of the lack of debts between $30 and $40, and between $82.90 and $114.00. I assume the first break to be the division between the Conservative and the Progressive factions. There is no clear separation between the Progressives and Mixed-bloods, although the latter (tentatively identified by surname) appear to have incurred some of the highest debts. This suggests the difference between the Progressives and Mixed-bloods was minimal. This is understandable. Because there were fewer White traders than Ojibway women who could marry them (Armstrong 1892), the difference between a Mixed-blood and a Progressive was largely a product of chance and due to forces outside the control of the individual Indian. The trader, not the Indian, made the decision as to which Indian woman he would marry.[11]

While individuals with non-Indian surnames also appear among the ranks of those with the lowest debts, all but one had incurred debts in the upper part of the range presented in Table 3. Intriguingly, the percentage of those with European-derived surnames within each group increases within each of these groupings (Group I: 5 of 28, or 18%; Group II: 3 of 10, or 30%; Group III: 4 of 7, or 57%). Thus, on the basis of two independent measures, the segmentation of the Indian community into these arbitrary groups is consistent.

Table 3. Categories of Indebtedness

Conservatives

Name	Amount	Name	Amount
Le lou cheux	$1.00	Tagamance	$3.00
Kay che in min ney	$3.00	Pansleek squaw	$4.00
Abretau wagewas	$4.50	Attaya	$4.80
Megeesee	$5.10	Quinisenshish	$6.00
Lhomme du Sault	$6.00	Waga-cootoonis kois	$8.00
Dee been dee	$8.50	Matt way na quette	$13.00
Sagataugan	$13.00	Wabekaakicke	$13.50
Caug waw	$15.20	Acinance	$16.50
The Bell	$19.00	Pay can nouch e	$19.40
o saw gee	$21.40	me gee since	$21.50
Benjamin Clutier	$22.00	Pin ny shish	$24.30
Antoine lendron	$26.00	Wah poose	$27.30
Match e gee shich	$28.00	Joseph Laundron	$29.00
Cay Kaik	$29.10		

(Table 3 continued)

Progressives

Name	Amount	Name	Amount
Pee way bic a kay	$40.50	Nay gan ash	$44.00
Naose ke tea yea	$51.90	Tayache	$51.90
Manog sid	$64.20	Puck go an go shick	$66.60
Champaigne	$71.00	Quinishashish Ojibway	$72.90
Young Wolf	$80.70	Little Frenchman	$82.90

Mixed Bloods

Name	Amount	Name	Amount
Quivisance Champaigne	$114.00	Ocupe wan	$115.10
Lhomme des been Deishi	$131.60	Homme des Pere	$162.20
Young MacGillvray	$164.40	Wa ba noo	$182.60
Miau wash	$212.10		

I base the idea that account books may imply psychological orientations on two assumptions. First, because the document is coeval with the community's fission, the extent to which an individual incurred a debt to the trader provides a rough indication of the extent to which White material culture attracted an individual at the time of the schism.[12]   I emphasize this is a rough indication because incurring a debt requires the lender's tacit agreement that the individual in question can incur the debt and the extent to which the lender is willing to take a risk that the debtor will repay him. Second, because the two resultant communities subscribed to very distinct philosophical orientations (Progressive and Conservative), other documentary sources giving names of individuals residing in a community can be used to identify individuals appearing in the account book, and determine whether a relationship exists between indebtedness and community of residence.

Using documents written between 1845 and 1847 (within four years of the establishment of the Catholic community, a period of time necessary because there was some movement of personnel between the two communities), I have been able to identify 20% of the individuals on this list. Those identified had among the lowest debts and became members of the Catholic mission; those with the debts between $40 and $80 became members of the Methodist mission.[13]   Mixed-bloods were divided between the two communities. I present a suggestion for this below.

The period after the mid 1840s was marked by massive alterations in the Upper Peninsula, occasioned by the rapid influx of Whites entering the area in search of mineral wealth and/or employment at the mines. Most of this development occurred on the east side of the bay. Traditional economic activities--hunting, trapping, and fishing were becoming more difficult to perform due to the encroachment of Whites. The lack of suitable soil upon which to develop subsistence agriculture further placed further pressures upon them to participate in the cash- and labor- markets. By 1875, they had learned enough about cash economy that they understood that the money owed them by the Federal Government could be invested in bonds and the community could use the accumulated interest to pay for their needs.

The Catholic Indians were not as affected by White encroachment for at least three reasons. First, evidence suggests they were less attracted that way of life. Second, the economic development occurring in the region did not take place on the west side of the bay. This further insulated them from White encroachment. Third, the Catholic Indians had sufficient land suitable for agriculture, upon which they could develop a self-sufficient economy. The absence of Whites on the western side of the bay also permitted them to continue to hunt and trap animals in the forests nearby. The development of economic self-sufficiency further insulated them from the impacts of White encroachment. So effective was this orientation that they were willing to forego their share of the $20,000.

I do not wish to leave the impression that the two communities were rigid structures. Individuals could, and did, from time to time, move from one community to the other. Although reports of these cases are relatively rare. This suggests that the majority of the individuals were relatively well adapted and fell within the normal range with respect to the extent to which community members as a whole were willing to take risks. Those who were less willing to take the risks inherent in a fluctuating capitalist economy, the Conservatives were members of the Catholic community. Those more willing to take these risks were members of the Methodist community.

The point that members could migrate between communities suggests there were some individuals who fell outside the norm of the bell-shaped curve. As external conditions changed, individuals assessed the extent to which they felt capable of successfully adapting to the new conditions. Those who felt they were ready to assimilate further into the White society either moved from the Catholic mission to the Methodist, or from the Methodist community to White communities. Those who were unable to do so, migrated from the Methodist to the Catholic community.

Especially poignant with respect to the hierarchist nature of the Catholic community was an instance in which a group of individuals left *en masse* the Catholic community in 1881 to establish their own community far away from the parental community. This event parallels the initial schism that occurred in 1832. Information gleaned from the field suggests that these individuals are even more Conservative in their orientations than were those living at the Catholic community (Adams 1988).

I mentioned above that Mixed-bloods became residents of both communities. I suggest this was a product of their demotion from integral to peripheral agents in United States - Native American relations. This sudden change affected Mixed-bloods in ways analogous to the concepts of hierarchists and entrepreneurs presented earlier (Douglas and Wildavsky 1982).

The hierarchists apparently became discouraged by their demotion and believed they had more in common with the Conservative group. Others, the entrepreneurs, became members of the Methodist community because they believed they had more in common with those who accepted more fully White values. Supporting such an interpretation is an incident occurring in the Methodist community in 1865. Mixed-bloods had enjoyed the right to vote in township elections for at least ten years and were now turned away at the polls. This caused much consternation among the Native Americans living on the east side of the bay. In a document detailing the situation are the following statements:

> At the polls when rejected one chief said to the other now let us return we have been trying to be white men for the past ten or twelve years & now we are cast off. What is the use to try--let us now do as formerly. Get drunk, kill steal take our drum-dance & put feathers in our head &c (Johnson 1919).

Because we do not know the identity of the disgruntled chief, we cannot know whether he moved to the other community. However, his willingness to state that they should "do as formerly" suggests his discouragement in `the American way' and that a lifestyle approximating traditional values was an option. This option was especially available due to the presence of the Catholic mission on the other side of the bay.

Conclusion

The members of each community had specific orientations and cultural patterns. The missionaries provided both groups with ideologies and programs which encouraged these orientations. One of these, the Methodist, became firmly absorbed by the dominant economy and became, in essence, dependent wards of the state. Its members were the 'entrepreneurs' of the nineteenth century. The other community, the Catholics, became self-sufficient. Its members, staunch supporters of the *status quo* were the 'hierarchists' of the nineteenth century. These orientations were further fostered by the Federal government when it withheld Federal assistance to the Catholic mission. Although these policies were designed to bring the two communities into a single body, they had the opposite effect.

The conceptualization of Methodists as Progressives (or entrepreneurs) and the Catholics as Conservatives (or hierarchists) is further reflected in the values inculcated by the denominations. Protestant denominations prided themselves in their perception of individual salvation and a direct, personal relationship with the Almighty God. Such a relationship releases individuals from the tenacious grasps of the community and allows them to strike out on their own. By contrast, the strict adherence to set ways (marked by the fact that there have only been three Vatican Councils during the past 2,000 years), and the strict adherence to a hierarchy is clearly evidenced among the Catholics. The values emphasizing community membership, rather than individualism, is similarly a reflection of hierarchist values and tendencies among the Catholics. The importance of community and conservatism was further emphasized by the migration of the ultra-conservative from the Catholic mission to what is now Hannahville in 1881.

The establishment and maintenance of a dual-community structure was a product of intra-community dynamics; that were products of the interplay of psychological and economic forces. These forces interdigitated with the psychological and economic pressures exerted upon the community from the outside. The combination of these internal and external psychological and economic forces caused groups of individuals to respond in one of two ways: They could either stay with the *status quo* or accept the opportunities offered by the White social and economic systems. The differences between the two orientations, here-- as at Oraibi (Sekaquaptewa 1972)-- resulted in the dissolution of what had appeared to be a "homogeneous" community.

The decision whether to be a hierarchist or an entrepreneur narrows the subsequent choices available to members of a given community in response to the interdigitation of further internal and external forces. This is because the orientations and methods used by one group defines membership in that community, and members of the other group are loath to adopt them (Kennedy 1982). In time, the members of the historically "homogeneous" community adopt two different cultural manifestations so that, from an archeological perspective, it is difficult to see that they were a single culture at a previous period.

The identities of the two factions are expressed by membership in Methodist or Catholic denominations. The differences between Methodism and Catholicism as ideologies are real and provide a structure for the behavioral differences of the two communities. But, underlying these ideological differences may be the personal orientations of those who opted to affiliate with one or the other denomination. These differing orientations may provide a deeper structure of organization analogous to deep structure in language (Chomsky 1981) of which the denominational differences are surface manifestations.

Notes

1. Acknowledgements. This research is derived from the author's doctoral dissertation (Adams 1988). The author gratefully acknowledges the financial assistance provided by Sigma Xi for two grants (1985, 1986) and the W.B. and Candace Thoman Foundation for Hunger and Famine Prevention. Dr. Joseph L. Chartkoff and Dr. Dwight B. Heath made useful comments on an earlier draft, for which I also express gratitude. I, alone, am responsible for any remaining errors.
2. Authors disagree when the Ojibway migration occurred. Two authors state the groups migrated before Whites arrived (Blackbird 1887; Warren 1957), while an ethnohistorian has more recently opined that the migration occurred in the late sixteenth or early seventeenth century (Danziger 1978).
3. There were differences among the various Protestant denominations in the relative importance placed on agriculture and industrial expansion. Presbyterians, for example, placed more emphasis on the latter, while Methodists placed more emphasis on the former (Tyrell 1979). This distinction is not of importance for present purposes. However, it may have had some bearing on individual/group responses.

4. The boundary between Canada and the United States was not formalized until the Webster-Ashburton Treaty was ratified in 1841 (Bald 1961; Johnston nd). The fear of Britain did not subside until after 1860. The fear underlay the claim of United States control up to 54' 40° in 1848 (Dunbar 1970) and was present on the eve of the Civil War: In 1861, the United States Interpreter wrote to the Commissioner of Indian Affairs:

> Mr Leach in his council with the Indians explained the policy of the Govt in the pending war and the relations of the Govt to the Indians [toward?] the same...They were entirely satisfied with his explanation and gave strong proofs of their loyalty. I have no hesitancy in saying that they are loyal, and the Department need have no apprehension of any trouble from that quarter (Ashneur October 17, 1861).

Nonetheless, six companies of soldiers were dispatched to the Upper Peninsula the following year because rumor held the Indians were to stage a revolt (Armstrong 1892).

Some authors have stated the danger was more imaginary than real (McClurken 1986; Calloway 1986). Whether material or not, the rhetoric helped shape United States foreign policy and lasted until the early 1860s (Helms 1975; LaFeber 1983). By then, the United States had attained an economic base so strong it vied with Britain for first place in the world (Rossiter 1971) and the fear of foreign intervention could no longer be justified--at least in the Northwest Territory.

5. The hatred toward Catholics was so intense that the Know-Nothing Party, established in the 1850s, had anti-Catholicism as its primary political plank (Anderson 1970).

6. I use the term `Mixed-Blood' to designate those individuals who shared Ojibway and White heritage. I capitalize it, as I do the terms White and Indian, to emphasize these are proper nouns.

7. In the interim, Michigan became the nation's 26th state and the Methodist Episcopal Church assumed control of the mission. As an indication of the demotion of Mixed-bloods, the missionaries appointed to the Methodist mission were Whites. No Native American filled the post of principal missionary in the community from then until at least 1881.

8. His death was attributed to sorcery by one of the medicine-men who had recently converted to Methodism (Brown March 9, 1843). The Methodist missionary intervened and saved the medicine man's life (Ibid.). Undoubtedly, the allegations of witchcraft and the missionary's intervention increased the social distance between the two groups.

9. The *reducción* in Latin America had two goals: to convert the Indians to Catholicism and to provide the Spaniards with a ready source of labor (MacLeod 1973). There is no evidence that Baraga intended to adopt the second objective in his program.

10. These terms are heuristic devices only that highlight specific features of the groups. With the possible exception of the Mixed-bloods, there is no indication

that the members of these groups regarded themselves in these terms. The term "Conservative" highlights those individuals who were more traditional in their cultural patterns than were the "Progressives." The latter group emphasized their ties to the White society and economy.

11. I read of one case in which an Indian woman asserted herself and became the wife to a particular trader (Armstrong 1892). However, Armstrong also states that her behavior astonished both the trader and the other Indians (Ibid.), suggesting that her action was anomalous.

12. The argument that the schism occurred due to social and economic considerations rather than religious is obviated by the frequent reports that doctrine had little, if any, importance to the Ojibway. Reports of individuals who crossed from one community to the other lends support to this interpretation (Adams 1988 Chapter IV). However, both missionaries had a role in the economic lives of the Ojibway because they offered them goods and services not available through the trader (Adams 1988; Siskind 1977).

13. There were exceptions to this general trend. For example, Wabanoo was a Full-blood (Walker December 29, 1829), but he had the second highest debt.

Chapter 14

Sacraments, Society, and Women

Mary Douglas

The sacraments raise controversy at every turn, no matter which one of the seven we think of. There is no end to hot debate on pastoral issues. For example, why has Penance taken a back seat of late? Is it because we sin less? Or do we have less sense of sin? If so, why should it be so? Or are we more forgiving and therefore take it for granted that God is more forgiving? As to the Eucharist, why cannot any one receive communion whether they are baptized Catholics or believing Christians or outright pagans? Would it not do them good, whatever their condition? Does Marriage really matter? Why does Ordination rule out Marriage? How often can the Last Sacrament be given? Why is Ordination the only gender-exclusive sacrament? I have left out Confirmation and Baptism, but we can ask why the Catholic Church institutes seven sacraments, while some Christian congregations just have Baptism, and others, Baptism and Confirmation, and some take everything in the world to be a potential sacrament?

I want to take the last two questions together, women priests (why not?) and the seven instituted channels of grace (why seven?), together with the claim of the Church to be universal. Universal means standing above local bias, resisting temporary pressures, recognizing a passing fashion for what it is, and thus standing for permanent truths for all times and places. The universal Church is old, but not a fossil, she must develop; truth is revealed gradually, the doctrines have to be unfolded. I understand that the work of the Holy Spirit is to safeguard doctrine and practice.

The professional anthropologist has to turn these questions into ones about the organization of religions in general. At the turn of the century comparative religions took a new turn at the hands of French scholars at the Sorbonne who were looking for a formula to explain the meaning of sacrifice in Hinduism, Judaism and Christianity (Levy, Mauss, Hubert, Loisy). Expanding the scholastic distinction between two worlds, one of natural events and the other of the supernatural, they developed what we can call the lightning conductor theory of sacrifice, which adapts quite well to sacraments in general. On this theory the profane world of human activity is distinct and separate from a sacred world invested with tremendous powers. On the one hand the Sacred is dangerous, its powers can be unleashed for untold destruction, on the other its powers are beneficent, and humans cannot do without harnessing them to their purposes. This two-way mediation between World 1 and World 2 is the object of religious organization. Apollo carries a quiver full of plague-bearing arrows. Jupiter is equipped with thunderbolts, the God of *The Bible* wields flood and fire and plague; the chastisement from World 2 strike the denizens of World 1 when they misbehave; the cult fends off the dangers and protects the innocent. This is what the equivalents of sacraments do in all religions. Calamity is warded off, good health and good harvests, regular seasons, prosperous times, these are channeled by sacrifices, blessing and other cultic rituals.

Nowadays we have no trouble in believing in the dangers all right, flood, famine, fire and earthquake are all around, but we are much less impressed by the power of cult to ward them off. The disbelief may be due to secularism, or to the coming together of different cultures. I suggest it is also due to a new way of life introduced and encouraged by advanced capitalist industrialism. We have been sucked away from our local origins; our primordial ties of family and township have weaker claims. We are on our own, no community umbrella is offering to shelter us; no one is trying to make us conform to community standards, or are we ourselves trying to make a community cohere around ourselves or persuading anyone else that their moral code needs tightening up. On the contrary, we are bending over backwards to be tolerant. In other words, there is no scope for us to warn each other against thunderbolts or plagues sent from heaven to punish our misconduct. Punishing is illiberal. The old tie between conduct and nature depends on a self-conscious, punishing community, and once that is dispersed, the lightning conductor model of divine intervention makes no sense. This is what the theologians have to consider. The sacraments are not justified by their making a channel between World 1 and World 2, because those sacred and profane worlds are not so distant as they used lo be, nor is the sacred so powerful; they are both lodged in the consciousness of the believer for whom the sacrament is a solace more than a protection. When the Church of Rome is asked to make an apparently minor adjustment to modern times, in respect of admission to communion, or confession, or ordination, this is the context. Will the change make it easier to dissolve the ties of community? And would that be a good thing? The meaning of the sacraments depends on the form of the social life that is being lived. I do not think that anyone nowadays would seriously argue that the meanings are in words and ritual actions and have nothing to do with the institutional background. The feminist critics of Rome have rightly drawn attention to constitutional problems. To support their case I need to say more about the forms of social organization in which religious ideas are fostered, for I believe it is by rearranging constitutions that problems such as that of the exclusion and subordination of women can be resolved.

The Missing Place for Women in a Hierarchical Community

The complaint is that the Catholic hierarchy is male, and there is no place for women in it. Polite verbal expressions of esteem for women are not relevant, and if the Church of Rome is hierarchical it would be irrelevant to mention that individual women have played important parts. Individuals as such do not figure in hierarchical constitutions. It is inconsistent to point to Hildegard and Teresa and other famous influential women without saying what supposing institutions they could rely on at the time. There is a real crisis for the Church, a radical challenge as to how to honor women and give them a voice. I can understand that the feminists should think that some dismantling of hierarchy would help their cause, but I disagree. Hierarchy is a system of buffers and protected areas, if they are dismantled the women are in the same case as they were before, but exposed to unbridled competition. The world of the individualist is much harsher on the weak, and by definition, women will be relatively weak in it so long as it is normal for most of them to be pregnant, to give birth, and to nurse and rear infants. For the same kind of reasons I do not think that ordaining women as priests will improve their general condition. Even if they were to take over the whole priesthood and feminize its organization, the men would be complaining of oppression. The situation could go on being very fraught.

My own idea is more radical. We, the women, should look carefully at the reasons given for rejecting ordinations of women. When we do this, we find the defense of hierarchy is a paramount concern. That being so, we are merely setting off the alarms by demanding equality. Instead we should see whether we cannot do better for ourselves by asking for a higher quality of hierarchy. There are many different kinds, and hierarchies tend to fall into traps of their own making. The worst for a Church is the trap of setting up a monolithic top-down command.

When we read the 1976 Declaration on the Ordination of Women (*Inter Insigniores*) we see that the authorities are much attached to the gender symbolism by which God is presented as masculine, and the Church herself as feminine. The three main arguments of the 1976 Declaration against the ordination of women were:

i) respect for the ancient traditions of the nuptial mystery. Christ as the Heavenly Bridegroom, the Church as the Bride.

ii) the idea of the 'natural sign':the teaching must be based on signs which are readily interpretable. The idea of biological procreation and the union between male and female are signs of God's intimate and loving relation to his Church. A man is an exemplar of masculinity which enables the priest to represent Christ in the mystery of God-made-man.

iii) the nuptial mystery is the way the Church has always seen her own identity. This links her identity with the Israel as the Bride of God. Israel was feminine, the Church is feminine, therefore the priest representing Christ has to be masculine. Their gender precludes women from being ordained.

The theme of the nuptial mystery is evidently a major myth, and it would be a mistake to argue with its details. Anthropologists would never ask for a myth to be tested against any facts at all: first, it is impolite, and second it is unproductive. If a myth claims to have continuity with *The Bible* it is pointless to show discontinuity. Never mind that the idea of the Church as the Bride of Christ was favored by the medieval Church. Never mind that

Israel in *The Bible* was continuously denounced by the prophets, as an unfaithful bride (Jer. 3.12, 14.22; 23.37; 3.18-20;31; Isa. 42-43;51; 65-66; Hosea 14). Admittedly this is not the advertised model, the Church as the spotless bride of Christ is represented by the Virgin Mary, but Israel is portrayed as a fallen woman, always about to fall again, and continually being forgiven by her Lord. And never mind the subversive claim that Magdalene gives better *New Testament* continuity with Israel than Mary. The time has come to be constructive.

As to the facts of sexual reproduction, we would not deny that the female role is to receive the seed and the male role to give it, we only need to know what these selected facts are doing in the argument. When we know that, we can use the myth for our own purpose.

The essential is that the universe in this myth is gendered: World 1 is female, World 2 is male. This is very commonly found in non-western religions, but not necessarily with the effect of relegating the feminine gender to the humblest position. Nor is it necessary for the gender assignments to be fixed to biological sex: masculine can change places with feminine, according to context. For anyone who is unfamiliar with this way of thinking, I strongly recommend Marilyn Strathern's book, *The Gender of the Gift* (1988) for an account of the dilemmas of postmodern feminist politics and her astute strategies for writing a book about relativising that escapes being relativised. The Papuan people she describes use gender as their main organizing principle, but she explains that this does not involve exploiting the female sex. According to their local theory the person is composed of multiple gendered parts which come to the fore or retreat into the background according to the stage of interaction. In every exchange the donors are male, the recipients female and in every exchange a person has to be engaged first as a same sex actor, but sometimes the mobilization is initiated in the male and sometimes in the female mode. In this case it is absurd to talk about gender as if it was only about the relations between men and women.

We could be creative in using some such strategy for ourselves. 'Come on! Gender is only a mode of comportment, a convention, that is all', we might say, were it not for the attachment expressed in *Inter Insigniores* to the idea of procreation as a natural sign. This is a myth in a different sense of the word, not a narrative to live by, but a wrong idea, a fallacy. We have to say bluntly that there is no such thing as a natural sign. It is an oxymoron, because the idea of nature is a cultural artifact. No sign conveys the same meaning to all peoples at all times, and any sign can convey many different meanings at any time. Signs are open; they only get a closed and stable meaning from the way they are institutionalized. The stabilizing of the sign and the stabilizing of the institutions are one interaction. But when all this is said and done, it has to be admitted that procreation comes near to the ideal of an eminently universal natural sign, which everyone can understand. Instead of caviling, we have to attend to what this natural sign is being used for. The Church is saying that she has long seen herself as a gendered hierarchy, that this is an essential part of her identity. The task for the women seeking to reform the Church in their own regard is to make use of the myths of gender, of natural sign, and, and of hierarchy, to achieve their ends.

Hierarchy and Sect

A comparison of forms of organization is essential to our topic, since the Women's Movement in the Church has complained bitterly against the blindness and constraints of hierarchy. To develop my thesis that hierarchy is not the enemy I revert to my favorite scheme (Douglas 1970) which compares four kinds of viable social organizations. They are extreme types:

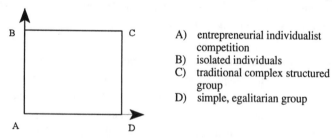

A) entrepreneurial individualist competition
B) isolated individuals
C) traditional complex structured group
D) simple, egalitarian group

Figure 6. Structure

One dimension gives structure, the other gives corporate inclusiveness. The scheme can be used to compare business organization, or academic, or professional, or types of farming community, and the extreme positions renamed according to context. For comparing religions we can rename them thus:

A) charismatic radio evangelist,
B) the private religion of the lone,
C) the hierarchy of the Catholic Church,
D) sectarian groups.

We can leave A) and B) out of what follows, because in a social environment of individualists there is not much interest in permanently instituted sacraments. Their religions generally take them to God without intermediary institutions. The contrast we shall examine between the two kinds of communitarian religions, the complex, traditionalist, highly structured organization of the Church of Rome or the Church of England, and any egalitarian dissenting Christian minority group or sect. What I am going to say is highly speculative, because, to my own chagrin, not much comparison of doctrines has been made along these lines.

First a caveat: each of these contrasted forms of religious organization is valuable. No outsider can use this scheme to say that one is right or the other wrong. What we will surely find that the adherents are deeply convinced that their form is the only right way to God. We will also find that in their history each of the extreme opposed types wobbles in its loyalty to its principles: the sect can find itself becoming hierarchical and the hierarchy can become quite sectarian. The Catholic Church behaves quite differently when it is well-established and not in fear of losing its young to other faiths, than it does when it is a dissident minority. Richard Griffith's (1966) account of French Catholicism at the turn of this century gives a painful picture of a sectarian religion fighting a losing battle against secularism, heroic, violent and absolutist. The comparison has to be careful. Each has its strengths, which make it specially fit for survival in specified conditions, and each has its weaknesses which may bring about its downfall.

The hierarchy tends to spring up spontaneously whenever people come together to organize some task that needs coordination. It does not necessarily have to subscribe to a particular set of ideals. It develops specialized roles, makes rules for sequencing, spacing, canonizing, and in the course of the work, ideals take hold of order, balance, symmetry and the integrity of the whole task. The sect also tends to spring up spontaneously, but it starts the other way round, with principles. A community develops around its ideals, which tend to dissent. It espouses equality in defiance of the stratified hierarchical community; simplicity, in rebuking the alleged artificiality and complexity of the hierarchy; sharing, in contrast to individual profit seeking in the individualist culture. And in being true to these principles, it develops a characteristic form of organization. If both are present in any community they play contrapuntal roles, the sect attacking the hierarchy for its inequities and pomp, the hierarchy fearing the sect's subversive influence. Such a community may be fortunate in that the dialogue of opposed cultures takes the usual normative debate to a high moral and religious plane; the debate polarizes ideals and each culture, by attacking the other, articulates its own identity and principles. We shall take them in turn, but what I will say below is highly speculative, because the comparative research on styles of thought and behavior as between sects and hierarchies, which I ought to have put in hand twenty five years ago, has not been done. Among the strengths of hierarchy are effective delegation and mobilization. Everyone has an assigned place, in a crisis every one knows what to do, (and no one has an identity crisis). Within any of the constituent units everyone knows their place and ambiguity is reduced to a minimum; but most hierarchies normally have multiple peaks of authority, and between the peaking subsystems there is ambiguity. Ingenious formulae are found for preventing conflict what is lower in one context, becomes higher in the other. Pope Gelasius in the fifth century had a formula for the mutual respect between the separate and balanced spheres of Pope and Emperor, the *auctoritaa* of the priest, and the *potestas* of the king (Dumont 1983:52). Something of the kind is spontaneously repeated in many multi-peaking forms of hierarchy. For example, the relation of wife to husband is expressed in demarcation of spheres, the same for the King and Commons, territorial chief and lineage chief: when the context shifts the precedence rules change. We can hardly insist too much that this experience of hierarchy is different from the common idea of hierarchy as a linear top-down command system (monolithic like General Motors was once supposed to be). At the end of this essay we shall raise it again, because the question of what the Church should be doing about its women has been blurred by a false idea of how hierarchies have worked in ancient civilizations (Douglas 1993).

The hierarchy is geared to the long view; it expects to reproduce itself for ever, and the expectation of stability is self-fulfilling. It has a vested interest in its traditions, and is a vehicle for their conservation. It has effective co-optative powers, it can absorb and contain diverse elements without splitting apart. Either it sets up rank orderings, or separate compartments and buffer zones. You remember the story about St. Peter taking a party of newly arrived Non-conformists on a guided tour of Heaven; in room after room they cheer and clap, exclaiming with delight at what they see; one door, however, he does not open and beseeches them to go by on tiptoe, making no noise; after they have got past, Peter explains:'that room is for the Catholics. They think they are the only ones here, and we don't like to tell them." A typical maneuver for a hierarchy.

Another hierarchical trick is to divide all members of the community into two or more responsible associations. For example, a man in some contexts is a member of his mother's group, in others of his father's, so that each person is linked to others in crosscutting ways, no one loyalty can absorb the others; or territory and lineage may be counterpoised affiliations. In several parts of Africa gender classification does this work of balancing the community. Everyone has two alignments, so that if strife breaks out, cross-pressures prevent an irreconcilable split.

There are many other features of hierarchy but the one I must take care to mention is that, as an upshot of the separating, ranking and balancing processes, the diversity of social life is fully articulated. Though there are words for the various positions, there is little need to spell out verbally what is happening: specific allocations in space indicate social place and sequencing; dress, gesture and body movement acknowledge it without verbalizing. Ritual choreographs each person's part in the ongoing cycle of generations. The insides of their minds are partitioned and furnished for the roles assigned to them in the cosmic drama. An articulated social system means an articulated mind set. The hierarchism is used to complexity, logical and practical, and experienced in playing around with patterns and positions.

The disadvantages of hierarchies are well-known. They can mobilize, but only slowly. They fall into the bureaucratic traps, over-formalization, routinization, emotional aridity and frustration. Their biggest danger stems from their habit of trying to control knowledge. New knowledge is an immediate threat to the carefully built complexity of the hierarchical system; the work of assimilating it is onerous; only too easy is the other solution, to apply censorship. The hierarchy always risks a danger that it has censored its essential information. While it is monitoring the maze-like warrens of its internal relations, the outside world may change so much that some essential supplies are cut or enemies make a surprise attack.

The sect is smaller. I start with its disadvantages so as to explain why it is difficult for it to encompass a large populations. Sects that seem in the course of history to have acted as aggressive imperialists, if they have lasted beyond the death of their founder, have generally modified their organization towards hierarchical structures. I have described the weaknesses of enclaves in *How Institutions Think* (Douglas 1986). The position of a dissenting minority group is essentially weak. There is reason to worry about losing members as some will always be tempted to defect to the larger, richer, established institutions, and there is no effective way of stopping the leak. Weak leadership follows on the difficulty of maintaining the boundary against the outside world, and the ever lively fear of defection. An egalitarian commitment is a response to the double effect of weak leadership and ineffectual boundary maintenance, a tactic to restrain free-riding as well as a principle. The organizational difficulties of egalitarian communities are compensated by a doctrinal focus on the evils of the outside world, meaning especially the hierarchies and the culture of entrepreneurial individualism. Given these difficulties, the sect is a fragile organizational form. Faced with threatened schism it tends to split. Sometimes this is turned to strength as when the parent group maintains good relations with the newly formed one. Confronted by ambitious leaders who would deny its ideals, the sect's main resource is to expel them; they cannot be demoted or punished, there is no upstairs or downstairs for them to be kicked to. The sect can look to eternity, but not plan for the long term. It is good at mobilizing a rush to the barricades, but bad at coordinating complex roles. It can muster for attack, but not for settled administrative cadres. Delegation is difficult. Ambiguity in personal relations has to be tolerated, but not ambiguous intellectual positions. The biggest disadvantage is the tendency to simplify divergent views and reduce disagreement to nonnegotiable black and white, right and wrong. The advantage of the sectarian enclave is its passionate devotion to equality. The ideal of equality is much more difficult to actualize in internal relations than is normally supposed. At every point of social life what we can call natural inequalities of endowments emerge, or initial first-comer advantages are there to be built upon, cornering a source of privilege can be too tempting. Equality requires constant vigilance if it is to be maintained over time (see Rayner, "The rules that make us equal" 1988). On the other hand, equality, as a rallying cry against the outside, has the power and appeal of simplicity. This gives the attack on hierarchy a strong cutting edge. The sect is the conscience of the community; powerless, it denounces the destructive quest for power; leaderless, it accuses the self-seeking of leaders; egalitarian, it inveighs against inequality.

When it comes to debating on matters of conscience, the two cultures have opposite styles. The hierarchism is good at splitting logical hairs and used to looking for compromise solutions. Hierarchical policy aims to keep everyone together, to maintain the integrity of the whole. If a schism threatens, the contenders are expected to find a *modus vivendi*, and logic will be engaged to invent a conciliating formula. Do not underestimate hierarchy's role in the development of doctrine: the doctrine of the Trinity is one such formula, "Consubstantial with the Father" is another, also the doctrines on the resurrection of the body, the virgin birth of Jesus, miracles, purgatory, the sacraments, or the role of Mary. Catholic doctrine as we have it now bears witness to the hierarchical bent for argumentation and a cumulative, incorporative style of thought. The doctrinal preferences of the sect are simpler, given its liking for simplicity in all things, its affection for the primitive Church, its dislike of artificiality. The sect is short on administrative infrastructure, it has not got the institutional support to sustain a complex argument; negotiation is not its forte; it is not interested in resolving doctrinal disagreements with complex compromises and paradoxical formulae which fudge the strong certainties of black and white.

If you accept these contrasting pictures of the two forms of organization, you will see why a hierarchical church should have seven sacraments. Rather it is surprising that Catholicism has not instituted seven more. And you can see why the Church authorities are dubious about reducing their hierarchical distinctions. It is not just traditions that are at stake.

Doctrine as a Way of Life

There is another issue. If we respect a religious institution, we cannot dismiss out of hand its claim to honor its continuity with its own past. The scholars at the Vatican see an element of betrayal in going back on what has been decided by their deceased predecessors. Any community has a certain way of perceiving its own historic identity. Telling its members to forget their common past and make new myths of present reality is the same as telling them to get lost, die off and disappear. You can do this if you basically dislike the institutions, but it would be easier to leave it. We can now return to the sacraments and the ordination of women. How can the Church keep the sacraments, all seven of them? How can she keep to her elaborated doctrines which testify to the intellectual tradition of argument and compromise? How can she keep the capability to renew herself without dissolving into fragments? For all this I believe she needs to keep her hierarchical conception of herself and of the world.

She is in charge of a truth. Some would maintain that the truth is held in a form of words. But I would demur. How can that be? The words themselves only make their sense in the institutions in which they are used? Can the charge to preserve the truth be performed by simply conserving and handing on the words? Are doctrines words? Or are they a way of life? We can take the spectrum of Christian Churches, and find in them all the possible ways of being organized, each form of life demonstrating a different way of meaning what is said.

When the Church holds on to a hierarchical conception, she might be saying that the organization is the message. In holding to the hierarchical ideal for herself, she is not necessarily saying that no other forms of organization are good and right. It could be that the worship of God is not complete without the whole spectrum of enacted ideas. It could also be that the others, the non-hierarchical ideas, need at least one extreme form of hierarchy for realizing their own identity of dissent. If they were all to got the same way, Catholic Church with the others, towards sectarian and individualist forms of religion, there would be a loss of dialogue and a loss of meaning.

The Catholic Church may be saying that her calling is to exemplify hierarchy and so to enshrine a certain message that can only be expressed in that form. Such a view would be a rather advanced position in semeiotics and epistemology. What, in that case, would the message be? What can the hierarchy do that the other forms of religion cannot? Perhaps the message is something about articulating a form of thought in a form of organization. Or perhaps about a machinery for self-renewal and survival, which is more difficult without an experience of complexity. Or something about reconciling opposed views. It would not be a matter of blindly holding on to the past. We run the risk to a certain extent of losing the capability for dealing with new problems. There's no chance that an egalitarian way of organizing would preserve that capability. Were it to be lost, the Church leaders could reasonably fear that what has been lost will be dissipated. The Church of the future could become more factious, more angry against backsliders, more convinced of sin, more intransigent, to the point of violence. The Church extols hierarchy. Sects deride it. When neither can go forward or back they must look for a way out. It needs to be thought out more carefully than I am in a position to do. I suggest a permanent commission on doctrine, empowered by the Pope, elected by a female franchise, for a term to be decided, according to qualifications to be decided. The Women's Commission on Doctrine should have real authority. Should they express doubts about a teaching on faith, morals or administrative and disciplinary matters, it would have to be taken seriously: the suspect ruling would have to be sent back to source and rethought, and it could not pass into practice without the agreement of the Women's Commission once they have queried it. I am not sure whether the women should have a special field of concern, such as matters affecting gender and procreation, or whether they should not be free lo initiate enquiries on anything that they find worrying, and take up questions and complaints from the laity worldwide. Above all, and perhaps the ma n thing, the Women's Commission should be seen to be effective. Perhaps they should be equipped with sanctions? I am told that one of the reasons why the women's wish to be ordained can be safely disregarded by Rome is that there is so much heavy Third World Catholic opinion against it. These will be societies which are used to hierarchy and to gendered organization in their own traditional lands, and which see with dismay the current trend to market individualism. Many of them would take to the idea of a high-powered Women's Commission, because of their experience of similar gender-balancing institutions. The demand for a powerful, fully accredited Women's Commission would call the hierarchical bluff. Agreeing to a Women's Commission on Doctrine would prove Rome's commitment to her own arguments against ordaining women, (natural signs, procreation as the model of God-to-people, the nuptial mystery, and continuity with the Old Testament). It would help the existing hierarchy to look to the quality of their present arrangements and to worry about their present tendency to operate a top-down command system. There is at present not lateral balance to check abuse of authority. It would be a way to institute countervailing powers by which information could come to the top from the bottom and the sides. At present it is only too easy to tell the women that they can never be priests, and not wait for a reply.

It would call the gender bluff. Rome says that the Church is a gendered institution, this is at the heart of her identity. Right! say the women, we like that idea, but when will you introduce gender as a principle of organization? It would call the bluff on natural signs. Right! say the women, procreation is fine as the model for the organization of men and women in the Church; we understand it very well, every one knows it takes two to procreate. When will the natural sign be serious, not just a form of words? In the strategy of debate, this suggestion would pull rugs out from under episcopal feet. How could the bishops object?

Bibliography

Adams, James L. 1976. *On Being Human Religiously*. Boston: Beacon Press.

Adams, Walter R. 1988. Fission, Maintenance, and Interaction in an Anishinabe Community on Keweenaw Bay, Michigan, 1832-1881. Ph.D. Dissertation. East Lansing: Michigan State University.

------. 1994. Sifting Through the Trash. In *Becoming Unbecoming, Unbecoming Becoming*, ed. Myrdene Anderson and Walter R. Adams, 63-87. American Journal of Semiotics, vol. 11 (1996).

------. 1995. Guatemala. In *International Handbook on Alcohol and Culture*, ed. Dwight B. Heath, 99-109. Westport: Greenwood Press.

Adewale, S.A. 1988. *The African Church, 1901-1986: A Synthesis of Religion and Culture*. Ibadan: Oluseyi Press, Ltd.

Aguirre Beltran, Gonzalo. 1967. *Regiones de refugio: El desarrollo de la comunidad y el proceso dominical en mestizo América*. Mexico City: Instituto Indigenista Interamericano.

Ajayi, J.F.A. 1965. *Christian Mission in Nigeria: 1841-1891*. London: Longmans.

Albanese, Catherine, L. 1988. Religion and the American Experience: A Century After. *Church History* 57 (3):337-51.

Allen, Paula G. 1986. *The Sacred Hoop: Recovering the Feminine in American Religious Traditions*. Boston: Beacon Press.

Anderson, Charles H. 1970. *White Protestant Americans: From National Origins to Religious Group*. Englewood Cliffs: Prentice-Hall, Inc.

Angrosino, Michael V. 1994. The Culture Concept and the Mission of the Roman Catholic Church. *American Anthropologist* 96 (4):824-33.

Annis, Sheldon. 1987. *God and Production in a Guatemalan Town*. Austin: University of Texas Press.

Anzaldua, Gloria (ed). 1990. *Making Face, Making Soul: Creative and Critical Perspectives by Women of Color*. San Francisco: Aunt Lute Foundation.

Armstrong, Benjamin G. 1892. *Early Life Among the Indians...* Ashland: W.W. Bowron.

Ashneur, Edward. 1861. letter to Commissioner of Indian Affairs, Frame 1071. NAM M234, no. Reel 406. Michigan State University, October 17.

Assinins, Edward. 1875. letter to E.P. Smith, Frames 279-80. NAM M234, no. Reel 411. Michigan State University, October 28.

Aveni, Anthony F. 1992. *Conversing with the Planets: How Science and Myth Invented the Cosmos*. New York: Kodansha International.

Ayandele, E.A. 1966. *The Impact of Christian Mission on Modern Nigeria.* London: Longmans.

Balandier, Georges. 1965. Messianism and Nationalism in Black Africa. In *Africa: Social Problems of Changes and Conflict*, ed. Pierre van den Berghe, 443-60. New York: Chandler.

------. 1970. *The Sociology of Black Africa: Social Dynamics in Central Africa.* Trans. D. German. New York: Praeger.

Bald, Frederick C. 1961. *Michigan in Four Centuries.* Revised and expanded. New York: Harper and Row.

Baraga, Frederic, Rev. 1844. letter to Robert Stuart, Frames 125-28. NAM M1, no. Reel 56. Michigan State University, May 20.

------. 1849. letter to William A. Richmond, Frames 81-82. NAM M1, no. Reel 61. Michigan State University, March 22.

Barnet, Richard J. 1995. *The Global War Against the Poor.* Washington, D.C.: Servant Leadership Press.

Barrett, David B. 1982. Mexico. In *World Christian Encyclopedia: A Comparative Study of Churches and Religions in the Modern World, A.D. 1900-2000*, ed. David B. Barrett. Nairobi: Oxford University Press.

Bast, William. 1956. *James Dean: A Biography.* New York: Ballantine Books.

Bastian, Jean-Pierre. 1985. Dissidence religieuse dans le milieu rural mexicain. *Social Compass* 32 (2-3):245-60.

------. 1992a. Les protestantismes latino-américains: Un objet à interroger et à construire. *Social Compass* 39 (3):327-54.

------. 1992b. La fonction sociale et politique des hétérodoxies religieuses en Amérique Latine. *Social Compass* 39 (4):543-51.

Bauer, H. 1988. *Utopia in the Desert.* Albany: State University of New York Press.

Bauers, S. 1992. Seasonal Adjustments. *The Philadephia Inquirer*, December 9, F1, F4.

Beals, Ralph L., Harry Hoijer, and Alan R. Beals. 1977. *An Introduction to Anthropology.* Fifth edition. New Yorki: Macmillan.

Beattie, John. 1964. *Other Cultures: Aims, Methods and Achievements in Social Anthropology.* New York: Free Press.

Beck, Peggy, Anna L. Walters, and Nia Francisco. 1977. *The Sacred: Ways of Knowledge, Ways of Life.* Tsaile: Navajo Community College Press.

Bednarowski, Mary F. 1989. *New Age Religions and the Theological Imagination in America.* Bloomington: Indiana University Press.

------. 1992. The New Age Movement and Feminist Spirituality: Overlapping Conversations at the End of the Century. In *Perspectives on the New Age*, ed. James R. Lewis and J. Gordon Melton. Albany: State University of New York Press.

------. 1993. Widening the Banks of the Mainstream: Women Constructing Theologies. In *Women's Leadership in Marginal Religions:*

Explorations Outside the Mainstream, ed. Catherine Wessinger, 211-31. Urbana: University of Illinois Press.

------. 1994. personal communication to M. Jean Heriot, November 19.

Belenky, Mary F., Blythe M. Clinchy, Nancy R. Goldberger, and Jill M. Tarule. 1986. *Women's Ways of Knowing: The Development of Self, Voice, and Mind*. New York: Basic Books.

Bellah, Robert N., Richard Madsen, William M. Sullivan, Ann Swidler, and Steven M. Tipton. 1985. *Habits of the Heart: Individualism and Commitment in American Life*. Berkeley: University of California Press.

Betts, George I. 1875. letter to Edward P. Smith, Frame 320. NAM M234, no. Reel 411. Michigan State University, March 2.

------. 1875. letter to Edward P. Smith, Frame 333. NAM M234, no. Reel 411. Michigan State University, March 29.

Billingsley, Andrew. 1992. *Climbing Jacob's Ladder: The Enduring Legacy of African American Family*. New York: Simon and Schuster.

Bishop, Charles A. 1974. *The Northern Ojibwa and the Fur Trade: An Historical and Ecological Study*. Toronto: Holt, Rinehart, and Winston of Canada, Ltd.

Blackbird, Andrew J. 1887. *History of the Ottawa and Chippewa Indians of Michigan.*. Ypsilanti: Ypsilanti Job Printing House.

Blackwell, James E. 1975. *The Black Community: Diversity and Unity*. New York: Harper and Row.

Bloomfield, Morton W. 1967. *The Seven Deadly Sins: An Introduction to the History of a Religious Concept, with Special Reference to Medieval English Literature*. East Lansing: Michigan State University Press.

Blum, William G. 1989. *Forms of Marriage: Monogamy Reconsidered*. Nairobi: Ameea Gaba Publications.

Bohannan, Paul. 1985. *All the Happy Families*. New York: McGraw Hill.

Bolen, Jean S. 1984. *Goddesses in Everywoman*. San Francisco: Harper and Row.

------. 1992. *Can Women Re-Image the Church*. New York: Paulist Press.

Bovee, Tim. 1992. Black Women Found Less Likely to Marry. *The Philadelphia Inquirer*, December 9, A3.

Boxberger, Daniel L. 1988. In and Out of the Labor Force: The Lummi Indians and the Development of the Commercial Salmon Fishery of North Puget Sound, 1880-1900. *Ethnohistory* 35 (2):160-90.

Bradley, Martha. 1993. *Kidnapped From That Land*. Salt Lake City: University of Utah PressBrigham Young University Press.

Brady, Ivan (ed.). 1991. *Anthropological Poetics*. Savage: Rowman and Littlefield.

Brady, Ivan, and Edith Turner (eds.). 1994. Special Issue: Humanism and Anthropology. *Humanism and Anthropology* 19 (1).

Briggs, Jean L. 1970. *Never in Anger: Portrait of an Eskimo Family*. Cambridge: Harvard University Press.

Bross, Rene. 1988. El hombre, su fe, su cultura, su religión. *La Iglesia en Amazonas* 42-43:89-95.

Brown, George W., Rev. 1843. letter to Robert Stuart, Frames 679-92. NAM M1, no. Reel 55. Michigan State University, December 29.

------. 1843. letter to Robert Stuart, Frames 205-06. NAM M1, no. Reel 54. Michigan State University, March 9.

Brujo, Benezer. 1992. *African Theology in Its Social Context.* Trans. John O'Donohue. Maryknoll: Orbis Press.

Bruner, Karen. 1993. Mystery Deaths in Brazil. *The Christian Science Monitor,* August 31, 6.

Buijtenhjs, R. 1984. Dini ya Msambwa: Rural Rebellion on Counter Society. In *Theoretical Exploratory in African Religion,* ed. W.M.J. van Bisnbergen and Matthew Schoffeleers. London: Kegan Paul International.

Burkhart, Louise M. 1989. *The Slippery Earth: Nahua-Christian Moral Dialogue in Sixteenth Century Mexico.* Tucson: The University of Arizona Press.

Burridge, Kenelm. 1991. *In the Way: A Study of Christian Missionary Endeavors.* Vancouver: University of British Columbia Press.

Calloway, Colin G. 1986. The End of an Era: British - Indian Relations in the Great Lakes Region After the War of 1812. *Michigan Historical Review* 12 (Fall):1-20.

Cancian, Frank. 1967. Political and Religious Organizations. In *Social Anthropology,* ed. Robert Wauchope, 283-98. Handbook of Middle American Indians, vol. 6. Austin: University of Texas.

Cannon, J. 1992. My Sister, My Wife: An Examination of Sororal Polygyny in a Contemporary Mormon Fundamentalist Sect. *Syzygy* 1 (4):315-20.

Cappelletti, E.J. 1994. Napoleon A. Chagnon's Column 'Covering Up the Yanomamo Massacre.' Letter to the Editor. *The New York Times,* January 18, A22.

Capps, Donald. 1989. *Deadly Sins and Saving Virtues.* Philadelphia: Fortress Press.

Cardozo, Jesus Ignacio. 1995. E-mail response to first draft of Salamone's mansucript (this volume).

Carrasco, Pedro. 1969. Central Mexican Highlands: Introduction. In *Ethnology, Part Two,* ed. Evon Z. Vogt, 579-601. Handbook of Middle American Indians, vol. 8. Austin: University of Texas Press.

Carrier, C.T. 1844. letter to Robert Stuart, Frames 601-04. NAM M1, no. Reel 55. Michigan State University, February 5.

Castañeda, Carlos. 1968. *The Teachings of Don Juan: A Yaqui Way of Knowledge.* New York: Pocket Books.

------. 1972. *Journey to Ixtalan: The Lessons of Don Juan.* New York: Washington Square Press.

Chagnon, Napoleon A. 1968. *Yanomamo: The Fierce People.* New York: Holt, Rinehart, and Winston.

------. 1983. *Yanomamo: The Fierce People*. Third edition. Fort Worth: Holt, Rinehart, and Winston.

------. 1988a. Life Histories, Blood Revenge, and Warfare in a Tribal Population. *Science*, February 26, 985-92.

------. 1993. Covering Up the Yanomamo Massacre. *The New York Times*, October 23, A13.

------. 1994. Letter to the Editor. *Interciencia* 19 (4):161-62.

------, Padre Jose Bortoli, and San Maria Isabel Eguillor. 1998b. Una aplicación antropologíca practica entre los Yanomami: Colaboración entre misioneros y antropólogos. *La Iglesia en Amazonas* 42-43:75-83.

Chance, John, and William Taylor. 1985. Cofradias and Cargos: An Historical Perspective on the Mesoamerican Civil-religious Hierarchy. *American Ethnologist* 12 (1):1-26.

Chaput, Daniel. 1970. Early Fur Traders on Keweenaw Bay. In *Baraga County Historical Pageant*, 20-22. Ishpeming: Globe Publishing.

Chinnici, Rosemary. 1992. *Can Women Re-Image the Church?* New York: Paulist Press.

Chomsky, Noam. 1981. Outline of the Theory of Core Grammar. In *Lectures on Government and Binding*, ed. Noam Chomsky, 1-16. Providence: Foris Publications.

Christ, Carol P., and Judith Plaskow. 1979. *Womenspirit Rising: A Feminist Reader in Religion*. New York: Harper and Row.

Clawson, David L. 1984. Religious Allegiance and Development in Rural Latin America. *Journal of Interamerican Studies and World Affairs* 26:499-524.

Cockburn, Alexander. 1991. The Bind That Ties. *Missionary Position*, October 14, 434-35.

Cohen, Eugene N., and Edwin Eames. 1982. *Cultural Anthropology*. Boston: Little, Brown.

Congar., Yves, O.P. 1987. Christian Theology. In *The Encyclopedia of Religion*, ed. Mircea Eliade, Charles J. Adams and et al, 455-64. New York: Macmillan.

Cooper-White, Pamela. 1995. *The Cry of Tamar: Violence Against Women and the Church's Response*. Minneapolis: Fortress Press.

Copway, George. 1851. *The Traditional History and Character of the Ojibway Nation*. Boston: Mussey and Co.

Cornell, George L. 1986. Ojibway. In *People of the Three Fires: The Ottawa, Potawatomi, and Ojibway of Michigan*, 75-108. Grand Rapids: Grand Rapids Inter-Tribal Council.

Coues, Elliott, ed. 1965. *The Manuscript Journals of Alexander Henry and David Thompson, 1799-1814. Vols. 1-II*. Minneapolis: Ross and Haines, Inc.

Cox, Harvey. 1991. Inculturation Reconsidered. *Christianity and Crisis*

51:140-42.

Crocker, J.C. 1982. Ceremonial Masks. In *Celebration: Studies in Festivity and Ritual*, ed. Victor Turner, 77-88. Washington, D.C.: Smithsonian Institution Press.

Crollius, Ary Roest, S.J. 1986. Inculturation: Newness and Ongoing Process. In *Inculturation: Its Meaning and Urgency*, ed. John Mary Walligo and David Giatri, 31-47. Kampala: St. Paul Publications.

Crooks, Ramsay. 1834. letter to Gabriel Franchere, Papers of the American Fur Company, Mss F-52. Clarke Historical Collection, no. Reel 3. Central Michigan University, October 20.

Crytser, Ann. 1990. *The Wife-in-Law Trap*. New York: Simon and Schuster.

Dalton, David. 1974. *James Dean: The Mutant King*. San Francisco: Straight Arrow Books.

Danziger, Edmund J., Jr. 1978. *The Chippewas of Lake Superior*. Norman: University of Oklahoma Press.

Deloria, Vine, Jr. 1992. *God is Red*. Second edition. Goden: North American Press.

Delumeau, Jean. 1990. *Sin and Fear: The Emergence of a Western Guilt Culture, 13th-18th Centuries*. New York: St. Martin's Press.

Desjarlais, Robert. 1992. *Body and Emotion: The Aesthetics of Illness and Healing in the Nepal Himalayas*. Philadelphia: University of Pennsylvania Press.

Diebold, A. Richard. 1964. Incipient Bilingualism. In *Language in Culture and Society: A Reader in Linguistics and Anthropology*, ed. Dell Hymes, 495-510. New York: Harper & Row, Publishers.

Dompier, J.R. 1969. Baraga Township Centennial--1869-1969: Captain James Bendry, Baraga's First Supervisor. In *First Annual Baraga County Historical Pageant*, 30-32. Ishpeming: Globe Publishing.

Donovan, Vincent J. 1982. *Christianity Rediscovered*. Maryknoll: Orbis Books.

Douglas, Mary. 1970. *Natural Symbols*. New York: Penguin.

------. 1986. *How Institutions Think*. Syracuse: Syracuse University Press.

------. 1987. The Debate on Women Priests. In *Essais sur le Rituel, Colloque du Centenaire de la Section des Sciences Religieuses*, ed. K. Scipper and A.M. Blondeau. Paris: Bibliotheque de L'Ecole des Hautes Etudes.

------. 1992. Hierarchie et voix des femmes. *Philosphie et Anthropologie. Paris, Espace International, Philosophie* 39:39-55.

------. 1993. *In the Wilderness*. Sheffield: Sheffield Academic Press.

------. 1995. The Gender of the Beloved. *Heythrop Journal* 36:397-408.

------, and Aaron Wildavsky. 1982. *Risk and Culture: An Essay on the Selection of Technical and Environmental Dangers*. Berkeley: University of California Press.

Dow, James A. 1974. *Santos y supervivencias: Funciones de la religión en una comunidad Otomi, México*. Mexico City: Instituto Nacional Indígenista y Secretaría de Edución Pública.

Dumont, Louis. 1970. *Homo Hierarchicus: The Caste System and Its Implications*. Chicago: University of Chicago Press.

------. 1983. *Essais sur l'Individualisme. Une perspective anthropologique sur l'ideologie moderne*. Paris: Editions du Seuil.

Dunbar, Willis F. 1970. *Lewis Cass*. Grand Rapids: William B. Eerdmans' Publishing Co.

Durkheim, Emile. 1915. *The Elementary Forms of Religious Life*. Trans. J.E. Swain. London: George Allen and Unwin, Ltd.

Earle, Duncan. 1992. Authority, Social Conflict and the Rise of Protestantism. *Social Compass* 39 (3):377-88.

Edgerton, Robert B. 1992. *Sick Societies: Challenging the Myth of Primitive Harmony*. New York: The Free Press.

Edmonson, Munro S. 1982. *The Ancient Future of the Itza: The Book of Chilam Balam of Tizimin*. Austin: University of Texas press.

Egan, Robert J. 1992. Who's Doing Catholic Theology? *Commonweal*, March 13, 13-19.

Eibel-Eibelsfeldt, I., and G. Herzog-Schroder. 1994. In Defense of Mission. unpublished manuscript.

------, and G. Herzog-Schroder. 1994. Letter to Bishop Ignacio Velasco, February 28.

Eisler, Riane. 1988. *The Chalice and the Blade: Our History, Our Future*. San Francisco: HarperSanFrancisco.

------, and David Loye. 1990. *The Partnership Way*. San Francisco: HarperSanFrancisco.

Eller, Cynthia. 1993a. *Living in the Lap of the Goddess: The Feminist Spirituality Movement in America*. New York: Crossroad.

------. 1993b. Twentieth Century Women's Religion as Seen in the Feminist Spirituality Movement. In *Women's Leadership in Marginal Religions: Explorations Outside the Mainstream*, ed. Catherine Wessinger, 172-95. Urbana: University of Illinois Press.

------. 1993c. Divine Objectification: The Representation of Goddesses and Women in Feminist Spirituality. Paper presented at the. annual meeting of the American Academy of Religion. Washington, D.C.

------. 1993d. New Religious Movements and Social Change: The Case of Feminist Spirituality. *Syzygy* 2:97-106.

Emerson, Dorothy M., (ed.). 1993. *Collegium: Association for Liberal Religious Studies*. Occasional Papers, vol. 2. Chicago.

Evans-Pritchard, E.E. 1958. Sin. Chapter in. In *Nuer Religion*, 177-96. Oxford: Clarendon Press.

------. 1963. Religion and the Anthropologists. Chapter in. In *Essays in Social Anthropology*, 29-45. New York: Free Press of Glencoe, Inc.

Ewing, Katherine P. 1994. Dreams from a Saint: Anthropological Atheism and the Temptation to Believe. *American Anthropologist* 96 (3):571-83.

Fadipe, Nathaniel A. 1970. *The Sociology of the Yoruba*. London: Ibadan

University Press.

Fairlei, Henry. 1979. *The Seven Deadly Sins Today.* Notre Dame: University of
    Notre Dame Press.

Fienup-Riordan, Ann. 1983. *The Nelson Island Eskimo: Social Structure and
    Ritual Distribution.* Anchorage: Alaska Pacific University Press.

Finkers, Jan. 1994. Antwoord Chagnon. *Don Bosco Nu* 53 (3):7-10.

Fischhoff, Baruch, Ssarah Lichtenstein, Paul Slovic, Stephen L. Derby, and Ralph
    L. Keeney. 1981. *Acceptable Risk.* Cambridge: Cambridge University
    Press.

Fisher, Elizabeth (ed.). 1994. *Rise Up and Call Her Name: A Woman-Honoring
    Journey Into Global Earth-Based Spiritualities.* Boston: Unitarian
    Universalist Women's Federation.

Flandrin, Jean-Louis, and Philip Hyman. 1986. Regional Tastes and Cuisines:
    Problems, Documents, and Discourses on Food in Southern France in
    the 16th and 17th Centuries. *Food and Foodways: Explorations in the
    History and Culture of Human Nourishment* Sample Issue:1-31.

Flora, Cornelia B. 1980. Pentecostalism and Development: The Colombian Case.
    In *Perspectives on Pentecostalism*, ed. Stephen D. Glazier. New York:
    University Press of America.

Fortes, Meyer. 1981. *Oedipus and Job in West African Religions.* New York:
    Octagon Press.

------. 1983. *Rules and the Emergence of Society.* London: Royal Anthropological
    Institute.

Foster, George M. 1972. The Anatomy of Envy: A Study in Symbolic Behavior.
    Current Anthropology 13:165-202.

Foster, Lawrence. 1991. *Women, Family, and Utopia.* Syracuse: Syracuse
    University Press.

Franchere, Gabriel. 1835. letter to William Brewster, Papers of the American Fur
    Company, Mss. F-52. Clarke Historical Collection, no. Reel 3. Central
    Michigan University, October 11.

Frazer, James G. 1963. *The Goldon Bough.* 1 volume abridged edition of 1922 2
    volume edition. New York: Collier Books.

Freidel, David, Linda Schele, and Joy Parker. 1993. *Maya Cosmos: Three
    Thousand Years on the Shaman's Path.* New York: William Morrow
    and Co.

Fuss, Diana. 1989. *Essentially Speaking: Feminism, Nature and Difference.*
    New York: Routledge.

Fürer-Haimendorf, Christoph von. 1967. *Morals and Merit: A Study of Values
    and Social Controls in South Asian Societies.* London: Weidenfeld and
    Nicolson.

------. 1974. The Sense of Sin in Cross-Cultural Perspective. *Man (N.S.)* 9:539-56.

Gaard, Greta (ed.). 1993. *Ecofeminism: Women, Animals, and Nature.*
    Philadelphia: Temple University Press.

Gadon, Elinor. 1989. *The Once and Future Goddess.* San Francisco: Harper and

Row.

Gans, Herbert H. 1979. Symbolic Ethnicity: The Future of Ethnic Groups and Cultures in America. *Ethnic and Racial Studies* 2 (1):1-20.

Garma Navarro, Carlos. 1984. Liderazgo protestante en una lucha campesina en México. *América Indígena* 44 (1):127-41.

------. 1987. *Protestantismo en una comunidad totonaca de Puebla*. México City: Instituo Nacional Indígenista.

------. 1992. Pentecôtisme rural et urbain au Mexique: Différences et similitudes. *Social Compass* 39 (3):389-400.

Geertz, Clifford. 1968. *Islam Observed*. Chicago: University of Chicago Press.

Gilligan, Carol. 1992. *In a Different Voice: Psychological Development and Women's Development*. Second edition. Cambridge: Harvard University Press.

Gitari, David. 1985. The Church and Polygamy. *Wajibu* 1 (1):15-17.

Goldschmidt, Walter. 1977. Anthropology and the Coming Crisis: An Autoethnographic Appraisal. *American Anthropologist* 79:293-308.

Good, Kenneth. 1987. Limiting Factors in Amazonian Ecology. In *Food and Evolution: Toward a Theory of Human Food Habits*, ed. Marvin Harris and E. Ross, 407-26. Philadelphia: Temple University Press.

------. 1989. Yanomami Hunting Patterns: Trekking and Garden Relocation as an Adaptation to Game Availability in Amazonia, Venezuela. Ph.D. Dissertation. University of Florida.

Goode, William J. 1964. *Religion Among the Primitives*. Glencoe: Free Press.

Goodykoontz, Colin B. 1939. *Home Missions on the American Frontier*. Caldwell: The Caxton Printers, Ltd.

Gossen, Gary H. 1974. *Chamulas in the World of the Sun: Time and Space in a Maya Oral Tradition*. Cambridge: Harvard University Press.

Gray, A.B. 1936. Letters from the Long Ago. *Michigan History Magazine* 20:185-212.

Greene, Robert A. 1991. Synderesis, the Spark of Consciousness, in the English Renaissance. *The Journal of the History of Ideas* 52:195-219.

Gregory, Wilton P. 1991. Toward a Promised Land. *America* 164 (14):411-15.

Griffin, Susan. 1992. *A Chorus of Stones: The Private Life of War*. New York: Doubleday.

Griffiths, Richard. 1966. *The Reactionary Revolution: The Catholic Revival in French Literature, 1900-1914*. London: Constable.

Grindal, Bruce, and Frank A. Salamone (eds.). 1995. *Bridges to Humanity: Narratives on Anthropology and Friendship*. Prospect Heights: Waveland.

Hall, Barnes M. 1856. *The Life of Rev. John Clark*. New York: Carlton and Porter.

Halloway, J.E. (ed.). 1990. *Africanisms in American Culture*. Bloomington: Indiana University Press.

Hallowell, A. Irving. 1939. Sin, Sex and Sickness in Saulteaux Belief. *The British*

Journal of Medical Psychology 18:191-97.

------. 1949. The Social Function of Anxiety in a Primitive Society. In *Personal Character and Cultural Milieu (Revised Edition)*, ed. Douglas G. Haring, 375-88. Syracuse: Syracuse University Press.

------. 1976. The History of Anthropology as an Anthropological Problem. In *Contributions to Anthropology: Selected Papers of Irving Hallowell*, ed. Raymond et Fogelson, al, 21-35. Chicago: University of Chicago Press.

Hare, Nathan., and Julia Hare. 1989. *Crisis in Black Sexual Politics*. San Francisco: Black Think Tank.

Harris, Marvin. 1984. Animal Capture and Yanomami Warfare: Retrospective and New Evidence. *Journal of Anthropological Research* 40:183-201.

Hausknecht, Douglas, and Kevin Casper. 1991. The James Dean Gallery. In *Retailing*, Fourth edition, ed. Dale M. Lewison. New York: Macmillan Publishing Co.

Heffner, Robert W. 1993. Introduction: World Building and the Rationality of Conversion. In *Conversion to Christianity:" Historical and Anthropological Perspectives on a Great Transformation*, ed. Robert W. Heffner, 3-44. Berkeley: University of California Press.

Heim, David. 1994. Sophia's Choice. *Christian Century*, April 6, 339-40.

Helms, Mary W. 1975. *Middle America: A Culture History of Heartland and Frontiers*. Englewood Cliffs: Prentice-Hall, Inc.

Herbert, Christopher. 1991. *Culture and Anomie: Ethnographic Imagination in the Nineteenth Century*. Chicago: University of Chicago Press.

Heriot, M. Jean. 1994a. *Blessed Assurance: Beliefs, Actions, and the Experience of Salvation in a Carolina Baptist Church*. Knoxville: University of Tennessee Press.

------. 1994b. El estudio de la "Nueva Era" en los Estados Unidos: Problemas y definiciones. Trans. Maria Julia Carozzi. In *El Estudio Científico de la Religión a Fines del Siglo XX*, ed. Alejandro Frigerio, 55-85. Buenos Aires: Centro Editor de America Latina.

------. 1996. Fetal Rights versus the Female Body: Contested Domains. *Medical Anthropological Quarterly* 10 (2):176-94.

------. n.d. Women's Encounters with the Sacred: Feminist Spirituality, the New Age, and Alternative Religious Experience. unpublished manuscript.

Herskovits, Melville .J. 1958. *The Myth of the Negro Past*. Boston: Beacon Press.

Herskovits, Melville J. 1952. *Economic Anthropology: A Study of Comparative Economics*. New York: Alfred A. Knopf.

Hertz, Robert. 1922. Le pécheé et l'expiation dans les sociétés primitives. *Revue de l'Histoire Religions* 86:1-60.

Hickerson, Harold. 1970. *The Chippewa and Their Neighbors: A Study in Ethnohistory*. New York: Rolt, Rinehart, and Winston.

------. 1973. Fur Trade Colonialism and the North American Indians. *Journal of Ethnic Studies* 1 (2):15-44.

Hillman, Eugene. 1975. *Polygamy Reconsidered*. Maryknoll: Orbis Books.

------. 1989. *Many Paths*. Maryknoll: Orbis Books.

------. 1993. *Toward an African Christianity: Inculturation Applied*. Mahwah: Paulist Press.

Hitt, Jack. 1994. Would You Baptize an Extraterrestrial? *The New York Times Magazine*, May 29, 36-39.

Hooks, Bell. 1990. *Yearning: Race, Gender, and Cultural Politics*. Boston: South End Press.

Hopgood, James F. 1991. Saints and Stars: Exploration of Two Types of Charismatic Movements. Paper presented at the. 90th Annual Meeting of the American Anthropological Association. Chicago, IL, November 20-24.

------. 1993. Memorabilia, Transformation and the Sacred. Paper presented at the 115th Annual Meeting of the American Ethnological Association. Santa Fe, NM, April 15-18.

------. 1994. "Obsession" and "Excess" in a Contemporary American Iconic Movement. Paper presented at the. 93rd Annual Meeting of the American Anthropological Association. Atlanta, GA, November 30 - December 4.

------. 1995. What Would Durkheim Say About James Dean? In *Sociology: A Global Perspective*, Second edition, ed. Joan Ferrante, 556-58. Belmont: Wadsworth Publishing Co.

Horgan, John. 1988. The Violent Yanomami: A New Study Rekindles a Debate over the Roots of Warfare. *Scientific American*, May, 17-19.

Husserl, Edmund. 1931. *Ideas: General Introduction to Pure Phenomenology*. New York: Macmillan.

Hyams, Joe, and Jay Hyams. 1992. *James Dean: Little Boy Lost*. New York: Warner Books.

Idowu, E. Bolaji. 1962. *Olodumare: God in Yoruba Belief*. London: Longmans.

------. 1973. *African Traditional Religion: A Definition*. Maryknoll: Orbis Books.

Ilogo, Edmund. 1974. Traditional Ibo Religious Beliefs, Practices and Organizations. In *Christianity and Ibo Culture*, ed. Edmund Ilogo, 34-55. New York: Nok Publishers.

Ingham, John M. 1986. *Mary, Michael, and Lucifer: Folk Catholicism in Central Mexico*. Austin: University of Texas Press.

Iñupiat Community of the Arctic Slope. 1979. *The Iñupiat View*. Anchorage: National Petroleum Reserve in Alaska, 105 (c), vol 1 (b) (U.S. Department of the Interior.).

Jackson, Michael. 1989. *Paths Toward a Clearing: Radical Empiricism and Ethnographic Inquiry*. Bloomington: Indiana University Press.

James, Bernard J. 1954. Analysis of an American Indian Village. Ph.D. Dissertation. Madison: University of Wisconsin, Madison.

Jamison, James K. 1948. *By Cross and By Anchor: The Story of Frederic Baraga on Lake Superior*. Peterson: St. Anthony Guild Press.

Jarvenpa, Robert, and Hetty Jo Brumbach. 1985. Occupational Status, Ethnicity, and Ecology: Metis Cree Adaptations in a Canadian Trading Frontier. *Human Ecology* 13:309-29.

Jezernik, Maksimiljan. 1968. *Frederick Baraga*. Studia Slovenica, vol. VII. New York: Studia Slovenica.

John Paul II. 1990. Redemptoris Missio. *Papal Encyclical*.

------. 1993. Veritatis Splendor. *Papal Encyclical*.

Johnson, Elizabeth A. 1992. *She Who Is: The Mystery of God in Feminist Theological Discourse*. New York: Crossroad.

Johnson, Ida A. 1919. *The Michigan Fur Trade*. Lansing: Michigan Historical Commission.

Johnson, P.O. 1865. Document 2, RG 44 B73. Records of the Executive Office, G.I.I. Correspondecne, Complaints Agaisnt County officers. Houghton County, L'Anse Township Election Inspectors, no. F20. Lansing: Michigan Historical Archives, April 10.

Johnson, Paul. 1979. *A History of Christianity*. New York: Atheneum.

------. 1994. Shamanism from Equador to Oak Park: A Case Study in New Age Ritual Appropriation. paper presented at the. annual meeting of the American Academy of Religion. Chicago, November 21.

Johnston, George. 1828. letter to Henry R. Schoolcraft, Frame 379. NAM M1, no. Reel 67. Michigan State University, March 12.

------. 1829. letter to M. Cadotte, Frame 47. NAM M1, no. Reel 68. Michigan State University, February 24.

------. nd. Reminiscence No. 4. George Johnston Papers, Mss F-52, no. Reel 9. Clarke Historical Collection: Central Michigan University.

Josefa, Vicente. 1988. La situación indígena: Punto de convergencia entre antropólogos y misioneros. Entrevista al Doctor Napoleon Chagnon. *La Iglesia en Amazonas* 42-43:85-88.

Keesing, Roger. 1981. *Cultural Anthropology: A Contemporary Perspective*. New York: Holt Rinehart and Winston (?).

Kennedy, John C. 1982. *Holding the Line: Ethnic Boundaries in a Northern Labrador Community*. Social and Economic Studies, vol. 27. Memorial University of Newfoundland: Institute of Social and Economic Research.

Kepp, Michael. 1993. President of Amazon Gold Miners Says He Will Quit Over Massacre. *American Metal Market*, August 26, 4.

Kilbride Philip L. 1994. *Plural Marriage for Our Times: A Reinvented Option*. Westport: Bergin and Garvey.

King, David (and, others). 1865. letter to William P. Dole, Frames 670-71. NAM M234, no. Reel 407. Michigan State University, January 7.

Kirwen, Michael C. 1987. *Anthropology and Divination*. Maryknoll: Orbis Books.

------. 1988a. How African Traditional Religions Assimilate Christianity. Unpublished manuscript.

------. 1988b. *The Missionary and the Diviner*. Maryknoll: Orbis Books.

Kirwin, Michael C. 1974. The Christian Prohibition of the African Leviratic Custom: An Empirical Study of the Problem of Adapting Western Christian Teachings on Marriage to the Leviratic Care of Widows in Four African Societies. Ph.D. Dissertation. Toronto: University of Toronto.

Klass, Morton. 1966. Marriage Rules in Bengal. *American Anthropologist* 68:952-70.

------. 1995. *Ordered Universes: Approaches to the Anthropology of Religion*. Boulder: Westview Press.

Kwyune, David. 1991. Interview. The Catholic University of East Africa, January 10.

LaFeber, Walter. 1983. *Inevitable Revolutions: The United States in Central America*. New York: W.W. Norton & Co.

Lambert, Bernard J. 1971. The Founding of L'Anse. In *100 Years of History--L'Anse-Skanee Centennial*, 5-12. Ishpeming: Globe Publishing.

Langness, Lewis L. 1975. Margaret Mead and the Study of Socialization. *Ethos* 3 (2):97-112.

Lanternari, V. 1963. *The Religion of the Oppressed*. New York: Alfred A. Knopf.

Laughlin, Charles. 1994. Apodicticity: The Problem of Absolute Certainty in Transpersonal Ethnology. *Anthropology and Humanism* 19 (2):115-29.

Lee, George W. 1880. Monthly Report for Month of August 1880. letter to R.E. Trowbridge, Frames 397-402. NAM M234, no. Reel 415. Michigan State University.

Lewis, James R. 1992. Approaches to the Study of the New Age Movement. In *Perspectives on the New Age*, ed. James R. Lewis and J. Gordon Melton, 1-12. Albany: State University of New York Press.

Lévi-Strauss, Claude. 1949. *Les Structures Élémentaires de la Parenté*. Paris: Presses Universitaires de France.

------. 1969. *The Elementary Structures of Kinship*. Revised edition. Ed. Rodney Needham. Trans. James H. Bell and John R. von Sturmer. Boston: Beacon Press.

Lindholm, Charles. 1990. *Charisma*. Cambridge: Basil Blackwell, Inc.

Littlewood, Roland. 1992. Putting out the Life: From Biography to Ideology among the Earth People. In *Anthropology and Autobiography*, ed. Judith Okely and Helen Callaway. London: Routledge.

Lombreglia, Ralph. 1996. The Only People for Him. *The Atlantic Monthly*, August, 88-93.

Long, William. 1993. Amazon Murder Mystery: Yanomamis Say Miners Killed a Clan of Indians. *Los Angeles Times*, August 30, A!

Lorde, Audre. 1984. *Sister Outsider: Essays and Speeches*. Trumansburg: Crossing Press.

Luhremann, Tanya M. 1989. *Persuasions of the Witches' Craft: Ritual Magic in*

Contemporary England. Cambridge: Harvard University Press.

Luzbetak, Louis J. 1988. *The Church and Cultures*. Maryknoll: Orbis Books.

Lyman, Stanford, M. 1989. *The Seven Deadly Sins: Origins of Religion*. Garden City: Doubleday.

MacLeod, Murdo J. 1973. *Spanish Central America: A Socioeconomic History, 1520-1720*. Berkeley: University of California Press.

MacNichol, Sally N., and Mary E. Walsh. 1993. Feminist Theology and Spirituality: An Annotated Bibliography. *Women's Studies Quarterly* 1 (1-2, 177-196).

Madsen, William. 1967. Religious Syncretism. In *Social Anthropology*, ed. Manning Nash, 369-91. Handbook of Middle American Indians, vol. 6. Austin: University of Texas Press.

Malefijt, Annemarie de, wal. 1969. *Religion and Culture: An Introduction to Anthropology of Religion*. London: Macmillan.

Malinowski, Bronislaw. 1948. *Magic, Science, and Religion*. Boston: Beacon Press.

Martin, David. 1990. *Tongues of Fire: The Explosion of Protestantism in Latin America*. Oxford: Basil Blackwell.

------. 1992. Evangelicals and Economic Culture in Latin America: An Interim Comment on Research in Progress. *Social Compass* 39 (1):9-14.

Marton, Yves. 1994. The Experiential Approach to Anthropology and Castaneda's Ambiguous Legacy. In *Being Changed By Cross-Cultural Experiences*, ed. David E. Young and Jean-Guy Goulet, 273-97. Ontario: Broadview Press.

Marty, Martin. 1987. Commentary. *Christian Century* 10:1127.

Maxwell, Judith M. 1990. The Specification of Genre in Mayan Discourse. paper presented at the Cleveland Conference on Maya Text Analysis. Cleveland.

Mbefo, Luke. 1987. Theology and Inculturation. *Cross Currents* 37:393-403.

McClurken, James M. 1986. Ottawa Adaptive Strategies to Indian Removal. *Michigan Historical Review* 12 (Spring):29-55.

McDonald, James H. 1993. Whose History? Whose Voice? Myth and Resistance in the Rise of the New Left in Mexico. *Cultural Anthropology* 8:96-116.

McFague, Sallie. 1982. *Metaphorical Theology: Models of God in Religious Language*. Philadelphia: Fortress Press.

------. 1987. *Models of God: Theology for an Ecological, Nuclear Age*. Philadelphia: Fortress Press.

McGee, R. Jon. 1984. The Influence of Prehispanic Maya Religion in Contemporary Lacandon Ritual. *Journal of Latin American Lore* 10 (2):175-87.

------. 1988. Ritual Use of Balché Among the Lacandon Maya. *Estudios de Cultura Maya* XVIII.

------. 1989. The Flood Myth from a Lacandon Maya Perspective. *Latin American*

Indian Literatures Journal 5 (1):68-80.

------. 1990. *Life, Ritual and Religion Among the Lacandon Maya.* Belmont: Wadsworth Publishing Co.

------, and F. Kent Reilly, III. 1994. Ancient Maya Astronomy and Cosmology in Lacandon Maya Life. unpublished manuscript.

Mead, Margaret. 1949. *Male and Female.* New York: William Morrow & Company.

Memorandum of Outstanding Debts of L'Anse Indians for the Years 1832-1834 with Jean Baptiste Dubay. 1834, Frame 37. NAM M1, no. Reel 54. Michigan State University.

Merkur, Daniel. 1985. *Becoming Half-Hidden: Shamanism and Initiation among the Inuit.* Stockholm: Almqvist and Wiksell.

Midgley, Mary. 1991. *Can't We Make Moral Judgements?* New York: St. Martin's Press.

Minh-Ha, Trinh. 1989. *Women, Native, Other: Writing Postcoloniality and Feminism.* Bloomington: Indiana University Press.

Mitchell, Don. 1993. Sightlines. *Anthropology and Humanism* 18 (2):80-81.

Mittelholtz, E.F. 1957. *Historical Review of the Red Lake Indian Reservation: A History of Its People and Progress.* Bemidji: General Council of the Red Lake Band of Chippewa Indians and the Beltrami County Historical Society.

Mohanty, Chandra T., Ann Russo, and Lourdes Torres (eds.). 1991. *Third World Women and the Politics of Feminism.* Bloomington: Indiana University Press.

Monaghan, John. 1990. Reciprocity, Redistribution, and the Transaction of Value in the Mesoamerican Fiesta. *American Ethnologist* 17 (4):758-74.

Muratorio, Blanca. 1980. Protestantism and Capitalism Revisited in the Rural Highlands of Ecuador. *Journal of Peasant Studies* 8 (1):37-60.

------. 1981. Protestantism, Ethnicity, and Class in Chimborazo. In *Cultural Transformations and Ethnicity in Modern Ecuador*, ed. Norman E. Whitten. Urbana: University of Illinois Press.

Musser, J. 1944. *Celestial or Plural Marriage.* Salt Lake City: Truth Publishing Co.

Nations, James D., and Ronald B. Nigh. 1980. The Evolutionary Potential of Lacandon Maya Sustained Yield Tropical Forest Agriculture. *Journal of Anthropological Research* 36 (1):1-30.

Needham, Rodney. 1962. *Structure and Sentiment: A Test Case in Social Anthropology.* Chicago: The University of Chicago Press.

Neitz, Mary Jo. 1990. In Goddess We Trust. In *Gods We Trust: New Patterns of Religious Pluralism in America*, Second edition, Second edition, ed. Thomas Robbins and Dick Anthony, 353-72. New Brunswick: Transaction Publishers.

------. in press. Constructing Women's Rituals: Roman Catholic Women and 'Limina.' In *Work Family and Faith: New Patterns Among Old Institutions*, ed. Nancy T. Ammerman and Wade C. Roof. New

Brunswick: Rutgers University Press.

Newman, Philip. 1994. personal communication to M. Jean Heriot, March 1.

Norbeck, Edward. 1961. *Religion in Primitive Society*. New York: Harper & Row.

Okite, Odhiamo. 1981. Less Joy, More Power: Africa's Independent Churches have Moved Out of the Parks and Into the Housing Estates. *One World* 65 (1):21-22.

Okullu, H. 1991. *Church and Marriage in East Africa*. Nairobi: Uzima Press.

Opoku, Kofi Asare. 1975. *Speak to the Words: Proverbs from Africa*. New York: Lothrop, Lee & Shepard Co.

O'Connell, Loraine. 1994. Almighty Goddess. *San Jose Mercury News*, April 23, 1C, 11C.

O'Connor, Mary. 1979. Two Kinds of Religious Movement Among the Mayo Indians of Sonora, Mexico. *Journal for the Scientific Study of Religion* 18 (3):260-68.

Paden, William E. 1992. *Interpreting the Sacred*. Boston: Beacon Press.

Parkin, David. 1985. Introduction. In *The Anthropology of Evil*, ed. David Parkin, 1-25. Oxford: Basil Blackwell, Ltd.

Parks, E. 1986. Could Canada Have Ever Been Our Fourteenth Colony? *Smithsonian Magazine* 18 (9, September):40-49.

Parsons, Talcott. 1958. Translator's Preface. Trans. Talcott Parsons. In *The Protestant Ethic and the Spirit of Capitalism, by Max Weber*. New York: Charles Scribner's Sons.

Peters, Bernard C., ed. 1983. *Lake Superior Journal: Bela Hubbard's Account of the 1840 Houghton Expedition*. Marquette: Northern Michigan University Press.

Phillips, Adedotun, and Eddy Ndukwu. 1987. *Structural Adjustments Programme in a Developing Economy: The Case of Nigeria*. Ibadan: Wemiloru Press, Ltd.

Pintchman, Tracy. 1994. Is the Hindu Goddess Tradition a Good Resource for Western Feminism? Paper presented at the. annual meeting of the American Academy of Religion. Chicago, November 20.

Pitezel, John H., Rev. 1857. *Lights and Shades of Missionary Life.*. Cincinnati: Western Book Concern.

Plaskow, Judith, and Carol P. Christ (eds.). 1989. *Weaving the Visions: New Patterns in Feminist Spirituality*. San Francisco: Harper and Row.

Polanyi, Karl. 1957. The Economy as Instituted Process. In *Trade and Market in the Early Empires: Economies in History and Theory*, ed. K. Polanyi, Arensberg and H.W. Pearson, 243-70. Glencoe: Free Press.

Pollitt, Katha. 1993. Are Women Morally Superior to Men? Debunking "Difference" Feminism. *Utne Reader* 59 (September/ October): 101-09.

Potts, Timothy C. 1980. *Conscience in Medievel Philosophy*. Cambridge: Cambridge University Press.

Priest, Robert J. 1993. Defilement, Moral Purity and Transgressive Power: The Symbolism of Filth in Aguaruna-Jívaro Culture. Ph.D. Dissertation.

Berkeley: University of California and Berkeley.

Prindle, Cyrus, Rev. 1842. *Memoirs of the Rev. Daniel Meeker Chandler: For Several Years Missionary Among the Indians at Ke-wa-we-non and Saut de St. Marie, Lake Superior.* Middlebury: Ephraim Maxham.

Prucha, Francis P. 1973. *American Indian Policy in the Formative Years: The Indian Trade and Intercourse Acts, 1790-1834.* Lincoln: University of Nebraska Press.

Radin, Paul. 1957. *Primitive Religion: Its Nature and Origin.* New York: Dover.

Ranck, Shirley. 1986. *Cakes for the Queen of Heaven.* Boston: Unitarian Universalist Association.

Ranger, Terence O. 1968. Connexions Between 'Primary Resistance' Movements and Modern Mass Nationalism in East and Central Africa, Part 1. *Journal of African History* 9 (3/4):437-53.

Rappaport, Joanne. 1984. Las misiones Protestantes y la resistencia indígena en el sur de Colombia. *América Indígena* 44 (1):111-26.

Rayner, Steven. 1988. The Rules that Make Us Equal. In *Rules, Decisions and Inequality in Egalitarian Societies*, ed. James M Flanagan and Steven?? Rayner. Brookfield: Gower Press.

Reilly, F. Kent. 1987. The Ecological Origins of Olmec Symbols of Rulership. M.A. Thesis. Austin: University of Texas.

------. 1990. Cosmos and Rulership: The Function of Olmec-Style Symbols in Formative Period Mesoamerica. Special Edition. In *The Emergence of Writing in Mesoamerica*, ed. Schmandt-Besserat, Denise and F. Kent Reilley, III, 12-37. Visible Language, vol. XXIX. Providence: Rhode Island School of Design.

------. 1992. *Workbook for the XVIth Maya Hieroglyphic Workshop at the Univeristy of Texas.* Austin: Department of Art and Art History and the Institute of Latin American Studies.

Rezek, A.I., Rev. 1906. *History of the Diocese of Sult Ste. Marie and Marquette.., Vol. 1.* Chicago: M.A. Donahue.

Richardson, Miles. 1994. Writing Poetry and Doing Ethnography: Aesthetics and Observation on the Page and in the Field. *Anthropology and Humanism* 19 (1):77-87.

Richmond, William. 1848. letter to William Medill, Frames 242-43. NAM M! no. Reel 40. Michigan State University, December 8.

Ricoeur, Paul. 1967. *The Symbolism of Evil.* Boston: Beacon Press.

Rose, Wendy. 1992. The Great Pretenders: Further Reflections on White Shamanism. In *The State of Native America*, ed. M. Annette Jaimes. Boston: South End Press.

Rosenau, Pauline M. 1992. *Post-Modernism and the Social Sciences.* Princeton: Princeton University Press.

Ross, Marc H. 1993. *The Culture of Conflict: Interpreations and Persepctives in Comparative Perspective.* New Haven: Yale University Press.

Rossiter, Clinton L. 1971. *The American Quest, 1790-1860: An Emerging*

Nation in Search of Identity, Unity, and Modernity. New York: Harcourt, Brace, and Jovanovich.

Ruther, Rosemary R. 1985. *Woman-Church: Theology and Practice of Feminist Liturgical Communities.* New York: Harper and Row.

------. 1992. *Gaia and God: An Ecofeminist Theology of Earth Healing.* San Francisco: HarperSanFrancisco.

------. 1993. The Woman-Church Movement in Contemporary Christianity. In *Women's Leadership in Marginal Religions: Explorations Outside the Mainstream,* ed. Catherine Wessinger, 196-210. Urbana: University of Illinois Press.

Salamone, Frank A. 1975. A Continuity of Igbo Values After Conversion: A Study in Purity and Prestige. *Missiology* 3:33-43.

------. 1986. Joans -of-All-Trades: The Dominican Sisters in Nigeria. *Missiology* 5:487-501.

------. 1991. Creole Performance and the Mass: The Creolization Process. *Studies in Third World Societies* 46:21-36.

------. 1991. Mixed Messages at the Mission. *Anthropos* 86:487-99.

------. 1994. Mixed Messages at the Mission. In *The Message in the Missionary,* ed. Laurie Klein and Elizabeth Brusco, 61-90. Williamsburg: Studies in Third World Society Press.

------. 1985. *Missionaries and Anthropologists: Case Studies.* Williamsburg: Studies in Third World Societies.

Salzmann, Zidnek. 1993. *Language, Culture, and Society: An Introduction to Linguistic Anthropology.* Boulder: Westview Press.

Sanneh, L. 1986. Reciprocal Influences: African Traditional Religions and Christianity. In *Third World Liberation Theologies,* ed. D.W. Ferm, 231-40. Maryknoll: Orbis Books.

Sarriss, Greg. 1993. *Keeping Slug Woman Alive.* Berkeley: University of California Press.

Schele, Linda, and David Freidel. 1990. *A Forest of Kings: The Untold Story of the Ancient Maya.* New York: William Morrow and Co.

Schimmel, Solomon. 1992. *The Seven Deadly Sins: Jewish, Christian, and Classical Reflections on Human Nature.* New York: The Free Press.

Schmidt, Wilhelm. 1935. *The Origin and Growth of Religion: Facts and Theories.* Trans. H.J. Rose. London: Metheun.

Schoeck, Helmut. 1990. *Envy: A Theory of Social Behaviour.* Indianapolis: Liberty Press.

Schoenfus, Walter P. 1963. The Chippewa Indians in Michigan and the Missionaries of the Methodist, Presbyterian, and Lutheran Churches, 1840-1855. Master of Arts Thesis. St. Louis: Washington University.

Schoolcraft, Henry R. 1840. letter to J. Hartley Crawford, Frames 242-43. NAM M1, no. Reel 38. Michigan State University, July 15.

------. 1958. *Schoolcraft's Expedition to Lake Itasca: The Discovery of the Source of the Mississippi.* Ed. P.P. Mason. East Lansing: Michigan

State University Press.

------. 1962. *The Literary Voyager or Muzzewniequn*. Ed. P.M. Mason. East Lansing: Michigan State University Press.

Scott, John. 1989. The Sociology of the Other Woman: Man-sharing. In *Crisis in Black Sexual Politics*, ed. Nathan Hare and Julia Hare, 105-09. San Francisco: Black Think Tank.

Sekaquaptewa, Emory. 1972. Preserving the Good Things of Hopi Life. In *Plural Society in the Southwest*, ed. Edward H. Spicer and R.H. Thompson, 239-60. New York: Interbrook.

Serbin, Ken. 1990. Amazon Gold Prospectors a Threat to Yanomami Indians. *National Catholic Reporter*, February 23, 7.

Sered, Susan S. 1994. *Priestess, Mother, Sacred Sister: Religions Dominated by Women*. New York: Oxford University Press.

Sexton, James. 1978. Protestantism and Modernization in Two Guatemalan Towns. *American Ethnologist* 5 (2):280-302.

Shifford, Patricia A. nd. A Study of Economic Change: The Chippewa of Northern Wisconsin, 1854-1900. unpublished manuscript. Department of Sociology and Northern American Studies, Northland College.

Shipps, J. 1985. *Mormonism: The Story of a New Religious Tradition*. Urbana: University of Illinois Press.

Shweder, Richard A. 1990. Ethical Relativism: Is There a Defensible Version? *Ethos: Journal of the Society for Psychological Anthropology* 18:205-18.

------. 1991. *Thinking Through Cultures*. Cambridge: Harvard University Press.

------, Manamohan Mahapatra, and Joan G. Miller. 1990. Culture and Moral Development. In *Cultural Psychology: Essays on Comparative Human Development*, ed. James W. Stigler, Richard A. Shweder and Gilbert Herdt, 130-204. Cambridge: Cambridge University Press.

Singer, Milton. 1980. Signs of the Self: An Exploration in Semiotic Anthropology. *American Anthropologist* 82 (3):485-507.

------. 1984. *Man's Glassy Essence: Explorations in Semiotic Anthropology*. Bloomington: Indiana University Press.

Siskind, Janet. 1977. *To Hunt in the Morning*. London: Oxford University Press.

Small, Jospeh D., and John P. Burgess. 1994. Evaluating 'Re-Imagining." *Christian Century*, April 6, 342-44.

Sommerville, Charles J. 1990. *The Rise and Fall of Childhood*. Revised edition. New York: Vintage Books.

Sosa, John R. 1989. Cosmological, Symbolic, and Cultural Complexity Among the contemporary Maya of Yucatan. In *World Archeoastronomy*, ed. Anthony F. Aveni, 130-42. Cambridge: Cambridge University Press.

Spicer, Edward H. 1971. Persistent Cultural Systems. *Science* 174 (4011): 795-800.

Spretnak, Charlene (ed.). 1982. *The Politics of Women's Spirituality: Essays on the Rise of Spiritual Power Within the Feminist Movement*. Garden City: Anchor Books.

St. John, John R. 1846. *A True Description of the Lake Superior Country...* New York: William H. Graham, Tribune Building.

Starhawk. 1987. *Truth or Dare: Encounters with Power, Authority and Magic.* San Francisco: Harper and Row.

Stock, Dennis. 1978. *James Dean Revisited.* New York: The Viking Press.

Stoll, David. 1990. *Is Latin America Turning Protestant?: The Politics of Evangelical Growth.* Berkeley: University of California Press.

Stoller, Paul. 1989. *The Taste of Ethnographic Things.* Philadelphia: University of Pennsylvania Press.

------, and Cheryl Olkes. 1987. *In Sorcery's Shadow.* Chicago: University of Chicago Press.

Strathern, Marilyn. 1989. *The Gender of the Gift: Problems with Women and Problems with Society in Melanesia.* Berkeley: University of California Press.

Stuart, Robert. 1844. letter to Frederic Baraga, Frame 421. NAM M1, no. Reel 39. Michigan State University, April 15.

------. 1844. letter to James Ord, Frames 404-06. NAM M1, no. Reel 39. Michigan State University, April 4.

Sudarkasa, Niara. 1982. African and Afro-American Family Structure. In *Anthropology for the Eighties*, ed. J. Cole, 132-61. New York: The Free Press.

Taussig, Michael. 1980. *The Devil and Commodity Fetishism in South America.* Chapel Hill: University of North Carolina Press.

Tax, Sol. 1978. A Community of Anthropologists. *Practicing Anthropology* 1 (1):8-9.

Taylor, Mark K. 1986. *Beyond Explanation: Religious Dimensions in Cultural Anthropology.* Macon: Mercer University Press.

Tracy, David. 1987. Comparative Theology. In *The Encyclopedia of Religion*, vol. 14, ed. Mircea ET Eliade, AL, 446-55. New York: Macmillan.

Treat, James A. 1992. Contemporary Native Religious Identity. Ph. D. Dissertation. Berkeley: Graduate Theological Union.

Truffaut, François. 1978. *The Films in My Life.* Trans. Leonard Mayhew. New York: Simon and Schuster.

Turnbull, Colin M. 1972. *The Mountain People.* New York: Simon and Schuster.

Turner, Paul R. 1979. Religious Conversion and Community Development. *Journal for the Scientific Study of Religion* 18 (3):252-60.

Turner, Terence. 1993. Brazil's Guilt in the Amazon Massacre. *The New York Times*, August 26, A21.

Turner, Victor. 1969. *The Ritual Process: Structure and Anti-Structure.* Chicago: Aldine.

------. 1977. Process, System, and Symbol: A New Anthropological Synthesis. *Daedalus* 106 (3):61-80.

------. 1985. Experience and Performance: Towards a New Processual Anthropology. Chapter 9. In *On the Edge of the Bush*, ed. Victor

Turner, 205-26. Tucson: University of Arizona.

------, and Edith Turner. 1975. *Image and Pilgrimage in Christian Culture: Anthropological Perspectives*. New York: Columbia University Press.

------, and -----. 1982. Religious Celebrations. In *Celebration: Studies in Festivity and Ritual*, ed. Victor Turner, 201-19. Washington, D.C.: Smithsonian Institution Press.

Tyrell, Ian R. 1979. Temperance and Economic Change in the Antebellum North. In *Alcohol, Reform, and Society: The Liquor Issue in Social Context*, ed. J.S. Blocker, 45-67. Contributions in American History, vol. 83. Westport: Greenwood Press.

Tysl, Robert W. 1965. Continuity and Evolution in a Public Symbol: An Investigation into the Creation and Communication of the James Dean Image in Mid-Century America. Ph.D. Dissertation. East Lansing: Michigan State University.

Un Grupo de Missionarios del Alto Orinoco. 1991. *Consideraciones a un documento de Charles Brewer Carias*. Pamphlet.

van der Geest, Sjaak, and Jon P. Kirby. 1992. The Absence of the Missionary in African Ethnography, 1930-1965. *African Studies Review* 35:59-103.

van Wagoner, R. 1986. *Mormon Polygamy: A History*. Salt Lake City: Signature Books.

Vatican II. 1965. Ad Gentes. *The Decree on the Church's Missionary Activity*, December 7.

------. 1965. Gaudium et Spes, No. 58.

Veatch, J.O. 1941. *Agricultural Experiment Station*. Special Bulletin, vol. 231, no. First revision. East Lansing: Michigan State University Press.

Vecsey, Christopher. 1983. *Traditional Ojibwa Religion and Its Historical Changes*. Philadelphia: American Philosophical Society.

Verwyst, Chrystosom. 1900. *Life and Labors of Rt. Rev. Frederic Baraga, First Bishop of Marquette, Michigan*. Milwaukee: M.H. Wiltzius and Co.

Viasta, Boa. 1993. Brazil Miners Grouse in Wake of Massacre. *American Metal Market*, October 20, 5.

Villacorta, J. Antonio, C., and Carlos A. Villacorta. 1933. *Codices Mayas: Dresden, Peresianus, Trocortesianus*. Guatemala City: Tipografia Nacional.

Viola, Herman J. 1974. *Thomas L. McKenney: Architect of America's Early Indian Policy, 1816-1830*. Chicago: The Swallow Press, Inc.

Vogt, Evon Z. 1976. *Tortillas for the Gods: A Symboic Analysis of Zinacanteco Rituals*. Cambridge: Harvard University Press.

------. 1990. *The Zinacantecos of Mexico: A Modern Maya Way of Life*. New York: Holt, Rinehart, and Winston.

Wafer, Jim. 1991. *The Taste of Blood: Spirit Possession in Brazilian Candomble*. Philadelphia: University of Pennsylvania Press.

Walker, M.M. 1829. Extracts from M.M. Walker's Journal, Frame 138. NAM M1, no. Reel 68. Michigan State University, December 25.

Wallace, Anthony F.C. 1956b. Revitalization Movements. *American Anthropologist* 58:264-81.

Warner, W. Lloyd. 1959. *The Living and the Dead: A Study of the Symbolic Life of Americans*. New Haven: Yale University Press.

Warren, William W. 1957. History of the Ojibways, Based Upon Traditions and Oral Statements. In *History of the Ojibway Nation*, 21-394. Minneapolis: Ross & Haines, Inc.

Washburne, Wilcomb E. 1971. *Red Man's Land / White Man's Law*. New York: Charles Scribner and Sons.

Weber, Max. 1946. The Protestant Sects and the Spirit of Capitalism. In *From Max Weber*, ed. Hans Gerth and C. Wright Mills. London: Routledge.

------. 1958. *The Protestant Ethic and the Spirit of Capitalism*. Trans. Talcott Parsons. New York: Charles Scribner's Sons.

------. 1963. *The Sociology of Religion*. Trans. Ephriam Fischoff. Boston: Beacon Press.

Webster, James B. 1964. *The African Church among the Yoruba, 1888-1912*. Oxford: Clarendon Press.

Wertime, Richard A., and Angela M.H. Schuster. 1993. Written in the Stars: Celestial Origin of Maya Creation Myth. *Archeology* 25 (July/ August): 27-30.

Wessinger, Catherine (ed.). 1993. *Women's Leadership in Marginal Religions: Explorations Outside the Mainstream*. Urbana: University of Illinois Press.

Whitehead, Barbara D. 1993. Dan Quayle Was Right. *The Atlantic Monthly* 172 (4):47-84.

Whiteman, Darrel (ed.). 1985. *Anthropologists and Missionaries*. Williamsburg: Studies in Third World Societies.

Wilkie, James W., David E. Lorey, and Enrique Ochoa (eds.). 1988. . Statistical Abstract of Latin America, vol. 26. Los Angeles: UCLA Latin American Center Publications.

Williams, Delores. 1989. Womanist Theology. In *Weaving the Visions*, ed. Judith Plaskow and Carol P. Christ, 179-86. San Francisco: HarperSanFrancisco.

Williams, Preston. 1990. A More Perfect Union: The Silence of the Church. *America* 162 (12):315-18.

Winokur, Lawrence A. 1993. Emissary from the Rain Forest. *The Progressive*, March 19, 14.

Wolf, Eric. 1969. American Anthropologists and American Society. In *Concepts and Assumptions in Contemporary Anthropology*, ed. Stephen A. Tylor, 3-11. Georgia: University of Georgia Press.

Wuthnow, Robert. 1994. *Sharing the Journey: Support Groups and America's Quest for Community*. New York: Free Press.

Wyllie, Robert W. 1980. *Spirits in Ghana*. Missoula: Scholars Press.

Young, Josiah U. 1986. *Black and African Theologies*. Maryknoll: Orbis Books.

Young, Kimball. 1954. *Isn't One Wife Enough?* New York: Holt.
Zablocki, Benjamin. 1980. *Alienation and Charisma*. New York: The Free Press.
Zimanawe, Cesar. 1990. Letter to Señor Chagnon. *La Iglesia en Amazonas* 11 (49):20.

Index

270

272

About the Contributors

Robert J. Priest (Ph.D., 1983, University of California, Berkeley) conducted 20 month of fieldwork with the Aguaruna-Jívaro of northern Peru between 1987 and 1989, with a dissertation, *Defilement, Moral Purity, and Transgressive Power: The Symbolism of Filth in Aguaruna-Jívaro Culture*. His publications include "Anthropologists and Missionaries: Moral Roots of conflict," in *Current Concerns of Anthropologists and Missionaries* (Karl Franklin, ed., Dallas: The International Museum of Culture) and "Missionary Eleotics: Culture and Conscience," *Missiology* 22: 291-315. He is currenlty Assoicate Professor of Intercultural Studies at Columbia International University in Columbia, South Carolina.

Morton Klass (Ph.D., 1959, Columbia University) is Professor of Anthropology at Barnard College, Columbia University. He has conducted research in India and among overseas communities of people of South Asian descent. His interests have been culture change, community structure, the caste system, and village-level religion. His most recent books are *Singing With Sai Babab: The Politics of Revitalization in Trinidad* (Westview Press, 1991, reprinted by Waveland press, 1996), and *Ordered Universes: Approaches to the Anthropology of Religion* (Westview Press, 1995).

M. Jean Heriot (Ph.D., 1989, University of California, Berkely) is an adjunct lecturer in the Department of Religious Studies at Santa Clara University. Concurrently, she is pursuing a Master of Divinity degree at pacific School of Religion in Berkeley. She has published an ethnography based on her dissertation fieldwork on a Southern Baptist Convention congregation, *Blessed Assurance, Beliefs, Actions and theExperience of Salvation in a Carolina Baptist Church* (Nashville, University of Tennessee Press, 1994). She was a visiting research fellow at the Center for the Study of American Religion at Princeton University in 1993-94, and is owrking on a forthcoming ethnography of women's religious experiences in the feminist spirituality movement and the New Age movement.

Edith L.B. Turner (M.A., 1980, University of Virginia) has been a member of the faculty of the department of anthropology at the University of Virginia since 1984. She has been in anthropology for 46 years. Her major interests are the Ndembu of Zambia, the Iñupiat of northern Alasak, the ritual of Irish farming communities, symbolism, ritual as perfornamce, and anthropological writing. Among her significant publications are *The Hands Feel It: Healing and Spirit Presence Among a Northern Alaskan People* (1996); *Experiencing Ritual: A New Interpretation of African Healing* (1992); "Poetics and Experience in Anthropological Writing (*Steward Journal*, 1990); *The Spirit and the Drum* (1987); and *Image and Pilgrimage* (with Victor Turner, 1978).

Frank A. Salamone (Ph.D., 1973, SUNY-Buffalo) is a Full Professor of Anthropology and Sociology at Iona College, New Rochelle, New York. He has conducted research in Nigeria, Kenya, Ghana, Venezuela and the United States. His interests have been religion and identity. He is now studying the religion and identity of his own ethnic group in his home town, Rochester, New York. He has published extensively on Italian americans in Rochester, New York, and is planning to publish a history of that group up to the endo of World War II. His latest book, *The Yanomami and the Interpreters: Who Speaks for the Yanomami?*, discusses the problems faced by this Venezuelan Indian group in the modern world.

James W. Dow (Ph.D., Brandeis University) is Professor of Anthropology at Oakland University and specializes in the cultures of Middle America. He has studied religion and economic systems there since 1963. He has published three books on the Otomí-speaking people of hte Eastern Sierra of Hidalgo, Mexico: *Santos y Supervivencias*, *The Otomí of the Northern Sierra de Puebla, Mexico*, and *The Shaman's Touch*. He has been a Fulbright Scholar and the recipient of a research award from the Society for the Scientific Study of Religion. He is the co-author of , and contributor to, *Class, Politics, and Populat Religion in Mexico and Central America*. Besides having an interest in the religions of Latin America, he is also interested in anthropological methods (both qualitative and quantitative), and is the administrator of the ANTHAP computer network serving the Societh for Applied Anthropology and the National Association for the Practice of Anthropology.

Olugbemi Moloye (Ph.D., 1985, University of Massachusetts) is on the faculty of the Sociology, Anthropology, and Criminial Justice Department at the Florida Agricultural and Mechanical University in Tallahassee, Florida. His publications have dealt with Yoruba culture, religion, indiegenous knowledge systems and politics. Dr. Moloye spent more than a decade at the Institute of Social and Economic Research in Ibadan, Nigeria, as a senior resarch fellow, where he conducted most of his research.

Philip Kilbride (Ph.D., 1970, University of Missouri) is Chair of the Department of Anthropology at Bryn Mawr College, Bryn Mawr, Pennsylvania and is the Mary Hale Chase Chair in hte Social Sciences and Social Work and Social Research. He has regularly conducted anthropological research in East Africa since 1969. Most recenlty, in 1996, he completed a National Science Foundation project on street children in Nairobi, Kenya. He is the author of, among other publications, *Changing Family Life in East Africa: women and Children at Risk* (written with his wife, Janet Kilbride, Penn State Press, 1990) and *Plural Marriage for Our Times: A Re-Invented Option* (Bergin and Garvey, Westport, 1994).

William Jankowiak (Ph.D., 1986, University of California, Santa Barbara) is an

Associate Professor of Anthropology at the University of Nevada, Las Vegas. He has conducted extensive field research in China, Inner Mongolia, and North America. He is the author of numerous scientific publications, including *Sex, Death and Hierarchy in a Chinese City* (Columbia University Press) and editor of *Romantic Passion* (Columiba University Press). Presently, he is working on a book about contemporary American polygamy.

Emilie Allen is a graduate student in the Anthropology Department at the University of California, Los Angeles. She has conducted field research in Belize and among a Mormon polygamous community in the Southwest. Presently, she is finishing her Master's thesis on sibling relationships in a polygamous family.

R. Jon McGee (Ph.D., 1983, Rice University) is an Associate Professor of Anthropology at Southwest Texas State University, in San Marcos, Texas. He began his research with the Lacandon Maya in 1980, and has continued this work to the present. His major publications include *Life, Ritual and ReligionAmong the Lacandon, Maya* (1990) and *Anthropological Theory: An Introductory History*.

James F. Hopgood (Ph.D., 1976, University of Kansas) is Professor of Anthropology and Department chair at Northern Kentucky University. He is the author of *Settlers of Bajavista: Social and Economic Adaptation in a Mexican Squatter Settlement* (The Ohio University, Athens, 1979) and many articles and essays. In addition to research on the Deaners, other iconic and quasi-religiouis movments, he continues research in Monterrey, Mexico, on issues of urban change and adaptation. He is a recent recipient of a Sasakawa Fellowship for study at the Japan Studies Institute, San Diego State University.

Walter Randolph Adams (Ph. D., 1988, Michigan State University) is a Research Associate at the Brown University Center for Alcohol and Addiction Studies. An applied anthropologist, he has conducted research in the United States, Mexico, Guatemala, El Salvador and Paraguay. In addition to conducting research on alcoholism, he is interested in developing theoretical frameworks that link the material and cognitive dimensions of culture. Some relevant publications include "Social Structre in Pilgrimage and Prayer: Tzeltales as Lords and Servants" in *Pilgrimage in Latin America* (N. Ross Crumrine and Alan Morinis (eds.), Westport, Greenwood Press, 1991: 109-122), "Political and Economic Correlates of Pilgrimage Behavior (*Anales de Antropología*, 1983: Vol 2: 147-171).

Mary Douglas (Ph.D., 1951, Oxford University) has written *Purity and Danger, Natural Symbols*, and other major works on symbolic anthropology. She has conducted extensive fieldwork in tropical Africa and is currently researching a major work on *The Bible*.